'Only in the dance is the mystic bond
between man and animals consummated.'

CURT SACHS, *World History of the Dance*

Steven Lonsdale

Animals and the Origins of Dance

with 116 illustrations

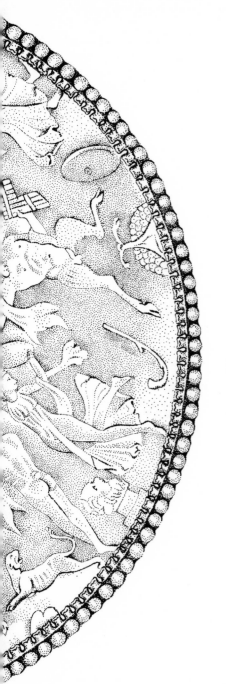

THAMES AND HUDSON

JHR
JHL

*Frontispiece: Dionysian revelry of maenads and satyrs
on the Neptune Dish from the Mildenhall Treasure,
British Museum*

*Page 6: Bushman rock painting of frog dance in which
the human figures seem to transform themselves
into frogs. After G. W. Stow in Dorothea F. Bleek's*
Rock Paintings in South Africa *(1930)*

*First published in the USA in 1982
by Thames and Hudson Inc.,
500 Fifth Avenue,
New York, New York 10110*

*Library of Congress Catalog Card
Number 81–51082*

*Typeset in Great Britain by Keyset Composition, Colchester, Essex.
Printed and bound in Great Britain by William Clowes Ltd, Beccles, Suffolk.*

CONTENTS

ACKNOWLEDGMENTS

Photographs:

Ardea, London 33; Arizona State Museum 59; Australian Information Service 18, 21, 29, 31, 36; Australian National Tourist Office 23; Ray Bishop, Wadebridge 58; Boston Museum of Fine Arts, Ross Collection 34; Robert R. R. Brooks 51; Cairo Museum 67; Cambridge, Haddon Library Collection, Museum of Archaeology and Anthropology 13, 14, 15, 25, 26, 27, 28, 30, 38, 44, 45, 46, 50, 53, 55, 57, 61, 77, 82; Canadian High Commission, London 42; Cologne, Museum für Volkerkunde 65; Colorado Springs Fine Art Center, Taylor Museum Collection, Gift of Alice Bemis Taylor 64; Delhi, National Museum 5; Documentation Française, Paris 37; Guatemala Museum of Archaeology and Ethnology 68; Hoa-Qui, Paris 56; Courtesy Dr Pascal James Imperato 16, 17; Indian Tourist Authority, London 80; Istanbul, Topkapi Museum 8; Institut National Géographique, Paris 7; Karlsruhe, Badisches Landesmuseum 4; R. Lannoy 35; Alfredo Linares 81; London, British Museum 2, 3, 6, 20, 43, 62, 63, 66, 74, 75; Tourist Development Corporation of Malaysia 79; Mansell Collection, London 24; Mexican National Tourist Council 47; New York, Metropolitan Museum of Art, Harry G. C. Packard Collection of Asian Art 76; Nuremberg Stadtsbibliothek 70; Courtesy John Picton 12, 41; Popperfoto, London 22, 32, 48; Portland Art Museum, Oregon 11; Roumanian National Tourist Authority 72; Singapore Tourist Promotion Board 69, 78; Sydney, Art Gallery of New South Wales 19; Tarquinia, National Museum 1; Washington D.C., Smithsonian Institution National Anthropological Archives 49, 60

Illustrations from publications:

E. S. Curtis, *The North American Indian* (1907–30), 39, 40, 54; D. F. Bleek, *Rock-Paintings in South Africa* (1930), 52; François Robichon de la Guérinière, *École de Cavalerie* (1733), 73; Nicholaes Witsen, *Noord en Oost Tartarye* (1705), 10

The author also wishes to express his thanks to the following:

Dover Publications Inc. for the quotations from George Catlin, *Illustrations of the Manners, Customs, and Conditions of the North American Indian. With Letters and Notes*; Johnson Reprint Corporation for the quotation from Edward S. Curtis, *The North American Indian*; Viking Penguin Inc. for the extracts from Joseph Campbell, *The Masks of God: Primitive Mythology*. Copyright © 1959, 1969 by Joseph Campbell. Reprinted by permission of Viking Penguin Inc.; Viking Penguin Inc. for the extracts from Frank Waters, *The Book of the Hopi*. Copyright © 1963 by Frank Waters. Reprinted by permission of Viking Penguin Inc.

Illustrations redrawn by Georgie Glen

FOREWORD

The purpose of this book is to introduce the reader to a little-known aspect of dance in ancient and ethnic cultures through animal myths, lore and art. The myths, many of which fall into the folkloric category of 'origin myths', incidentally shed light on the origins of all dance. Since the creators of these animal myths and dances are the people, an organization of the material around the seasons of life from birth to death suggested itself. Death, the final season, is followed by a survey of four major animal figures in the dance: dog, cat, horse and bird.

An earlier consideration of attitudes towards animals in ancient Greece led to the present work on animal dances. It does not pretend to be an anthropological or historical study of dance, although I am deeply indebted to the many ethnographers, folklorists and dance historians who helped me navigate and dock in so many foreign ports around the world. But in a sense, the anthropologist and dance specialist can add little to the meaning which is conveyed most subtly and directly by the dances themselves. Throughout the book it has been my attempt to let the myths speak for themselves. Except where indicated in the text, these are retold in the author's words.

I would like to thank warmly all those who have contributed in countless unseen ways to this undertaking. I am most grateful to the anthropologist and art historian Dr Werner Muensterberger, and to the dance historian and General Director of the New York City Ballet, Lincoln Kirstein, who invited me to give a series of lectures based on the theme of the book to dancers at his company's official school. The ancient historian and specialist in magic Professor Morton Smith, of Columbia University, kindly offered perspective comments based on his reading of a draft of the manuscript. The staffs of the obvious libraries and museums in London, Washington DC and New York City facilitated research with swift and intelligent service. Within the Research Libraries of the New York Public

Library I would like to single out for thanks Genevieve Oswald, Curator of the Dance Collection, and her staff; Elizabeth Roth, Keeper of Prints; and Robert Rainwater, Print Specialist, for his devoted and unstinting yielding of time.

Herakles wrestling with Proteus, the 'old man of the sea'

Dance (English), *danse* (French), *Tanz* (German), *dands* (Danish), and *dans* (Swiss and Dutch), are probably all related to the Sanskrit *tan*, which means 'stretching', and to the Greek *tenein* ('to stretch') and Latin *teneo*. The word 'dance' therefore carries notion of tension and its opposite, release.

I Prologue: Animal Shapes and Rhythms

'*Dionysos is beguiled even by the dancing herds of beasts . . .*'
PINDAR, fragment 61

Like leprechauns, dancers and 'shape-shifters' in mythology are difficult creatures to tie down. In a state of perpetual motion, these tireless, agile beings hold secrets to the universe which can be extracted only if human guile can trick them to stand still momentarily. Included among such creatures are satyrs and silens, who were envied in ancient Greece for their prophetic gifts. The goat-men were believed to dance in the countryside, along with herds of wild beasts, in honour of the god Dionysos; only under extreme duress would they reveal their wisdom to mortal men. King Midas of Lydia managed to catch a silen by plying him with wine; when asked to tell the true meaning of happiness, the silen replied laconically: 'best of all is not to be born, but once having passed through the gates of birth, next best is to die young.'

The dancing goat-man symbolizes the curious combination of bestial and human movement in animals and dance, which have been intimately connected by the strands of mythology from time immemorial. This can be illustrated by looking beyond animals and men to two dancing gods from East and West with animal attributes. In Greek seas, the shape-shifter Proteus travelled about with the secrets of the deep, as well as with his flocks of seals, for the 'old man of the sea' was a herdsman. Greek heroes like Herakles, sent on difficult missions to far-away places, were advised to ask Proteus for directions. But before he would divulge the desired information, it was necessary to wrestle with the god. This was difficult since, when grasped, the sea-prophet assumed innumerable shapes; lion, boar, snake, leopard, water and tree are mentioned in Homer's account in the *Odyssey* of the struggle between Menelaos and the slippery wrestler. Pollux, a scholar and rhetorician of the second century AD, mentions in the fourth book of the *Onomasticon* the *morphasmos*, described as the 'imitation of all sorts of animals'. According to a contemporary of Pollux, it was a humorous dance in which, as the name (from Greek *morphé*, 'form') implies, the dancer suggested the shapes of various animals one after the other. The legend of Proteus may have been derived from an earlier, imitative animal dance, as Lucian, the author of an early treatise on dance, hints when he says, 'Proteus is nothing but an imitative dancer'. Indeed, mimetic animal dances, from owl-hunting dances, to ritual bear dances, and the burlesque portrayals by choruses of animal dancers in classical comedy, were widespread in ancient Greece and Rome. Proteus, from which the term 'protean' is derived, is the prototype of the shape-shifter who could conjure up, in the words of an Athenian tragic poet, 'as many different figures and manifestations as the sea has waves in the great floods of winter'.

Shiva in Hindu mythology is called Nataraja, the Master of the Dance. Like Proteus and the satyrs, it was hard for Shiva to be caught – even by his wife Parvati, who, in a fit of pique, claimed she could dance as well as he. The gods assembled to judge the contest, in which she carefully imitated Shiva's every step. Finally, however, he lifted his leg higher than feminine modesty would permit, thus preventing her from winning the contest. The *rishis*, or holy sages, also found it impossible to subdue the dancer, whose ascendancy to godhead is related in the *Koyil Puranam*. In the company of Vishnu, disguised as a beautiful woman, the young god went to visit the *rishis* in order to teach them the truths of the universe. But the sages received them with noisy curses and tried to turn them away. When their threats failed to make any effect, the *rishis* unleashed a monstrous tiger forged out of sacrificial fires. But Shiva quickly subdued the big cat, effortlessly removed the animal's pelt with the nail of his little finger and flung it around his neck as a cape. The *rishis* next launched a terrible snake against him, which he threw around his neck like a garland. Then Muyalaka, a dwarf, ugly and black all over, rose up against the god with a club. Shiva merely stepped on the creature's back and began dancing; and as he danced, the gold vault of the heavens opened up, revealing Chidambaram or Tillai, the centre of the universe, and the other gods assembled to watch him set the rhythms of the universe in motion, while the *rishis* threw themselves down at Shiva's feet and adored him. Ever after, this animal-tamer danced with the tiger's cape and snake garland, and he can be seen in many Hindu works of art performing on the back of the dwarf or serpent in this costume.

These same animal attributes, snake and wild cat, were also worn by the maenads, the female counterparts of satyrs; like satyrs, they worshipped Dionysos, who was believed to be incarnate in a variety of animal species, including snake, panther, lion and bull. Clad in panther skins, the maenads hunted down wild animals; entwined with snakes, they ingested the prey's entrails in orgiastic dances, in the belief that by swallowing the god, they became one with him.

Can we catch the divine shape-shifters and dancers from East and West for a moment to extract some meaning from the connection between animals and dance? Dance is a superior type of movement elevated above everyday human existence. It is a magical activity which empowers the dancer to transform human flesh into whatever he chooses: leopard, snake, boar, baboon. Dance, furthermore, embodies a force capable of creating and destroying or, in the animal metaphor, taming. Shiva, for instance, created the universe after subduing tiger, snake and the sub-human dwarf in his dance of splendour. But animals too have unique movements which capture human imagination and inspire imitation. There is something uncanny about the compulsive regularity of animal movement that impresses man. The same fascination with sure, precise, athletic and rhythmic motion that impels the visual artist to capture the animal in action through works of art carries over into dance in choreographic imitations. Animals incorporate certain forces or qualities admired by humans, such as strength, speed, courage, or magical power over evil. These and other animal attributes may be controlled and harnessed through dance. Proteus assumes the fierceness of the lion, the strength of the boar, the slipperiness of the snake, in order to elude his opponent. Shiva's animal emblems, snake and tiger, are tokens of his conquest through dance; worn on his body, the wild animals lend him a more terrible aspect. In addition, animals are vehicles for attaining some end, dance being the prime mover. Snake and panther, for example, bring the dancing maenads closer to achieving union with Dionysos, who is flattered by their exotic prayer, as indeed he is 'beguiled even by the dancing herds of beasts'.

Proteus' ability to transform himself at will is a highly desirable talent for the large class of hallowed shape-shifters, the shamans of tribal societies. In time of need, the shaman, the virtuoso dancer of the tribe, communes through ecstatic dances with his animal familiars in order to grasp the secrets of the tribe's gods. His animal helpers serve as vehicles to transport him to the pinnacle of ecstasy in dance, from which he climbs, in a state of trance, to divine heights; and if the god is himself conceived as an animal, as is so often the case, it behoves the shaman to dance in his animal form.

In any form, what god is not tempted then to dance with his own image portrayed with such compliments as only the sculptor of dance can pay? The icon fascinates, for in its protean complexity it catches, as it turns, the light of myriad fires, warming, while seductively casting a series of cool glances. The danced image is irresistible. Through his ecstatic prayer the dancer himself moves closer to immortality: in dancing the god, he *becomes* him.

In dance man can lose himself, becoming momentarily whatever he wishes; buoyed up as he is above gravity, he is transported, etherealized. Tribal people require very little to attain this blissful, otherworldly state. They brush easily with divinity. A corridor between earth and heaven, mortal and immortal, is maintained by servicing, magically, whatever is patent around them: rocks, roots, leaves, streams, wind, stars, and most commonly animals, which can serve as totems.

If there is some explanation to be offered as to why animals are so widely used to effect metamorphosis in dance, perhaps it is the emotional bond existing between human and animal kingdoms and man's participation in animal nature. Man experiences an extreme degree of familiarity with animals, on the one hand, and hostility towards them, on the other. His earliest relationship was intimately and inescapably bound up with the animal population on which he first depended and later thrived: he has been both master and slave. But never in the long process of differentiating himself from animal species did he slough off his debt to the animal kingdom. Nor could he repudiate his essential biological kinship with other creatures. Man is an animal. Paradoxically, the animal dancer exhibits infinite superiority over the beast while at the same time humbling himself before the animal model, his god. His sense of mime and powers of imagination combine in a complex and seemingly endless array of patterns to serve, honour and reflect the infinite mystery that is the dumb beast. His quest is ultimately a spiritual one for instinctive origins. And if the dance returns the performer to his earliest rhythm, the danced animal image confirms the link to his animal brethren ineradicably residing within him in the form of animal instinct.

The Prehistoric Origins of Animal Dances

The connection between animals and dance, found in myths and folktales, stretches back to the beginnings of human existence. Historically, or rather prehistorically, evidence for the origins of

Palaeolithic masked dancers from the Cavern of Teyjat in France

dance lies literally buried in the bowels of the earth, in the caves dating back to the Stone Age. Like impressionist paintings stored in a bank vault, the colourful murals of the caves at Lascaux, Trois-Frères, or Altamira, among others, have restricted access. Only after winding down tortuous paths, creeping along the ledges of precipices, and scaling rocky surfaces, is the persistent adventurer rewarded with the splendour of the underground galleries, filled with paintings of bison, buffalo, ibex, horses, stags and aurochs painted one on top of the other in vibrant colours. Clearly some emotion stronger than fear motivated Stone Age artists to descend into the womb of the earth to impregnate her with acts of pictorial magic. The animal portraits convey an impression of awe and wonder about the majesty of these stolid beasts. Some paintings show the animals in a free, natural state, while others portray them from the hunter's point of view. Many of the paintings have a target drawn near the animal's heart which is pricked with a barb and streaming with blood. The act of killing starts underground; like putting a curse on an enemy or sticking a voodoo, the artificial wound would help to bring success to the hunter above ground. The overall meaning of the paintings is fairly clear: the multitude of animals represented below the earth reflects early man's anxiety and desire to ensure and control *above ground* the capture, and in turn the replenishment, of game on which he was so dependent.

Pictorial magic worked its effect, as did dancing sorcery. As the painted image was believed to destroy and restore animals, so pantomime provided a plastic facsimile to manipulate the game. There are fragmentary but unique records of the first steps man took in dance in approximately thirty-five representations of shamans found in the cave- and rock-paintings of northern Europe and Africa. Some shamans hold dancing sticks or music bows, and in several instances the dance movements of these early magicians are unmistakable. The dancers are disguised as birds, cattle, reindeer, or a composite of animals, as for example the 'Sorcerer' of Trois-Frères, probably the first prehistoric masked dancer. He is both man and beast: thick and sprawling antlers sprout between stag's ears; two bulbous eyes stare out over a thin nose. A massive beard and mask cover the mouth. At the other end of his body, the bushy tail of a horse sways above a feline phallus hanging backwards through muscular thighs. The front paws dangle in mid-air like those of a kangaroo, and the hind, human legs shift steps in a style, as the Abbé Breuil suggested, reminiscent of the cakewalk dance. In a freak survival in the cave of Tuc d'Audoubert are fifty fossilized heel-prints of a youth no more than fifteen years old imprinted onto a clay surface before a recess containing a model of copulating bison. The unusual position of the foot suggests that the youth was imitating in a dance the movements of the hoofed animal.

Much of prehistory is dance history, and much of dance history is prehistory. The sure conclusions that can be drawn about either are few; but it is probable that the close, almost symbiotic bond between man and animal was forged in early dance imitations of animals. The mystical dances of shamans and shape-shifters before the animals were flattering and seductive, like Orpheus' music; through dance the shaman felt out the vibrations of the animal world, and hovering above the beasts, discovered their precise rhythm, brushed against them and conversed, then seduced, harnessed and controlled their power. These curious flirtations between animals and dancers dressed as animals have persisted universally from the Stone Age to modern times. In certain areas the continuity of rituals from Palaeolithic times is striking. Jean Laude, in *The Arts of Black Africa*, cites paintings recently found in Algeria by Gérard Bailloud and others which prove the antiquity

Rock picture found in Aouanrhet, Algeria. The heads of dancers and hunters were represented in this epoch by circular discs; the figure on the left has stylized flowers sprouting from arms and legs and wears a severely abstract mask

of rituals including initiation, agricultural and mortuary rites, still practised with masks by the migratory populations.

In the human cycle, the connection between animals and dance begins in childhood. To the child, it is obvious, the imitation of animals comes as second nature. The following free adaptation of the 'Dancers' myth of the Onandaga Indians of North America illustrates how readily the very young amuse themselves by mirroring their environment in dance, here to their peril. A tribe was compelled to seek new hunting-grounds in a wild, distant territory, near Bear Lake. Busy with setting up their camp, they had little time for their children.

The children were growing lonesome, and to amuse themselves they went to a clearing in the forest where they made up dances about the deer and fish, the squirrels, the bluejay and the bear. They were especially fond of imitating the great birds which soar high in the sky, the eagle, hawk and falcon. They loved their dances and nothing could stop them.

One day a frail old man approached their dancing-ground. He was dressed in white feathers and his hair shone like silver. If his appearance frightened them, his words haunted them as well. For he said, 'Stop your dancing, or evil will come to you.' Then he disappeared. But little did the children heed the old man's warning, and they continued to take turns imitating the animals. The next day the man reappeared and repeated his warning, and the next day, and the next. The children danced on merrily.

Soon the children forgot about the old man. One day a little boy suggested that they have some food when they next met to dance. All the children agreed to ask their parents for a contribution to the little feast. But the parents didn't like this idea at all. One said, 'If you want to eat, you will have to stay home like everybody else.' Another parent said sternly, 'This is nonsense. You will waste good food. I will give you nothing.' The children gathered the next day the same as before, but they were disappointed. A little to eat after each dance would have made them very happy.

On a certain day the children were all in a circle dancing like birds. Their heads were growing light with hunger, and as they danced they rose little by little into the air. One of them said, 'Do not look back, for something strange is happening!' An old woman at the camp dropped her work as she saw them rising like smoke and called them back, to no avail. They kept circling slowly above the lake, beyond the beeches and the pines, up into the open sky. The woman alerted the parents of the children. When they saw what was happening they rushed into the lodges and brought out food in great quantities. Holding it outstretched in their arms, they piteously begged the children to return. But they would not and in fact could not return.

One child did look back and fell through the sky like a falling star. The others reached the sky, and are now a constellation. Each falling star recalls the story to the tribe, and they see in the ever-twinkling stars a merry band of dancing children.*

In this haunting tale, the children of Bear Lake, neglected and restless, try to make themselves feel important and at home in their unfamiliar environment. Instinctively, they turn to dancing among themselves. But their games come to have an intoxicating effect. Disregarding the words of the old man, the children flirt with danger until finally, their heads swimming with hunger, the band of children are beckoned by an invisible Pied Piper to join in the eternal, cosmic dance. Although at first punished for their little animal dances, they are later rewarded and immortalized by their dance that defies gravity. Significantly, it is imitation of animals which first inspires their movements.

Aristotle, in the fourth book of the *Poetics*, states that imitation is natural to man from childhood; that he learns at first by mimesis; and that no one can fail to be pleased by watching imitations of various phenomena. Australian Aboriginal parents make the most of the principles of imitation to teach their children the lore of the tribe. Whereas the children of Bear Lake danced in direct imitation of the animals, Aboriginal children are taught to dance like animals by mimicking an instructor. Like Proteus, the teacher is a versatile imitator of animals, capable of gliding from one role to the next. For the children, the animal characters take on a much greater significance than the animals in human situations of children's books and cartoons. The Aboriginals believe that in 'Dreamtime' the animals created the physical features of the world, the hills, rock, trees, lakes and sea. In their dances and songs the children learn to pay homage to these landscape architects and guardians at natural shrines where the animals are believed to reside in spirit. The children's dances, reported by W. Lloyd Warner and discussed in the next chapter, prepare children for the time when they undergo ceremonies appropriate to the various phases of initiation.

*The constellation, called Ootkwatah by the Onandaga, is the Pleiades. Greek lyric poets lengthened the name to Peleiades, meaning 'doves', referring to the birds which seem to flee before the hunter Orion. The lyric poet Alcman in his 'Partheneion' compares a band of dancing maidens to these winged stars.

Do Animals Dance?

In the case of both Palaeolithic man and the children of Bear Lake, it was taken for granted that some correspondence between the movement of animals and the systematic choreography of dance existed. Most would reject this assumption, calling it a projection of a strictly human activity onto animals: how could animals be said to dance in our sense of the word? People are nevertheless aware that animals communicate without words. Movements, smells and inarticulate sounds suffice for staking out territory and food, and for mating. For example, it has recently been discovered that certain male spiders meet the challenge of mating, without being accidentally eaten by the female, by attaching to her web a 'mating' thread which the male twangs and drums, thereby transmitting unmistakable courtship vibrations. Indeed, some animals receive messages from distant quarters. To cite another example, scientists now believe that baby turtles receive the 'celestial imprint', the pattern of the night-time sky, as soon as they are hatched. This programs turtles with information that will allow them, years later, to come back to their place of origin and lay eggs. Honey-bees scout for available pollen, then return to the hive, where they communicate the precise direction and distance of the hunting-ground to the gatherers. The Viennese scientist responsible for this discovery, Karl von Frisch, described their system of communication in *The Dance of the Bees* as a tactile sort of circle dance. Direction, measured in relation to the position of the sun on the horizon, is described in the 'dance' by the number of circles completed. Distance is described by the speed at which the bee dances: the further the pollen source, the faster the bee must dance. The gatherers absorb this information by encircling the scout who, in dancing, brushes against them.

But do animals express anything more than vital information in their rhythmic movements? The psychologist Wolfgang Köhler reported that the anthropoid apes in his laboratory in Tenerife performed round dances with gay abandon; and in the forest, apes have been observed 'dancing' and shouting in defiance of thunderstorms. They reportedly have a penchant for costume as well and entwine themselves with vines and twigs.

Animals fiercely compete for a mate in dance-like movements. A male adder will shield its mate against the approaches of other males in a fight that looks very much like a martial dance. With heads raised and swaying above the ground, the two opponents throw a series of coils around the other, in an effort to constrict it. The encounter may last for several minutes, during which the partners draw back now and again to rear their bodies. Birds are especially given to selecting a suitable partner in dances. In Australia, the bower birds, discussed below in 'Courtship and Mating Dances', construct areas for mating display called by the Aboriginals 'dance huts'. Long-necked cranes pair off to mate in a ritual closely resembling an erotic dance: the male takes the lead, enticing the female by advancing and rubbing his wings rhythmically against her body. The rite is imitated with moving realism by pairs of marriageable girls in the Watusi Crane Dance. The stilt birds have the most impressive and ordered mating behaviour. They appear to dance in the manner of a quadrille: scores at a time line up in antithetic rows, advance, bow to one another, withdraw, exchange partners, and repeat the sequence, until pairs locked in embrace withdraw to mate. These and other rituals not only serve to perpetuate the species, but also demonstrate, in their stately and elaborate attention to arrangement, the same passion for order found in the choreography of folk dances, such as the square dance.

The instances of such marked and consistent dance patterns are admittedly rare, but the question of whether animals do or do not dance should not be rejected out of hand as anthropocentric projection. Such projection is the explanation for quite a different sort of animal dance, those of bears and monkeys which are trained, often by a cruel human hand, to entertain at fairs or in the circus. But the circus animal's dance amuses precisely because its movements are human, and therefore unnatural. In conclusion it can be said that the configuration and rhythmic regularity found in the behaviour of certain animal species do correspond closely to our notion of an ordered choreography. Yet, however graceful or structured its movements are, the dancing animal is severely restricted by comparison with man, who can impose a seemingly infinite array of rhythmic patterns and shapes on his dances. Man is the supreme dancer.

Animal Origin Myths for Dance

The imaginative mind of tribal peoples attributes magical powers to animals' capacity for non-verbal communication. Animals, they believe, are capable of influencing weather, the growth of crops, or even the will of the supernaturals. If man can succeed in imitating the animal's gesture language in dance, he too may acquire the power of persuasion and access to privileged information.

Whether animals do or do not dance, tribes believe they do, some to the extent that they invent myths telling how they learned to dance from animals. Among ancient and tribal peoples, the need to order and to explain how things got to be, and why we do what we do, has prompted ingenious and – from a narrative point of view – charming explanations in myths. This holds true for dance; and myths about the animal origins of human dance are the most frequent explanation. The Iowa Indians said that they acquired dance by spying on the forest dances of turtles; and the Dogon of Mali to this day practise a kind of dance divination based on the primeval dance of Yurugu the fox, who, in revealing to man the future of the world, provided the model for all subsequent Dogon dances. The concluding pair of myths in this chapter, the wagtail's dance drum and the spider's dance, furnish additional examples from African folklore.

The following myth may serve to demonstrate the type of explanation offered, as well as the interpretation, application and realization of the myth in dance drama.

According to the beliefs of a tribal society in Nigeria, a tortoise demolished the world in a dance of destruction. This dance is the kernel of the foundation myth of the *ekine* masquerade society of the Kalabari and forms the core of their Tortoise Masquerade, studied by the anthropologist Robin Horton. Ikaki, called the 'old man of the forest', was a supernatural tortoise living behind the ancient village of Olomo. He rarely allowed himself to be seen, but now and again would appear at the edge of the forest to dance, and whenever he did, the people of the village gathered to watch. They took great pleasure in his dance and pestered him to come back again and again. Each time, the tortoise warned the people in a little song not to touch him. 'Remember my words. Don't any of you touch me. Chief Tortoise, Chief Grey Hair.' Heedless of the warning, the people persisted in calling Ikaki back, until one day he appeared with a fancier dance than ever. As he danced, he sang, 'Amegage. Human meat, yum, yum. Amegage. Human bones, yum, yum.' In his dance he lifted his right legs, and all the people living to the east died; as he lifted his left legs all the people living to the west died. Then Ikaki crept back into the forest and was never seen again.

Later, the few survivors left on earth banded together; deeply impressed by the tortoise's dancing, they thought to imitate it. But they feared what might happen when it came to the lifting of the leg: surely this would cause additional deaths. So they consulted the great oracle of Chuku which advised them to make certain changes and to observe certain rules; and if they did these things, all would be well. Mindful of the oracle's instructions, the people started performing the Tortoise Masquerade in the village of Olomo; and it continued there until the town was later destroyed by war. The tradition was kept alive, however, by the people of Kula, who had seen the play. Then the Ikaki play spread to towns like New Calabar.

Today, at Buguma, one of the daughter settlements of New Calabar, the Tortoise Masquerade is preserved by the *ekine* society, whose members are known as *Sekiapu*, 'Dancing People'. The masquerade takes place in July during the dry season when the people need to be 'cooled down'. The performance consists of a series of farcical episodes interspersed with dances, of which the first is the original, destructive dance. This is a solo dance performed by a man wearing a tortoise mask, not over his face, but on top of his head, in the Kalabari fashion. His dance is accompanied by the Master of the Drums, who strikes up the rhythm known as 'Ikaki Ada'. The fatal lifting of the legs mentioned in the myth takes on a burlesque note later in the play when the onlookers tease the old man about the size of the calabash between his legs. The appendage represents an unfortunate malady, elephantiasis of the scrotum, which afflicts sorcerers and other evil people. The encumbrance, however, does not keep Ikaki from dancing; in fact he ends up by lifting his robe, removing the testicles, and dangling them before the women, who feign horror! The play ends with an elephant-hunting pantomime in which the tortoise conquers the lord of the forest.

The brilliant balletic spectacle that has grown out of the myth of Ikaki's dance of destruction is a social metaphor for the importance of dominating negative, asocial impulses. The Kalabari mock the tortoise out of fear of what he represents – the sociopath who preys on society. Like trickster figures in the folklore of other cultures, the reptile is greedy, lewd and amoral: he pushes his actions beyond the normal limits of society. He is the reverse image of laudable human conduct. But the 'old man of the forest' is also cunning and capable, and powerful, like his dance. One may ask why the lumbering tortoise is chosen instead of an animal known for its man-eating violence, such as the leopard. In many cultures the tortoise and sea-turtle are creatures suspected of deceit, in part

because of the mysteries concealed in the shell. Throughout West Africa the tortoise is greatly feared for its powers of witchcraft, which can be infinitely more destructive than physical violence.

Near Nigeria, in the Ivory Coast, the Baule tell another type of animal myth, recorded by Hans Himmelheber, which accounts for the origins of dance masks, the single most important element of disguise in animal dances. One day an old man was wandering in the thick forest near his village. With him he carried his gun, in case there might be game to shoot at. He wandered for a long time but saw no animals at all until he came to a clearing; beyond the clearing was a lake, one of the many lakes in the forest. Through the trees he witnessed a most remarkable sight. For along the shore of the lake the water animals had all gathered to dance. The spectacle amazed the old man, who stole from tree to tree to get a closer look without being seen. When he neared the dancing-ground he studied their every movement and memorized them. Then the man took out his gun and shot at the animals, who fled back into the water. But in their haste and terror the masks which they were wearing fell to the ground. The tribesman walked up to the shore and gathered up the masks, which he placed in his backpack. When he returned to his village he told the people what remarkable things he had seen. Without giving them time to ask questions, he distributed the dance masks one by one and taught his people the dance of the water animals.

The Baule myth is an example of a standard folkloric motif about the origins and acquisition of masked dance. The motif is found in North American as well as in West African folklore. It includes a wandering tribesman, and his total surprise at seeing dance for the first time, particularly as performed by animals. He becomes jealous of their activity and steals the masks and dances for his own people.

Nowadays Baule masks are carved from wood. Animal masks are usually circular in shape with prominent features like horns added to the 'face'. Masks of human faces are stylized by rounded foreheads, semicircular eyebrows, slit noses, and small, open mouths; sometimes these human features are combined with animal attributes. A mask may, for example, be surmounted by bull horns or a pair of birds facing one another. The divinity who protects the village is Goli, embodied in a round mask representing a stylized water buffalo. His attendants are Gouli and Pondo. They move about in a crouching posture, covered with skirts of pine-apple fibre and antelope hide, and mock people's weaknesses.

The benefits of disguise for the animal shape-shifter are obvious. Since he wants to use the animal's power or magic, the best way is to become the animal, and the mask is the most convincing means of transforming identities. Whoever puts on a mask obscures the most telling part of the body and assumes the identity of the mask. This amounts to an act of deception: to the spectator, the performer is recognizable only as the object represented through the mask. This is crucial for the effectiveness of the dance charm: if the wearer is recognized, the spell is broken. The spell is worked through the dancer's masks, the receptacle for the spirit. When the dancer sets the mask in motion on top of his body, the spirit is drawn into the mask, which also acts like a lightning rod to insulate the dancer against an overload of supernatural energy. Once it enters, the dancer achieves his goal: he becomes possessed by the spiritual power.

A mask is itself like a spiritual being with a life-cycle of its own. Careful prescriptions govern the choice of material and the manufacture of these sacred objects. Masks, for example, may be made only at appointed times of the year. But there is more freedom in choice of materials, including shells, beads, noodles, grass, twigs, pebbles, metals, rocks, acorns, corn husks, jade, stone, clay, horn, feathers, etc. Usually only the male members of a tribe make masks; the women and children are prohibited from seeing them, on pain of death, until the ritual performance. Once produced, the mask may have to undergo an 'incubation' period. Balinese masks live in jars; and the Dogon store their masks in the back room of the chief's house, where they are fed on daily blood sacrifices of chickens and other animals. After performance the mask may have to be burned or ceremonially buried: the life-cycle of the mask culminates in the dance where it enjoys a brief apotheosis.

To the Westerner, dance masks are known mainly as stationary objects on display in ethnographic museums. In this orphaned state the mask fails to reflect the full scope and intensity of its former life. What a haunting or hilarious object the mask becomes in motion! The grotesque features, the disregard for proportion between wearer and mask, and the cumbersomeness of this extra head baggage are striking. Dogon dancers, for example, wear certain masks that tower some thirty feet into the air. The Bobo, who have plays with an interesting variety of animal masks, make a butterfly mask that is whirled, like a huge propeller, to activate a rain charm; and their dancers tickle the clouds with their tall masks, to make the sky weep with laughter.

Bushman painting from Medekane

Movement itself is a form of disguise, and an animal dancer may require no costume whatsoever to evoke a portrayal. In animal mimicry, a special type of pantomime practised by hunting tribes, a high premium is placed on the accuracy of movements, and, where masks are lacking, of facial gestures. The performers are critically judged, sometimes in contests, by the verisimilitude of their imitation in relation to the animal model. The Bushmen of South Africa practise animal mimicry to an uncanny degree of accuracy, as do the Javara of Upper Volta. A Javara dancer can perfectly reproduce the behaviour and antics of the stork, crocodile and antelope, to name a few in his repertoire. From South America along the Amazon, K. T. Preuss has provided an entertaining account of the animal pantomimes and accompanying lyrics performed by the Bororo the night before they set out on a hunt. In North America, as well, Blacks on southern plantations performed animal mimicry. Their repertoire included the Buzzard's Lope, the Turkey Trot, Snake Hip, and Pigeon Wing. Not all animal mimes bear a resemblance to their animal counterparts. Some come to have a metaphorical meaning, and the dance gesture is only vaguely reminiscent of the animal's movement. This is especially true of many animal dances of the Indians of North America, where the animal elements are retained in stylized steps and partial disguises, such as feathered head-dresses. Here the meaning of the dance depends upon a shared understanding of the tradition.

Aniela Jaffé, in *Symbolism in the Visual Arts*, states that 'dancing was originally nothing more than a completion of the animal disguise by the appropriate movements and gestures'. Conversely, the origin of costume can be linked to animal dances, where the addition of horns, fur, feathers, monkey hair and so forth increases the similarity of the dancer to his model. These and other animal parts may be worn by animal dancers; cowrie shells, trinkets, anklets, branches, twigs, vegetable fibres, and all manner of organic materials also fill out the disguise. In some tribes the entire body of the dancer must be covered from head to foot in order to protect him from the adverse effects of magic conjured up during the ritual. In Upper Volta, tradition dictated that every dancer of the Bobo must be covered from head to toe with Karite leaves; all the villagers lined up at dawn to pick the leaves for the costumes. In the Hornbill Dance of Zaire, which emphasizes the separation of the sexes, the male participants distinguish their territory (the forest) from the women's (huts in the village) by clothing their entire bodies with leaves, vines, twigs, and hides of forest animals – all this in addition to the striking mask of the hornbill, a species which immures the female in a tree when she is about to give birth. (See below, Chapter XII) In masquerade the coincidence of male dancers disguised as women and animals is frequent enough to make one speculate that both are regarded as the original source of fertility magic, which the males steal and appropriate for their use in exclusive rituals.

Rhythm-makers: Animals and Dance in the Tribal Life-cycle

If mime, disguise and gesture are the primary accessories of the animal dance, rhythm, in common with all types of dance, is its underlying essence. Rhythms make up the code through which signals among man, animals and divine masters are transmitted. Regular movements, of course, are to be found everywhere. The heavenly bodies whirl inexhaustibly until one, like the ascending child in Bear Lake who looked back, loses balance and becomes a falling star; in our solar system, the nine planets perform a dance around the sun – a circle dance, the oldest known configuration. It is shown in a Stone Age cave-painting, where eight maidens dance around a youth while an aurochs and another four-legged animal look on. Orbiting around the sun, our own planet sets in motion the wheel of seasons, known in the Renaissance as the 'Dance of the Hours'. Everywhere in nature, eternal movement arrests the human eye: the lapping of the sea against the shore, the dartings of a lizard's tongue in quest of a fly, the flapping of a hummingbird's wings, the wagging of a dog's tail, the pawing of a cat, the rush of a brook, and even the currents of the winds, made visible by the trees. Man by nature is a rhythmic being. He walks, breathes and sings rhythmically; his heart beats, an internal drum. At the centre of the universe, man embodies its rhythms. He is the time-keeper, the inventor of the drum.

1　The Greek heroes Menelaos and Herakles pinned down creatures of land and sea to extract secret information. On the inside of an Attic black-figure Kylix cup (Greek, mid-6th century BC), Herakles wrestles with Triton while the Nereids encircle them in a dance. Like Proteus, Triton is a sea-god capable of assuming slippery shapes to elude his opponent.

2　Satyrs perform an acrobatic dance. Endowed with attributes of the goat, satyrs were thought to enhance fertility in the natural world through erotic dances. The harvesting and trampling of grapes by satyrs was, like dancing, a scene frequently portrayed on wine vessels of the Classical period. Psykter by Douris, *c.* 490–480 BC.

3 *Above left*, dancer with wings, on a Corinthian aryballos, *c*. 590–580 BC. Such figures were to appear in the choruses of plays like Aristophanes' *Birds*.

4 *Above right*, a hybrid from Greek mythology related to the satyr is the centaur, portrayed here with the ears of a goat, its upper limbs those of a man, and its lower those of a horse. The centaur was both bellicose and benign. Interior of a red-figure cup signed by Phintias, *c*. 510 BC.

5, 6 The creative and destructive powers of the dance are embodied in Shiva, Master of the Dance. *Below*, Shiva's twilight dance; Chamba painting, late 18th century. *Right*, Indian bronze, 13th century AD.

7–11 Pictorial magic is conveyed by the Stone Age artists in their rock paintings of bison at Lascaux, in France. The stark magnificence of these beasts suggests the awe in which they were held. Communication with the animal spirits was a function of the shaman, the magical healer. *Opposite below*, ecstatic dance of shaman with animal spirit in a Turkish 15th-century illuminated manuscript. *Above*, the Sorcerer of Trois-Frères, after Breuil; the dancing shaman is disguised as a composite animal. *Above right*, Siberian shaman dancing. *Right*, shaman of the Tlingit, Alaska, as owl-man; the owl is the natural guardian of the shaman.

12–16 The mask, known to Westerners mainly as a stationary museum artifact, has a life of its own. In motion it can be hilarious or haunting; the mask attains its apotheosis in dance. *Left*, Igbirra tribesman from Nigeria carving a wooden mask. *Below left*, North American Indian bird/bear dancer. *Below right*, sawfish dancer from the Torres Straits. After use some masks are ceremonially burned or buried; some are stored in sacred enclosures. *Opposite*, mask house in New Ireland, Melanesia. *Opposite below*, Tyi Wara dancers of the Bambara from Mali.

Stone age cave painting at Cogul in Spain

Rhythms communicate, affect emotions and bodies, earthly and heavenly, and infect. Like infectious laughter rhythms spread; like a disease they are communicable. They get under the skin. Animals and men catch rhythms from one another, so says an African myth illustrating the inescapable ties between humans and animals. As the Abron of the Ivory Coast tell it, in a myth collected by Alexander Alland, Jr, a woman's dance infects a spider, who returns the disease to man.

One day a spider was wandering through the forest and heard a woman singing. Attracted by the beauty of her song, the spider approached and addressed the woman, who, as the spider made out, was also dancing. 'What a wonderful voice you have,' he said to the woman. 'Would that I could sing and dance like you.'

'Do you really?' asked the woman. 'Well, then gladly will I teach you. But you must do as I do and sing my song.'

She continued dancing and singing. The spider did as the woman did and sang her song. And as the spider danced and sang, sores that covered the woman's body began to heal, and soon the spider found its body covered with them. When the woman's sores were completely healed, she stopped dancing and singing. But the spider could not, since it was in great pain. The woman returned to her home and the spider went on its way, dancing and crying out in

< Baboon dancer of the Bambara tribe of Mali.

pain. Soon it came to a village. When the villagers heard the
spider's song, they came out to greet it.

'How beautiful your song is, spider!' they said. And then one of
the women said, 'Indeed, and how well he dances.' The villagers all
agreed. 'We would love to sing and dance like you,' said another,
and again the villagers nodded their heads. The spider saw its
chance. 'I will teach you, then,' said the spider to the assembled
villagers. 'You must listen carefully to my song and imitate my
dance.' The people watched and listened very carefully as the
spider performed. After a time one member of the village caught
the hang of it and started dancing and singing. Another joined in,
and then another, until finally, the whole village was dancing. But
the spider stopped dancing and singing because as the people
danced, the sores on its body gradually healed and disappeared,
and reappeared on the legs and arms of the people. Once the spider
was completely free of its sores, it turned to the band of dancing
villagers. 'Thank you,' it said, and disappeared into the forest.

The myth implies that the transmission of song and dance is
more than simple mimicry; these activities are shared, like a cold.
We speak of a 'catchy' tune, or 'contagious rhythms'; and folk-
medicine advises those who wish to get rid of a tune on the brain to
sing it aloud until someone else contracts it. Dance rhythms also
are contagious. As dance defies gravity, its rhythms surpass
boundaries human and animal. They can seduce, magnetize and
mesmerize the unsuspecting. A curious historical parallel to the
Abron myth is the tarantella, the Italian spider dance. The purpose
of the tarantella was to cure tarantism, an epidemic dancing mania
prevalent from the fifteenth century to the seventeenth and long
supposed to be caused by the bite of the tarantula. To purge the body
of the poison, it was thought necessary to dance recklessly and
demonically for hours on end, to the clack of castanets and the
shimmy of tambourines. Intended as a cure for the afflicted, the
tarantella resulted in infecting the spectators with a desire to join the
dance. According to some reports, nonagenarians threw away their
canes to participate in the delirium.

The Abron myth entitled 'How Man Got Sores' similarly
accounts for the origins of disease as well as for the origins of song
and dance. But at least along with sores, man acquired the uplifting
experience of dancing, through which he may, incidentally, com-
pensate for pain and loss. This mixture of pleasure and pain is
surely preferable to the dilemma presented in an animal myth from
nearby Zaire about a tribe whose creator forgot to invent the drum,

leaving the people with no means of expressing their joys and sorrows in dance. In the Kongo-Fiote myth recorded by R. E. Dennett and entitled 'Nchonzo Nkila's Dance Drum', the wagtail represents man.

Nzambi Mpunga was a proud and powerful princess, and what was more, she had created the world and all the people in it. But poor Nzambi forgot to make a drum for her people, so they could not dance. Nchonzo Nkila, a certain little bird with a long tail that always thumped against the ground when he walked, lived in a small village near where Nzambi had established her court. This bird set about to make the first drum, and he laboured day and night until it was finished. When Nzambi heard the sound of the drum she was indignant. 'What?' she said to her people, 'I, a great princess, cannot dance because I forgot to make a drum, while this little wagtail dances on into the night? Go now, antelope, and tell wagtail that the Mother of All Things wants his drum.'

The antelope lost no time in going to the village; and when he found the wagtail he said, 'Lend it to me, that I may dance.'

'Of course,' said the wagtail.

The antelope took the drum and beat on it several times. But instead of dancing, he ran off with the bird's prized possession. Wagtail lost his temper and ordered his people to pursue the antelope. They killed him, cooked him, and made a meal of him.

The people at the court were wondering what could be taking antelope so long. Kivunga, the hyena, was sent to the village. When he learned what had happened to the antelope, he rushed back and told everything to Nzambi, who fell to weeping piteously. Now she would send Mpacasa, the wild ox, on a mission to retrieve the drum. But the ox suffered the same fate as the antelope. Nzambi was inconsolable. She cried out to her people in the midst of her tears, 'Can no one help me get the drum?'

Finally an ant came forth saying, 'Grieve not, Nzambi. I will fetch the drum for you.'

'And how will you do that?' asked Nzambi incredulously. 'You are so small.'

'That is precisely why I alone can do it,' the ant answered.

So the ant went to the village and waited until all the people were asleep. And when they were all in bed and snoring loudly, the ant carried away the drum without a single soul seeing him. Nzambi was seized by a fit of rapture when she saw the drum. She ordered all her people to assemble and led them in a great dance while she beat upon the drum.

When Nkila heard the sound of the drum he awoke and looked about for it; but it was not to be found. So Nkila called a meeting of all the birds to decide how to resolve the dispute. They would go to the town of Neamlau, a great prince who would act as judge. They sent a messenger to summon Nzambi, who promised to be there.

Two days they waited, and on the third Nzambi arrived with a train of counsellors. The various people took their places before Neamlau and his council of elders. Nkila was the first to speak. 'O Prince! I made the drum and now Nzambi Mpunga has taken it away from me, for which reason, let her now speak.'

Nzambi replied, 'O Prince! My people wished to dance, but we had no drum, therefore we could not. But since ant brought back the drum we could dance, and we are very happy. O Prince! Surely I, who am the Creator of All Things, have the right to the drum.'

Neamlau and his council of elders retired to drink water.

When they returned Neamlau said, 'You ask me to judge, and my judgment is this. It is true that Nzambi is the Mother of All Things, but Nkila did make the drum. When Nzambi made us, she left us to live as we chose, and she did not give us drums at our birth. We make our drums for our dances. Although we all belong to Nzambi the drums are not hers, since she did not give them to us at our birth. Therefore Nzambi has no right to the drum.'

As the myth shows, the drum was invented by the wagtail for the use of the people and not the princess. Throughout Black Africa, as in Indonesia where the sound of the gamelan is so prevalent, the pre-eminence of rhythm is felt. The drumbeat is the heartbeat of the tribe. Dance and the drum herald life's important events – the birth of a child, the coming of age and marriage of a youth, the outbreak of war, the death of a warrior or elder. From village to village the drums serve as a telegraph system to announce market days, for example, or the arrival of an itinerant band of actors. In many West African tribes the subtle beats of 'talking drums' are a poetic language expressed by the hands of the bard. Without a drum there is no poetry, no drama, no dance.

Zoomorphic drums are common in traditional Africa. The wooden drums from the Ubangi Valley are shaped like cattle; and a stylized cow's body serves for the slit-drum of the Yangere in the Republic of Central Africa. A conical cylinder drum from the Baga of Guinea sits in the saddle of a horse; in a frieze around the body of the drum birds dance in antithetical pairs. Special drums imitate the sounds of animals. The friction-drum produces a boom resembling the roar of a wild animal and has acquired the name 'leopard-drum'. In the belief that a woodpecker's insistent rattling calls the rain, woodpecker rain charms are played on the hollow wooden drums which accompany rain dances. Clearly a fundamental link between the rhythm of man and animals is expressed through the dance drum, in Africa as elsewhere.

Dance is a rhythmic activity which marks the cycles of a man's life, from beginning to end: his birth, his coming-of-age, and the various stages of entrance into adult life and the world beyond. The first stage is often a hunt accompanied by a 'preparation' dance in which the young hunter imitates his prey; proof of ability to provide for the tribe permits the young hunter to marry and practise the art of the warrior. War and wedding dances alike are part of his repertoire. For women, mating and fertility dances are important for increasing the population of the tribe and, by extension, the crops and flocks. An individual continues to dance throughout his lifetime – as long as he is physically able. But in many cases when an elder can no longer perform his tribe's dances, he dies socially. Death, the final season, is also marked by dancing. The living honour the dead in funeral rites; in their dances, the mourners infuse the dead with their energy, conveying them to the world beyond. The ceremonies at which dances are performed are cyclical, timed to the wheel of seasons, the migratory and repro-ductive activities of game. Rituals for hunting, capturing, planting, reaping, mating, and so on, are in turn seasonal, and all are accentuated by the metronome of dancing feet. In all types of dance rituals, animals play an important role. Through the rhythms of animals and dance, man controls and is mesmerized by the natural and supernatural world. He is both master and slave.

One is left with the question posed by King Midas to the first animal dancer encountered, the satyr. What indeed is the meaning of happiness? One may pose another question which brings the cloven-hooved goat-man closer to the animal dance in the Christian tradition of the Middle Ages. For can one not see in the satyr a direct line of descent from Satan? Like the satyr, the Devil is a rakishly handsome man with at least one cloven hoof, a long tail, horns or goat's ears. Both are master musicians – the satyr plays the lyre or pipes, the Devil the violin. Both scamper in dance-like movements of the goat, performing caprioles. In theatrical embodiment Satan and the satyr again coincide. The Devil, dressed in a furry skin, not unlike the satyrs, performed wild antics, pantomimes and dances akin to those enacted by the chorus in the Greek satyr play. The dramatic effect was one and the same: as Silenus and the satyrs mocked the

statuesque hero of the satyr play, so Satan and his minions, the
vices, tempted and tripped up the main characters such as Adam
and Eve through mimes and dances in Christian miracle plays.
Like the Roman *stultus* or *stupidus*, himself cousin to the cloven-
hooved satyr, the Devil was essentially a dancing clown. Owing to
injunctions against dancing laid down by the Church Fathers from
St Augustine onwards, the Devil alone was allowed to be portrayed
dancing; but this only served to gain the performer of bawdy
dances and capers increased popularity.

The split between Satan and satyr ultimately lies in the interpretation placed on the performer's cloven hoof. In the eyes of the
Christian church, the Devil's hoof was a deformation and an
abomination, a confirmation of his powers of evil, death and
destruction. The cloven hoof of the satyr, on the other hand, merely
underscored his link with the natural world and animal fertility.
In this respect Satan and satyr stand diametrically opposed. The
satyr, like the Roman faun and the medieval Wild Man, enhanced
the natural world through his sexual omnipotence. Happily he
enlivened and fertilized the community at large with his erotic
energies, whereas the Devil was associated with the destroyer, the
Grim Reaper. The satyr symbolizes Eros, Satan, Thanatos. That the
Devil alone was allowed to be portrayed dancing can be explained by
the Church's rejection of the erotic element that is the undercurrent
of all dance. Ultimately this attitude would divorce dance from
religious expression in the West, recalling the myth in which the
Creator forgot to make the dance drum.

In retrospect, the satyr's laconic and pessimistic response to King
Midas is a reminder that earth-bound mortals are severed from the
land of the blessed engaged in eternal dance. Escape from earthly
tasks and mortal burdens can come through dance. Throughout the
present survey the overriding question will be: What are the roles of
animals and dance in human expression in the widest sense, to
include personal, social, mythical and religious experience?

*Silvanus and a goat
engage in winter-
versus-spring contest
in symbolic dance
terms. Wall painting
at Herculaneum after
engraving from
Piroli's* Antiquities
(1804–5)

II The Waters of Birth: Fish and Snake

Dance to your daddy,
  My little laddie,
Dance to your daddy,
  My little lamb;
You shall have a fishy
  in a little dishy
You shall have a fishy
  When the boat comes in.

Dandling song, England

When the child in your womb
Already leaps and bounds,
Let not your look stop,
Young mother,
Let not your look stop
On the trailing tortoise

Song of the pygmies of the Gabon forest

The lyrics of the English dandling song, with its charming promise of a 'fishy', call to mind the familiar sight of the parents bouncing the child on their knee, which serves here as the youngster's imaginary boat, or, more often, as the saddle for the 'rocking-horse jig'. Although an infant lacks co-ordination to dance on his own, strong, insistent rhythms excite him. So the mother lifts the baby high in her arms for a dizzying and exhilarating fling, singing, 'dance little baby, dance up high,/Never mind baby, mother is by;' or she rocks her child to sleep to the slow waltz rhythms of the lullaby. These vicarious dances of infancy are clearly one of our earliest experiences, and we return instinctively to them whenever we dance.

The song of the pygmies of the Gabon forest warns the mother with child to avoid the tortoise when she is about to give birth, since it can bring bad luck. And she knows well when this time is coming because the child inside her is already dancing in leaps and bounds. Dance, then, begins in the pre-natal state, according to the beliefs of the pygmies, who dance spontaneously on every occasion from human birth to the burial of elephants. When a child is born the father dances to the sound of the tom-tom to herald his off-spring's birth, while members of his family sing and clap in a circle around him. Once she has given birth, the mother joins in with the tribal dances. Papoose-style, she carries the baby on her back, and already the dance education of the child has begun.

Aboriginal drawing of Yurlunggur the snake as a huge womb with children. After Meerloo, Dance Craze and Sacred Dance *(1962)*

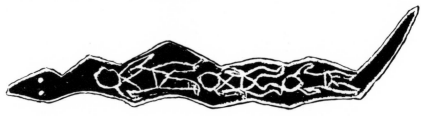

The pygmies of Gabon are not alone in thinking that dance originates in the womb. The Dogon of Mali in West Africa, the New Irelanders in the South Pacific, the Australian Aboriginals, and certain tribes in Tanzania are among the numerous peoples who share a belief in pre-natal dance, expressed in the recurring symbols of hairless, smooth-skinned creatures. Fish and snakes – creatures known for their swimming motions – represent the foetus in dance motion in dance, myths and art. Like the unborn child, fish and snakes are unarticulated, mysterious beings, who live in dark and inaccessible areas. The watery haunts of fish are associated with the amniotic fluid in which the foetus floats; and the cavities of both snake and fish serve as symbols for the child-bearing womb.

Fish dances represent dramatically the beginnings of life in many parts of the world. For the Dogon, the fish is a symbol of the human foetus; once every sixty years Dogon dancers dressed as fish enact the regeneration of mankind in the great Sigui festival. In New Ireland human birth is simulated through a shark-hunting pantomime which ends with a magical transfiguration. The rite reflects the content of the following myth by which the origin of dance is accounted for.

One day all the fish and sea-creatures assembled at the edge of the sea. The catfish danced with the crocodile, the turtle danced with the dolphin, and the squid danced with the eel. All the sea-creatures were proud and eager to display their talents, since it was they who had invented the dance. But the birds who gathered in the bush to watch the dances were not at all pleased. In fact they were extremely jealous of the sea-creatures and tried to break in on them. But the crocodile would not think of yielding his dancing partner, the catfish, to the sea-hawk, nor the turtle his partner the dolphin, to the cassowary. Finally, in exasperation, the birds flew off to the bush where they snatched up their spears in their crooked talons. When they were fully armed they returned to the shore and drove the sea-creatures back into the water. Then the birds, imitating the fish, began dancing. Much later, the people learned to dance from the birds who had stolen dance from the sea-creatures.

In New Ireland the virtuoso dancer is called simply the 'finest thing in the world'. Many myths and dances express gratitude to the dancing birds from whom the islanders derive the mainstay of their art and ritual. It is clear that they identify themselves with the exotic birds living around them, many species of which eat sea-creatures. Tribes name themselves after species of birds which serve as totem animals; and like the spear-carrying birds of the myth, they hunt at sea with spears for fish, an important staple in their diet.

But the indigenous tribes of New Ireland also recognize their own aquatic origins. They believe that men hunting at sea once fell overboard and were transformed into the sharks and other marine animals. In the shark-hunting pantomime, the virtuoso of the tribe plays the role of a hunter, and four other dancers play the parts of sharks. The hunter supports on his head a huge mask made from sea-weed and grass and wears a tight-fitting red shirt over his body.

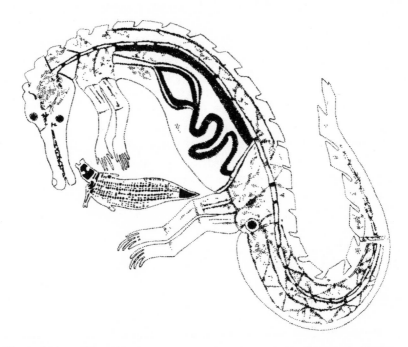

The catfish/crocodile motif appears in various Oceanic myths. Aboriginal bark painting

In his left hand he carries a net which he manoeuvres about, as if lowering it into the water to catch a shark. The four shark dancers imitate the animal, keeping a cool lookout, listening carefully, paddling through the water, twitching, and at rest. Suddenly the lead shark grows suspicious, and becomes especially attentive. The other sharks rally to his side and encircle the fisherman in his 'boat'. He goes through the motions of enticing the shark to swim into a rope noose, pulling the net over the head, and finally spearing the shark. The hunter returns with his prize; the lead shark dancer then lies down flat on the ground. Next, a most remarkable act of transformational magic takes place. The hunter casts his net in wide arcs over the spectators, letting it rest on the head of the shark. The dancer strokes and tickles the shark with the fingers and palm of his hand – on the belly, chest and shoulders – until gradually the shark comes back to life. His limbs twitch, and the joints twitch; then you see under the dancer's costume the big toe wriggling, and then the elbow, the knees, and so forth, until finally the shark sits upright. The hunter strokes him on his back along the spinal cord and the dancer hurls off his costume and rises – not as a shark but as a man reborn! The dance drama of death, transfiguration and rebirth is complete.

The shark-hunting dance has a more or less practical purpose of reassuring hunters that when they kill a shark, they will not be punished by the spirit of the shark, which was, after all, formerly a man. But of greater interest is the symbolic meaning of the ritual. The impact of the dance can be understood by returning to beliefs expressed in the myth of origin for dance. There the sea-creatures crawled to shore for their dance performance; and the ability to dance passed from fish, to birds, and at last to mankind. Taken together, the myth and dance affirm a belief in the gradual evolution of man from the sea, the mother of all things. A similar belief was expressed in the dance origin myth of the Baule, where the water animals left their natural habitat to dance on land; and, it will be recalled, the water animals were likewise driven back to the water once the tribesmen had appropriated their dances. Dance in these myths, it would seem, is a metaphor for life, and for the evolution of higher beings from sea-life – a belief, incidentally, that parallels what is known from a scientific point of view about the earliest land-creatures which gradually crept to life on land from the sea. Here mythical intuition has seized upon a scientific truth. Dance is life, and the transmission of dance is a symbol for the evolution of all animate beings from the sea, the waters of birth.

Birth of the Garuda. Drawing after Meerloo, from a sculpture in Tibet

Although the dance of the snake is not so obviously related to
birth as is that of the fish, the snake as a symbol of birth is
nevertheless ancient and widespread. Indian sculptors often
depicted the birth of Buddha from the Cosmic Serpent; Shiva
dancing the world into being is shown festooned with his serpent
garland. A Tibetan sculpture of the birth of the Garuda represents
the bird-god magically killing a snake at his birth. And Herakles'
labours really began in the crib when he was forced to wrestle with
snakes sent by hateful Hera at his birth.

Birth might be characterized as a convulsive dance which liberates
the wriggling child from the mother. The Dogon specifically
connect the movement of the snake with the rhythmic vaginal
spasms of childbirth. According to Dogon belief, the serpent
Nummo regenerated itself by swallowing the skull of the first
serpent ancestor. From within its womb, the Nummo then spewed
forth the skull in a vomiting gesture which represents the contractions
of labour. In recounting the tale of this magical self-regeneration,
Dogon story-tellers elaborately compare it to a dance. For it is the
Nummo, they believe, who in turn taught people to dance – in
other words, to reproduce mankind.

The meaning of an Australian Aboriginal snake initiation dance can be understood in the light of a Murngin myth from Arnhem Land called 'The Wawilak Sisters and the Yurlunggur Snake'. At the beginning of the world the Wawilak Sisters set off on foot towards the sea, naming places, animals and plants as they went. Before their departure both had had incestuous relations with men of their own moiety. One of them was pregnant and the other already had a child. After the birth of the younger sister's child, the two continued their journey until they came to a water-hole where the great snake Yurlunggur lived. The elder sister polluted the water with menstrual blood. This enraged the python. Yurlunggur emerged and caused a deluge of rain and a world-wide flood; then he swallowed the women and their children. And when the snake raised himself the waters covered the entire earth and its vegetation; but when he lay down again the great flood receded.

The tale of the great python's anger has inspired propitiatory rites throughout Aboriginal Australia, reported by W. Lloyd Warner. To appease Yurlunggur, young novices in the Gunabibi ceremony are first offered to the great snake and later reborn. The initiates, all male, are led to a secret place; the women are told that their sons have been swallowed by the python in order to avoid total destruction by flooding. The youths remain thus in seclusion for several months until they are transferred to a trench representing the snake's body; it is also believed to contain the Wawilak Sisters and their children inside. Here the initiates are covered with bark and told to sleep. The rite culminates in showing the women the rebirth of the novices. To bring this about, a group of men dance around two cylindrical representations of the python. Meanwhile, the women are lying down near by covered with mats. At a given signal two men begin crying like a new-born baby; the women are now allowed to sit up as they watch the 'twice-born' youths emerge from the snake's body. The men continue dancing with the movement of a snake around the initiates until the serpentine spell completely restores them to life.

The Gunabibi and other related ceremonies include cycles of dances which teach children about the mating and reproductive activities of totem animals. First the male of the species is danced, then the female, and finally their offspring. A snake, for example, catches a mate, and then their children, the issue of their reproductive activities, join in; the lizard, pigeon, honey-bee, turtle, and all the animals follow in turn. Afterwards, all animals represented in mating dances gather with two water snakes in a well, repre-

senting the hole defiled by the blood of the Wawilak Sisters, and
dance. Meanwhile, outside the well a female snake moves about
and lays eggs. At the sight of this, many other snakes are drawn to
one another; they copulate and lay eggs in the well. In the course of
the dancing the eggs are broken and children of the snakes emerge.
The children watching the ceremony are told that the totemic snake
is 'the same as man'.

Snake-handling ceremonies and dances involving live snakes
occur in all parts of the world, most frequently in the context of
initiation cults. The meaning of these rituals naturally varies from
people to people, and in many instances their significance is
obscure, even among the participants. The snake as a symbol of
birth, however, suggests that the rites recall in a tangible way the
trauma of birth. Initiation ceremonies have as their chief goal
testing the courage of the candidate; in a snake-handling ritual the
ability to handle or dance among dangerous snakes thus proves the
novice's ability to overcome any fear, including the most fundamental birth trauma.

The image of the snake lies dormant in the many serpentine
dance rounds which imitate the continuous coiling and uncoiling of
the snake. Performed in chains, these are group dances of sometimes impressive numbers; in Nyassa up to four hundred men and
boys took hold of one another and danced rapidly with snake movements until they sank to the ground in one exhausted heap. In most
cultures the meandering configuration in dance has taken on a
metaphorical or symbolic significance (especially in relation to the
mystery of the labyrinth), but its ultimate origin in the animal
dance is not entirely lost: serpentine rounds tend to be performed
in the context of fertility ceremonies where the snake as the life-
giving phallic symbol so naturally belongs. The sixteenth-century
Spanish priest and pioneer ethnologist Sahagún describes an Aztec
fertility dance to charm the corn goddess as 'one single big snake';
and in the course of the ceremony the goddess herself is called
'Seven Snake'. But dances such as this are better left to be
discussed below under fertility dances, where animals coax the
earth and her servants to bear.

Dances in the Lives of Children

An African folktale collected by Leo Frobenius, entitled 'The
Night Escapade of the Flute Player', tells of a young boy who is

*Two members of the disciplinary Dukduk
secret society from New Britain, Melanesia.*

forced to accompany the forest animals' dances on his flute, which
was a present from his father. When asked what profession he
would follow, the boy replied that he would like to play the flute,
and the father, who was a kindly farmer, brought home on the
following day a flute for the lad. One day the boy left the flute in the
forest where he had been practising. When he discovered the flute
missing, he insisted on retrieving it, though it was nearly dark.
Disregarding his father's warning to wait until morning, he set out.
The moon was shining brightly, and when he reached the spot
where he had left the flute, he could see the forest animals gathered
round. One animal after the other was trying to make the flute
sound, but none succeeded. The animals noticed the boy near by.
The Elephant said, 'Come here, lad! Is this not your flute? Show us
how it is played!' The frightened boy took the flute and began
playing. Then the Elephant said to him, 'We all wish to dance!'
And he instructed the Ape to stand next to the boy so that he could
not escape.

As the boy played the flute, all the animals began to dance. They
danced harder and harder, until they were all exhausted. Then the
Ape spoke, saying, 'Now play for me! I want to dance a little too.'
The Ape danced. And after the other animals had caught their
breath they came back for more dancing. The Leopard started
dancing away, and so did the rest of the animals, including the
Ape, who did not keep watch as he had been told. When they were
all lost in a whirl of movement, the boy ran home to the farm as fast
as his legs would carry him.

For children, dance can be a constant and irrepressible means of self-
expression, a release of excess energy, and an escape into the world of
make-believe. The children of Bear Lake turned to dance as an
impromptu form of recreation while their parents were busy. Their

dances were spontaneous and natural, in the sense that they responded to the movements of the animals in their new, natural environment. The imitative talents of a child, perhaps his most effective way of coping with the world during his formative years, lend themselves perfectly to dance, allowing him to become whatever he wishes – a crow, bear, witch, scarecrow, boar, waterfall, or devil. Dance is an exuberant form of play, and an integral part of games, such as 'Cat and Mouse', 'Wolf and Geese', or 'Bunny in the Ditch' – games which reproduce the predator's pursuit of its prey in the animal world. Clearly, the imitation of animals in games and dances comes as second nature to children.

But dance can also be dangerous and overwhelming for children, as the folktales and myths point out. Children are impressionable and easily led astray by seductive rhythms, like the children who follow the Pied Piper of Hamelin into the mountain pass. Dance can easily get out of hand. The children of Bear Lake discovered this when they disregarded the old man's warnings. In the 'Night Escapade of the Flute Player', the unrestrained and demanding dances of the forest animals leave the little flautist feeling helplessly trapped: the folktale in fact reads as if it were a child's nightmare.

In traditional societies, parents use the animal dance as a means of punishing and correcting behaviour through fright. Masks naturally add to the effect. The masks, called discipline masks, are common in China, Africa, the South Seas and North America; although usually intended to align the behaviour of youngsters, the mask can be used to police adult conduct as well. For instance the Dukduk, a secret society in New Britain, is famous for its five-foot monster masks which appear every month to judge and punish all offenders. For children, masks representing frightening animals are used to create a lasting impression; threatening elements of the animal's anatomy, such as the eyes of an owl, the sharp beak of the hawk, or the horns of a bull are emphasized; sometimes the features are combined into a hybrid or monster. To impersonate the ogre, the parents or a specifically designated member of the tribe dress up. The masked dancers either single out those children whose behaviour needs adjustment or inspire terror in the lot of them. The most mischievous are snatched up by the dancing apparitions, who flog the children on the spot; or more effectively, the child is taken away and punished in an unknown locale as a lesson to the remaining children.

Children seven to eight years old were kidnapped during the Shaman's Dance of the Nootka Indians of the North-west Pacific Coast. The adults impersonated supernatural creatures of frightening aspect: wolf, bear and Wild Man. These ancestral spirits swooped down into the audience, abducted specially selected children and hied them away to their ancestral homes. There they were punished and then instructed about hereditary privileges: the ceremonies ultimately had the purpose of transferring rights of heredity from parents to children. In a typical scene from the Shaman's Dance the spirits tracked down the children. Some represented supernatural bears, others the Wild Man of the Forest. When these creatures descended among the children in the audience, the adults feigned great terror, and at the height of the confusion the designated children were swept off to distant quarters.

'Parachicos', literally meaning 'for children', is a kind of horse dance practised in Mexico during the fiesta of Chiapa de Corzo in Chiapas. Older members of the tribe put on terrifying masks with animal attributes and mount on horseback. They seek out the naughty children, who see the masked, hoodless rider gesticulate ominously at them. To the frightened child, the rider-horse pair seem to be a single haunting apparition.

In New Mexico, children of the Hopi are initiated into the mysteries of the Kachina cult by adults impersonating the Crow Mother, who has a sharp beak for a nose, and her two warrior sons – called Hu – with bulls' horns and tails. The indoctrination is part of a children's initiation ceremony, not to be confused with puberty initiation rites. Kachinas, as works of religious art, are dolls carved from cottonwood, painted, dressed and ornamented; as the names 'Crow Mother', 'Screech Owl', or 'Butterfly' Kachina indicate, the dolls are often animal spirits. Hopi men dress themselves to mirror the Kachinas and impersonate their spirits in dance. Sometimes called the common denominator of Hopi religion, the Kachina cult comprises an extended family of supernaturals embodying the spirits of living things, as well as of ancestors. Individual Kachinas are responsible for specific functions such as bringing the clouds and rain, distributing food, receiving prayers, providing entertainment, or enforcing order and discipline.

Once a year during the Powamu or 'Bean Dance' festival, Hopi parents tell children of a certain age that the Kachinas are not actual spirits but rather men of the village who take on a spiritual identity, as we tell our children that Santa Claus is really just the man down the road wearing a red suit. But for the Hopi children the indoctrination takes on a ritual form in a purification dance which involves whipping. The Hu Kachinas, resembling great buffalo bulls, carry in their hands sharp whips which are made from the blade of the yucca plant.

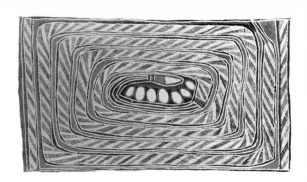

18–20 Animal dances of birth may re-enact aspects of creation myths or they may take the form of transformation dances whereby the performer, disguised as a creature symbolic of birth, such as the snake or fish, emerges as a human being.
Left, Aboriginal bark painting depicting man with traditional birth symbols: fish, turtle and snake.
Above, the great rainbow snake, lying at the bottom of the water-hole, as described in the myth of 'The Wawilak Sisters and the Yurlunggur Snake'. *Below*, Herakles wrestling with the snakes sent by Hera at his birth.

21–24 Ghosts, bogeymen and the Devil have all been invoked by parents to instil discipline in unmanageable children. The dancing animal as monster is especially effective. Sometimes, too, fearful masquerades are performed for the improvement of parents themselves. The animal may also serve as guardian or as a model for the child's learning of its tribe's dances. *Opposite (above)*, Aboriginal children being taught to imitate the brolga bird; *(below)* Sri Lankan devil dancers exorcising evil spirits. *Above*, a Western relic of the flagellation dance seen in this Austrian treatment of the St Nicholas legend. *Right*, witch dancer having snatched the dead child in the Balinese Tjalonarang dance drama.

25 In ancient and traditional cultures the turtle and tortoise are ambivalently admired and feared for the unknown secrets locked in their shells. Cutting open the turtle, as performed by these Torres Straits islanders, is one way of defusing the mysterious power.

26 Young Aboriginals in mimetic animal dance as part of initiation rite. 19th-century watercolour.

27, 30 Aboriginal Red Kangaroo initiation dance ceremony. *Below left*, initiates lie on mound from which kangaroo totem will emerge. *Below right*, kangaroo totem which represents for the initiated the penis of the ancestral kangaroo, but for the uninitiated the tail.

28, 29 The mystery of the bull-roarer being unfolded to Aboriginal initiates. Up to this point they had believed the sound emitted by the bull-roarer to be that of animal spirits. *Below*, Aboriginal kangaroo dancers.

31 Among the Australian Aboriginals, corroborees were originally held during the rutting season as marriage ceremonies in which pairs of animals were imitated in the dance. Now, when performed, they have become a more general display of virtuosic dance talents.

32, 33 *Below left*, girls of the Watusi, Zaire, perform an imitative crane dance in anticipation of courtship. *Below right*, in the dance of the cranes the male advances, covers the female with his wing, retreats, and then repeats the action.

34 *The Hour of the Cow Dust*, a late 18th-century Indian painting. In ancient India, indeed as in certain rural areas today, the cow and bull participated in courtship and marriage rituals. If the boy can wrestle the bull and dance on its back, he is worthy to protect his wife; the girl's tending of the animal shows that she can take care of a husband.

35 A bride in her ceremonial attire attended on her marriage day by birds. Indian painting from the Agra district.

36 Part of the long Aboriginal funerary process includes a dance before the animal totem of the deceased who is thereby united with his animal origins. **37** *Below left*, funeral dance of the Awa mask society of the Dogon of Mali, as prefigured in their mythology by the destructive dance of Yurugu the Fox. **38** *Below right*, the interchangeability of life and death is emphasized in the Swaihwe mask of the Salish of the North-west Pacific coast. The dancer performs at critical times such as following the birth of a child or a death.

The mighty pair dance around each child candidate four times, cracking their whips in the air, and leaping high to make their deadly snake rattles sound around their ankles. At the end of the fourth turn, the Kachinas hustle the initiate into an enclosed area containing a sand-painting. Next to the painting stands the ominous Crow Mother, Amgwusnasomtaka of the sharp beak. In her hands she holds more yucca whips, two of which she gives to the Hu Kachinas, with the order to beat the child. The child is held and repeatedly whipped until the blade is worn, whereupon the Crow Mother supplies her sons with fresh whips. Once the child has been sufficiently beaten, Crow Mother submits herself to the same treatment. Afterwards she explains the meaning of the sand-painting. The mystery of the Kachina having been unveiled, the child takes comfort with Ongchomo Kachina, who sympathizes with the children. From this time onwards Hopi boys and girls must learn the spiritual significance of the Kachinas through drawings, carvings and, for males, participation in the dances. A male Hopi is ordinarily eligible to dance a Kachina some time in his tenth year.

Flagellation dances occur in many parts of the non-Western world. The practice survives in the West in the legend of St Nicholas, who is said to beat wicked and greedy children with his staff. New Ireland, in the South Seas, has its own Santa Claus figure. An old man wearing a mask combining bird, fish and other animal attributes runs from house to house yelling and shaking rods which represent snakes. He squats, jumps up and dances and then squats again. The parents push their children towards him as he squats so that they may be touched by the old man's lucky charms; the parents allow themselves, not their children, to be beaten by him, in the belief that it makes them stronger parents.

Dance, in addition to its punitive value, plays a positive educational role in the lives of children. The function of animal dances in the sex education of Australian Aboriginal children was discussed above. There the very young learn about other aspects of life in animal dances by mimicking a dancing instructor. A dance song collected by A. Elkin, entitled 'How the Children Learn', describes the setting and content of the lessons. The songs resemble Aesop's fables in their use of animals and in their moralizing tone, but in Australia the children act out the content of the tale as well. The song names the dance master 'Badjeru'. The children's eyes light up when he begins telling the tale of the bird and the fish, or the turtle and the wily porcupine. As he recounts the stories he dances out each animal's part.

The lesson is indelibly imprinted on the children by its night-time setting around a fire. Dance stick in hand, Badjeru calls the children to attention in the outdoor classroom. In the background loom the shadows of trees, and the waves lap against the nearby shore. The captive audience of children, all lined up on a bench of driftwood, rise and mimic Badjeru as he tells the tale of bird, fish and tree, who were punished like people for their sin. Next Badjeru recounts the story of how the porcupine got its quills and why turtles live underwater. Turtle and Porcupine were at one time brothers. But Turtle and his cronies took up spears and ganged up against Porcupine. Now Porcupine, wearing his barbed coat of arms, limps feebly on the earth, while Turtle's people are con-demned to live underwater. When mimicking the turtle the children lie prone on the ground; to represent the porcupine they move their bodies in a slow zigzag movement. The Aboriginal dance song shows that children are taught the activity of dance through imitations of animals – animals which will become important in their future lives as species to be hunted, and as totems to be danced in the Intichiuma increase ceremonies. The animal dance is a means of transmitting tribal lore and, incident-ally, ethics. The fable and dance of Porcupine and Turtle has a simple moral: thou shalt not kill.

Children, because of their greater vulnerability to spirits, must be protected. Their souls are not yet completely formed and therefore fall easy prey to spirit possession. Dances to ward off the kidnappers – evil charms, diseases, sores, warts, demons and devils – are widespread. In the American West, for example, parents from the Luiseño tribes had their children dance in imitation of animals known for their protective powers. A child thereby acquired a personal animal guardian.

In Bali, parents fear that their children will be consumed by demons called leyaks. Like the Greek monster Lamia, leyaks have a perverse penchant for the flesh of young children. So real is the fear of a child being devoured that Balinese parents give their young disagreeable names to keep leyaks away. Leyaks, it is believed, were originally human beings who have the power to transform themselves into animals – snakes, pigs, wild boars, horses, monkeys, or tigers – in order to bring evil to people. Leyaks are present everywhere, in a crooked smile, in the way a dog's tail hangs weirdly, in the gait of a chicken crossing the road or in an upside-down image in the eye. At night leyaks lurk about the graveyard. But the graveyard is the centre from which all magic is worked in Bali, as elsewhere. The two major Balinese witch dramas, the Barong and the Tjalonarang, are staged in or near the village graveyard. It is here that the witches' masks are displayed and recharged with magical powers.

Tjalonarang is a favourite Balinese dance drama performed at times of illness, especially when children are sick. The plot of one such drama, recorded by Beryl de Zoete, is concerned with the semi-historical events in the life of King Erlangga who became the greatest king in Java in the eleventh century AD.

Tjalonarang lived in a village with her only daughter, Ratna Menggali, the most beautiful girl in the land. But no man dared marry her because her mother practised witchcraft of an evil sort. This angered Tjalonarang, who made repeated offerings to Durga, wife of Shiva, who finally allowed Tjalonarang to destroy the land. The next day pestilence broke out, and the people suspected that it must be the doing of the witch since she could be seen dancing furiously and non-stop at the cross-roads. King Erlangga sent many soldiers to her house, but vicious flames darted from her nostrils and burned them up. That night Tjalonarang gathered her disciples in the graveyard and proclaimed, 'Beat the drum, and let us dance one by one.' First Gujang danced, then Gandi. Then Larong danced. Her movements were like those of a tiger crouching before the spring, and her eyes gleamed red and huge. Woksira danced naked, except for the hair which hung down on either side. Mahisavadana danced with her legs close together, clutching at the air with her fingers as if they were birds' claws.

The pestilence spread, and people who fled along the road were pursued by leyaks. King Erlangga consulted the magician, Mpu Bharadah. The magician decided to have his son marry Tjalonarang's daughter and find the secret of her mother's magic. The son duly married the daughter and waited until the mother was out of the house. When he asked his bride the source of the mother's evil, Ratna Menggali pointed to a book kept in a box. But she said that he must not read it. While Ratna Menggali was busy tending to the tasks of the house the magician's son opened the box, took out the book and read it, learning it by heart as he went along. He hurried home and related to his father the content of the book.

The magician went around the village, cured the sick and raised children from the dead.

Durga appeared to Tjalonarang and warned her that her end was near. Then her disciples informed her of Bharadah's arrival. The magician, standing outside her house, called to the witch, 'Your only salvation is death.' The witch ran out of the house and stood near the magician. 'Is my sin so great? Free me, holy man. Have pity on me.' But when she saw that Bharadah was not moved she threatened to kill the saintly man. She began to dance, her hair hanging loose and her eyes ogling. As she danced she said, 'I will kill you, Bharadah, even as I now kill this child.' And with a single glance the child was burned to ashes. Bharadah said 'You can destroy, but can you bring to life again?' She tried in vain. But Bharadah effortlessly brought the child back to life. Then the saint said, 'Even so you shall inflict no evil on me.' From the jaws of the witch fire escaped, and from the eyes, ears and nostrils. Flames leapt at the body of the saint, but he was inviolable. Then the magician destroyed the witch by a spell. At the last moment Tjalonarang made peace and was shown the route to heaven.

The performance of the Tjalonarang dance drama takes place at night near the village graveyard. In the centre of the performance area stands a tree, representing the cross-roads at which Tjalonarang and her disciples danced their dances of destruction one by one. When Tjalonarang arrives on the scene her disciples, called the Sisias, are already engaged in an eerie orgiastic dance. Tjalonarang reproaches them for not wreaking more havoc in the land. The Sisias remove the white turbans covering their heads to reveal their animal manifestations. They have become leyaks. In this new guise they go out to destroy the land utterly.

The next scene shows the results of their activities. A man enters in consternation, claiming that he has seen leyaks. He is followed by his old pregnant wife and a servant. A witch-doctor is summoned, but a leyak, wearing a mask with tusks and a great horse's mane, steals up behind the pregnant woman. In her fright the woman gives birth to a stillborn child. Leyaks more mischievous than before snatch away the corpse and quarrel over it. This scene never fails to amuse the audience, who roll on the ground and laugh in high-pitched tones. The parents feign terror, as they snatch children to safety from greedy leyaks in the nick of time. Sometimes a small naked boy accompanies a leyak. With his face whitened and wearing a tail, the child goes about pinching victims in the audience at random and with wild abandon.

III   The Ovens of Youth: Initiation and Puberty Dances

In Polynesia among the Tikopia the expression 'ovens of youth' refers to initiation ceremonies of the young. The kindling of the ovens, called *punauma*, takes place after a boy has completed his first torchlit fishing expedition in a canoe at the age of ten. Upon his return the parents prepare and present him with vast quantities of food cooked in large ovens. Before the feast, the initiate is fed knowledge about the history and codes of conduct of the tribe, about their dances, and about sexual matters. He also undergoes a super-incision operation (cutting the upper foreskin only). Together these experiences constitute the kindling of the ovens, and to say 'his ovens have been kindled' means that a boy has successfully completed the initiation ritual. The last phase of the ritual is the feast itself. The eating of food prepared in the large ovens confirms that the initiate has mastered the ingredients that go into the recipe for adulthood. Symbolically, the food gives him sustenance to meet the increased demands of his new life. In addition to eating rituals, dances frequently accompany the final stages of initiation, at that time when the novice is accepted back into the tribe as an adult member. Both activities confer energy on the initiate when he most needs it. The tribes of Andaman Islanders, as will be seen below, combine eating and dance rituals in their Turtle initiation ceremony to reward and fortify a successful candidate.

Prior to being taken back into the tribe the initiate will be separated from his people, sometimes for a year or more. He learns to fend for himself in the wilderness during this time, much like an animal. Initiates will often be disguised as wild animals and take on their habits, eating roots and plants, or tracking down voracious predators. Their very survival may depend on their success in carving out an independent existence in the forest. Towards the end of the period of seclusion the candidates will be terrorized. Now it is the older tribesmen who assume the guise of a frightening animal or spirit, making themselves completely unrecognizable by dance masks used only in secret rites. Like animals travelling in a pack they

chase the initiates to dark, confined areas or specially constructed huts. From within, the initiate hears the noise of feet padding ominously to the chanting sounds of the bull-roarer, which imitates the cry of the animal spirit. The bull-roarer is a flat, oval slab of bone, stone, or wood, tapered towards the end, with a slit to allow the air to pass through. When swung, it makes a low, moaning noise like an anguished bull. Against this backdrop 'ghost stories' are told. In the South Pacific, novices of the Bibinga are told that the bull-roarer is really the voice of Katajaline, a spirit who lives in an anthill, and who eats boys. In parts of New Guinea, the bull-roarer is said to be a monster who swallows boys and vomits them up. Once they feel that the boys have been amply terrified, the men allow them to emerge. They show the dance masks and bull-roarers up close, explaining that these are not spirits and ghosts after all. Once privy to this information, the boys will themselves be permitted to wear the masks, and together with the men stand at the edge of the forest and terrorize the women in the village, who are forbidden to see masks except on such occasions.

*Bullroarer
from West
Kimberley in
Australia*

The fresh responsibilities and obligations that fall on new adult members of a tribe, as they shift from a posture of dependence to independence, are intense. They become the providers, and as such are expected to marry and raise children in order to ensure the continuity of the tribe. They must also learn to provide for the material well-being by sharing in the tasks of agriculture and hunting. Male members are obliged to transfer skills of the hunt to warfare when it becomes necessary to defend the village. In the metaphor of dance, this new degree of independence means establishing one's own rhythms, and, conversely, allowing the tribe's rhythms to shift the candidate's shape.

Becoming a member of the tribe also means acquiring traditional lore and tribal customs. An initiate is expected to have a thorough acquaintance with rhythmic codes and gestures and how tribes dance to get what they need. Initiation ceremonies too are sexual rites coinciding with the onset of puberty. Learning the codes of a tribe means knowing about love-making. The phrase 'birds and bees' takes on an almost literal meaning in copulation dances where older members act out the sexual intercourse of animals' dances, as is commonly done among the Aboriginals of Australia and the Bushmen. The girls' Gemsbok Dance of the Kalahari Bushmen provides an interesting example. When a group of girls has reached menarche, a puberty initiation dance is organized. The most honoured and sexually potent Bushman is chosen to lead the dance.

He wears on his head a pair of horns, those of an eland, a large variety of antelope. The girls undergoing the rites have their faces painted white with the markings of the gemsbok, a smaller variety of antelope. To seduce the girl, the man dressed as the bull eland hides in the bushes until a chorus of singing and clapping women announces the arrival of the first candidate. The women dance admiringly around the girl, and in turns show off their buttocks. The bull at this point emerges from the bushes and breaks in on the circle. He stomps up to the girl, butts his horns against her body, and lifts up his robe to display his genitals. At the completion of the ceremony the girls are considered marriageable.

In Australia imitative dances of totem animals are performed for novices at initiation rituals just prior to the circumcision ceremony. The dances instruct them about the sacred history of the animal ancestors in Alcheringa, or 'Dreamtime': their wanderings, creations, reproductive activities, and their role in establishing the litany of rites. In one tribe, for example, three dances are displayed before the initiate. The Red Kangaroo Dance is performed because it is believed that the Red Kangaroo circumcised youths in Alcheringa; the Hawk Dance, because the Hawk-man was responsible for reinstating circumcision after the custom had fallen into disuse; the Bat Dance, because the Bat-men had instructed the people about the finer points in the ritual procedures. Initiation ceremonies among the Aborigines are often extremely painful ordeals: teeth are knocked out, fingernails ripped off, and blood drawn from wounds inflicted all over the body. But by identifying with the animal who has authorized these actions, the older men are capable of executing what otherwise they could not; the initiators disguise themselves as the totem animals, and the shifting of identities enables them to repress feelings of guilt about their violent treatment of the novices. According to their lore the animal's precedent justifies, in fact dictates, their actions.

Novices learn through dances how to hunt animals and also how to replenish the supply of game and totem animals. Imitative kangaroo dances are especially interesting because of the mystery of the ceremony on the one hand, and their explicit sexual nature on the other. The kangaroo is a species of prime economic and ritual importance to the Aboriginal. Because of the seriousness attached to kangaroo ceremonies, few outsiders had actually witnessed a kangaroo dance until T. G. H. Strehlow, son of the collector and compiler of Aboriginal songs, saw a performance in 1933 at Alice Springs. The ceremony, called Utnitjija, was a variation of the

Intichiuma increase ceremony, and several novices were on hand. As a preparatory gesture, the initiated kangaroo 'totemites' tracked down the locale of the kangaroo ancestor, whose outward form was visible in a rock promontory. Here it was believed that the ancestor came to a final rest. Close to the rock an artist from the tribe traced the outlines of the kangaroo on the ground. This was supposed to attract the spirits of other kangaroo ancestors residing nearby. Blood drawn from the totemites was used to fill in the shallow depression or 'soak', which represented the vagina. This hole was ultimately designed to receive the ceremonial *para*, a conical-shaped hood worn on the head of the kangaroo actors. The initiated knew that the *para* symbolized the penis of the ancestral kangaroo, but the non-totemites still had it backwards, since they were told that it represented the tail of the kangaroo!

The chief of the kangaroo clan, Ekuntjarinja, performed the first in a series of imitative kangaroo dances. With his back to the ground-painting the chief lay down to impersonate the ancestor Krantjirinja. The head was cradled in the crook of his arm, and he gave the impression of having slept the sleep of death for several centuries. He was recognizable by the red *para* on his head and two long white strips of bird down. It was night, and out of the stillness came a slow, steady throb, as from a huge heart, as the oldest member of the clan smote the earth resolutely with a red-ochred shield. From the still form signs of life became perceptible. The head lolled from side to side, and little by little he raised it up from the crook of the arm, then let it sink back to its pillow. He shook himself gently to stir the blood, and with great effort turned over on to the other side to face the ground-drawing. He placed both hands flat on the ground and dragged his body forward. In a squatting position he imitated the action of the kangaroo grazing, but in slow-motion, as if he were barely aware of being awake. After several minutes of slow and measured movement he reached the ground-painting, oblivious to all but himself. He approached the soak, knelt down and placed his hands on either side of it, and bent his head down until his chin grazed the edge of the hole. He withdrew a little, fell on his side, and assumed his original sleeping position.

For the next fifteen days the initiated, and then the uninitiated, repeated the slow awakening dance; afterwards the performer would sneeze into the soak. The onlooking totemites stripped off the white feathers from the body of the dancer and placed them down the soak. After the last initiate had impersonated the kangaroo ancestor the totemites took the *para* and knelt down behind one another in a close file. They passed the *para* between their legs until each man had handled it. In single file they advanced on their knees and thrust the *para* into the soak as the culminating act to the symbolic insemination of the kangaroo ancestors.

Initiates are expected to attain certain moral, intellectual and spiritual qualities. Among the Senufo of the Ivory Coast, the buffalo is the symbol of intellectual and physical perfection. Adolescents undergo a period of apprenticeship with a creature known as Nasolo, who represents the buffalo. The *kagba* phase of the initiation ritual takes place in a sacred grove. Two dancers don a light wooden frame similar to that of a hobby-horse. At the front of the frame is attached a wooden head combining attributes of the crocodile and antelope. The body of the hulking beast, which is as much as fifteen feet long, is woven from grass and painted with geometric patterns. Below hangs a fringe. At the rear end is a stylized tail of plaited raffia. It appears at first sight that Nasolo wanders aimlessly, but in fact he moves with great precision from area to area in the grove under the guidance of an interpreter, Kodalu, who presents him to the initiates. Nasolo does not speak the language of humans but roars like a lion aided by an instrument blown by one of the dancers inside.

The initiation ceremonies examined thus far have concerned exclusively either boys or girls. In the tribes of the Andaman Islanders, a pygmy-like race inhabiting the Andaman Archipelago in the Bay of Bengali, youths of both sexes undergo the same turtle-initiation ceremony. The Andamanese, in fact, make no pronounced distinction between male and female, as reflected in their mythology which is free of compensatory or tendentious reference to women. These remarkable people, studied by the Cambridge anthropologist Radcliffe-Brown, have preserved their Stone Age ways intact into the twentieth century. The social life of the Andamanese is rudimentary. They hunt and fish for their food and cook it. But there is no organized government, except a loose tribal structure where the older men and women regulate daily affairs. Groups of forty to fifty Andamanese live in eight to ten open-fronted huts placed about the dance area, the focus of their habitation. After daily chores these people dance. The women keep rhythm, slapping their thighs, while the men dance around the fire. Often they dance until dawn appears, in the belief that their dance magically restores the daylight, as the myth below will demonstrate.

Andamanese mythology reflects a concern about the adverse powers of natural forces, especially excessive rains and cyclones which occur during the monsoon. The chief mythological character is the north-west monsoon, a spider named Biliku. Biliku is female and married to Tarai, the milder south-west monsoon. The ancestors of the Andamanese were a group of animal ancestors descended from Biliku. Later they became distinguishable from man by the discovery of fire, which burned and left markings on some of the animal ancestors. Sea animals were created, according to an Andamanese myth recounted by Radcliffe-Brown, by Sir Lizard in a stormy dance. Sir Lizard decided to hold a great dancing party. He became so wild at the dance that nobody could hold him, and as he was very strong the people were badly frightened. When they caught his arm, he threw them away so violently that they fell into the sea where they were turned into all sorts of fish and turtle. At last Berep, a small crab, caught the reptile's arm and stopped him.

In addition to a dread of cyclones, the Andamanese have anxieties about the harmful effects of certain animals they eat. This fear can be explained by their belief in the human origins of animals. A number of stories like Sir Lizard's Dancing Party tell of fishermen capsized at sea who became turtles. Another story tells about Lady Civet, the wife of the first man. Like Circe she changed some ancestors into pigs, who in turn jumped into the ocean and became dugongs. Killing and eating the animal incarnation of humans can therefore be highly dangerous, especially to initiates.

The Andamanese hold a firm and solid belief in the protective power of story-telling, dances and ceremonial costumes, and use them to avert adverse natural and spiritual forces. A corpse, for example, is clothed for burial in the white costume worn by dancers. An initiation ceremony of the Andamanese protects the young from the avenging power of the turtle. Prior to this a young person, either male or female, must abstain from eating turtle for a year or more, and then at a specified time take the first meal under ceremonial protection. The means for protecting the initiate against the power of the turtle flesh include ornamentation, songs and dances, which initiates are expected to improvise.

The power of song and dance to protect the initiate is illustrated by an Andamanese myth which tells how the animal ancestors were delivered from the most elemental anxiety, fear of the dark. Like many tribal peoples the Andamanese are terrified of darkness. They believe that the sun must be reborn each day; and they have faith that their recreational dancing around the fire after chores magically urges this rebirth. The following myth tells about an idyllic womb-like state, a golden age, when only daylight was known.

A mythical creature named Da Tengat, a spider created by the spider goddess Biliku, was a renowned and crafty hunter. One day Da Tengat was roaming through the forest. And as he wandered, he asked all the plants and animals their names. Suddenly, he took two arrows from his quiver, strung his bow, and shot them at random. He found that the first arrow had stuck in a yam. He spoke to the yam, asking, 'What is your name?' At first the yam did not answer. Tengat turned to go away. When he had gone a few steps he heard the yam call back, 'My name is gono.' Tengat replied, 'Oh, I didn't know. Why did you not say so before?' Then he found his second arrow in a large lump of resin. He took the arrow, and as he was going away, the resin called him back, saying, 'Here! My name is tug; you can take me along with you.' So Da Tengat put the yam and the resin in his pack. He also found a cicada, an insect famous for its shrill song, and took it along too. When he reached his tribe, he taught them how to cook the yam by burning the resin, and they feasted. But the cicada he crushed to death. The cicada screamed, and as his shrill cry pierced the air, the whole world grew dark for the first time ever.

All the creatures were frightened, since before they had known only the bright light of day. They took turns singing, thinking maybe their songs could bring the cicada back to life. But still darkness hung. Da Tengat, though, made his way in the darkness to the lumps of resin. He taught the others how to make torches. Next he showed them how to sing and dance at the same time. One by one, the creatures danced and sang, holding up high their torches. When they were all dancing in full swing, all the torches ablaze, dawn rose. And from that time onwards day and night succeeded one another. To this day the Andamanese dance late into the night in the belief that the energy of the dance urges the first rays of sun to shine down and warm the earth.

The myth explains how night came to be, and how the ancestors learned to dance from a spider. The emphasis in the myth on the preserving power of dance carries over into initiation ceremonies where imitative turtle dances defend initiates against the power of the sea-creature when they take the first meal. What does the turtle represent to the Andamanese? Practically, it is an important staple food used as a protein supplement to a mainly vegetarian diet. But according to belief, turtles represent transformations of fishermen who fell overboard. That men engulfed by the sea should have been changed into sea-turtles carries a certain logic. The sea is a vast, unknown body with murky depths; and the turtle, itself a large reptile, is something of a mystery, for all that it contains locked in its shell: there are dark and unknown regions there, like the night.

Could the sea-reptiles not represent the collective fears the initiate has in the face of his forthcoming adulthood, along with the increased responsibilities and obligations this brings? Like the animal ancestors of the golden age the initiate is being nudged forth into the world which contains night and day, good and evil. Also, one should not dismiss the possibility that eating turtle flesh is a covert form of anthropophagy, a well-known type of tribal worship through which the worshipper gains control over his enemy in the act of eating his flesh or a symbolic substitute.

The following description of the turtle initiation ceremony demonstrates how dance and song help the initiate to achieve autonomy by conquering fears about the unknown. When a boy or girl reaches puberty, the elders of the tribe forbid him or her to eat the meat of the turtle for a period of one to two years. This happens when the girl first begins menstruating, and when the boy has undergone a painful process of scarification to his back. The young person is further set apart from the community by not being allowed to dance: he is fundamentally excluded from a society in which dance is the strongest expression of unity.

At a time chosen by the elders, a turtle-hunt is organized. When a large number has been caught, everyone returns to the village. As in Polynesia, the women busy themselves with the preparation of turtle soup in the 'ovens of youth'.

Each initiate is meanwhile placed apart from all other members of the tribe in a hut. All ornaments – necklaces, belts, earrings, and so on – are removed, and the young person is stripped naked. In the hut he or she sits in a nest of hibiscus leaves, facing the open sea with a fire burning at the feet. One of the elders enters and rubs the fat of the turtle on the initiate's lips, and then smears the rest over the body. The old man places a chunk of turtle meat in the initiate's mouth. The young person must remain thus covered with hibiscus leaves in the hut for forty-eight hours, forbidden to speak or move; they are thought to be in a state of half-death. The hibiscus leaves have the magical property of protecting them from the first contact with turtle meat. So potent are the leaves that they can bring bad luck to a fisherman in the company of a recent initiate. A hunter returning empty-handed blames a boy named Keti in a song improvised to accompany a mimetic dance that acts out his unsuccessful turtle-hunt. 'Keti who just went through the ceremony of turtle-eating was with me, and wearing the leaves of the hibiscus tree tucked in his waistband, my turtle was ashamed to come near him; my turtle was ashamed and hid on account of the hibiscus.'

After lying in the hut for forty-eight hours, the initiate runs to the sea and washes. He puts on ornaments more elaborate than before, a necklace called the centipede creeper and a studded belt, both of which carry enhanced powers of protection. The dance follows. One of the older men takes in his hand a stick used for keeping time on a wooden sounding-board. The initiate stands in the midst of six older men. The dancers flex their hips and bend forwards so that the back is arched and parallel to the ground, in imitation of the shell of a turtle. The hands are raised to the nape of the neck. The dancer jumps up and down, and at every eighth jump brings his hands forward, down and back, then sweeps the ground next to his feet. The pawing arm movements reproduce the motions of the turtle swimming through water. As in the myth of origin for night and day, the initiate both sings and dances. He must improvise a song about the turtle-hunt. In the following example the performer describes the moment just before the kill, when he speaks to the man manoeuvring the boat with a pole: 'This is the right place, there are his breakers; / Stop here. / Pole for me slowly, / Pole for me slowly.'

The activity of the performance marks the rebirth of the young initiate after the forty-eight-hour period of restriction. The placement of the older dancers in a circle around the young dancer emphasizes his re-entry into the midst of the tribe, now as an adult member. The initiate has conquered any fears of passing into adult life by eating and *dancing* the turtle; the sea-creature which was created by Sir Lizard's commotion is now mastered by ordered movement. He traps the power and fears anchored in the turtle with the rhythm of song and dance, his netting. The tremendous energy of the youthful *tour de force* pumps fresh blood into the community.

As examined in the previous chapter, dance is an activity closely associated with the pre-natal and natal states of life; fish and snake are commonly the creatures symbolizing this earliest experience. Similarly dance nurses the novice, who has lived apart from the tribe in a quasi-animal state and endured a period of half-death, back to life. In the case of the Andamanese, the turtle dance is the vehicle of birth; the initiate is a reincarnation, as it were, of the drowned mariner. Just as the 'ovens of youth' in Polynesia are a kind of womb through which the initiate is restored to life, so dances of animals regenerate.

IV The Choreography of the Hunt

Bushman rock painting

In the vast expanses of Montana ringed about by the Rocky Mountains, the Blackfoot Indians kept close stock of the comings and goings of the great buffalo herds. One of the techniques for slaughtering the hefty animals was to drive them to the edge of a cliff and make them leap to their deaths, much as Palaeolithic hunters had done some 30,000 years ago. A myth about a maiden who cannot rid herself of an undesirable husband, who happens to be a buffalo bull, ends with a description of a type of hunting dance used to 'resurrect' game slain in the hunt. 'Once upon a time' – according to a Blackfoot story retold by Joseph Campbell – 'the hunters could not manage to make the buffalo fall over the cliff; something had gone wrong, and the people were starving. When driven toward the cliff the beasts would run nearly to the edge, but then, swerving to right or left, would go down the sloping hills and cross the valley in safety. So the people were hungry, and their case was becoming serious.

'And so it was that, one early morning, when a young woman went to get water and saw a buffalo, feeding on the prairie, right at the edge of the cliff above the fall, she cried out, "Oh! if you will only jump into the corral, I shall marry one of you."

'This was said in fun, of course, not seriously. Hence, her wonder was great when she saw the animals begin to come jumping, tumbling, falling over the cliff. And then she was terrified, because a big bull with a single bound cleared the walls of the corral and approached her. "Come!" he said. And he took her by the arm.

'"Oh no!" she cried, pulling back.

'"But you said that if the buffalo would jump, you would marry one. See! The corral is filled." And without further ado he led her up over the cliff and out onto the prairie.

'When the people had finished killing the buffalo and cutting up the meat, they missed the young woman. Then her relatives were very sad, and her father took his bow and quiver. "I shall go find her," he said; and he went up the cliff and over, out across the prairie.

'When he had travelled a considerable distance he came to a buffalo wallow – a place where the buffalo come for water and to lie and roll. And there, a little way off, he saw a herd. Being tired, and considering what he should do, he sat down by the wallow; and while he was thinking, a beautiful black and white bird with a long graceful tail, a magpie, came and lighted on the ground.

'"Ha!" said the man. "You are a handsome bird! Help me! As you fly about, look everywhere for my daughter, and if you see her, say to her, 'Your father is waiting by the wallow.'"

'The bird flew about and did as the father bid. He saw a girl among the buffalo herd, and perching on the back of the sleeping bull, whispered in the girl's ear, "Your father is waiting by the wallow."

'"Go back and tell him to wait," the girl said.

'Then the bull awoke and said to the girl, "Take this horn and get some water."

'The woman took the horn and went to the wallow. "Father!" she said. "Why did you come? You will surely be killed!"

' "I came to take my daughter home," the man replied. "Come let us hurry!"

'"No, not now! They would pursue and kill us. Let us wait till he sleeps again."

'She returned to the bull with the water. He drank and exclaimed, "Aha! There is a person close by here."

'"No, no, no one!" she protested.

Buffalo being chased over a cliff. From E. S. Curtis' Indian Days of Long Ago *(1914)*

'The bull drank more water. Then he got up and bellowed. What a fearful sound he made. All the bulls bellowed back, then pawed the dirt, rushed about in all directions, and coming to the wallow found the poor man who had come to seek his daughter. They trampled on him, and trampled on him again, so that soon not even a small piece of his body could be seen. His daughter wailed, "Oh, my father. My poor father."

'"Aha", said the bull. "You are mourning your father. And so, perhaps now you can see how it is with us. We have seen our mothers and fathers, many of our relatives, hurled over the rock walls and slaughtered by your people. But I pity you. I shall give you just one chance. If you can bring your father to life again, you and he may go back to your people."

'The woman turned to the magpie. "Pity me. Help me! Go and search in the trampled mud. Try to find some little piece of my father's body and bring it back to me."

'The magpie picked around, and finally he found a small piece of a bone, a joint of the father's backbone.

'The girl placed the particle of bone on the ground, and covering it with her robe, sang a certain song. Removing the robe, she saw her father's body lying there, as though dead. Covering him with her robe again, she resumed her song, and when she next removed the robe, her father was breathing, and after a time he stood up.

'The buffalo were amazed. The magpie was delighted. "We have seen strange things today," the bull husband said to the others of the herd. "The man we trampled to death into small pieces rises from the dead. The people's holy power is strong."

'He turned to the young woman. "But now before you and your father go, we shall teach you our dance and song. You must not forget them.

'"For these would be the magical means by which the buffalo killed by the people for their food should be restored to life, just as the man killed by the buffalo has been restored."

'All the buffalo danced; and as befitted the dance of such great beasts, the song was slow and solemn, the step ponderous and deliberate. And when the dance was over, the bull said, "Now go to your home and do not forget what you have seen. Teach this song and dance to your people. The sacred object of the rite is to be a bull's head and buffalo robe. All those who dance the bulls are to wear a bull's head and buffalo robe when they dance."'

This delightful myth of the origin of the Blackfoot Buffalo Dance, told from the point of view of the animals, says something

Nineteenth-century depiction of the Bison Dance. Drawing by George Catlin

about the mutual respect and reciprocity expected between hunters and animals. There is a bargain between man and the animal: if you take the life of an animal, you must later return it. The myth shows the magical power of song and dance to give back life, to regenerate. Like the song of the people, the dance which the buffalo teach the maiden restores life. Such dances, belonging to the brand of magic called restitutive, ensure that the hunted game will not perish, leaving the people without a food supply.

In tribes like the Blackfoot Indians, hunting is favoured over agriculture either by choice or necessity, and survival may depend primarily on acquiring sufficient meat from the hunted game. Amidst the urgency of this precarious pursuit a cult has formed: hunting is essentially a religious rite of sacrifice. Hunters pray to the guardian spirit of the hunt to send enough game for the hunters to make a good catch. But the guardian himself usually belongs to a species of hunted game, and this presents a diplomatic problem. The killing of one of his kind is seen as a necessary sacrifice, but one requiring ritual appeasement. Without this apology, the guardian may refuse to encourage the hunted game to reproduce for subsequent hunting seasons. The hunter must therefore remain on good diplomatic relations with the animal ambassador. Hunting songs and dances like those of the Blackfoot serve effectively to maintain this harmony. Although no less integral to the hunter's technique than tracking and the act of killing, the songs and dances lend to the activity of hunting a distinctly religious flavour.

Hunting is man's oldest cult. In the Palaeolithic era, it may be assumed, there were hunting myths as well, which may have resembled the Blackfoot myth, if not in tone, at least in content; unfortunately such myths, if they existed, are lost. It is known, however, that Stone Age hunters practised hunting-magic in underground caverns – recesses which sometimes required several hours of tortuous travel along steep, twisting paths to reach. In the inner sanctum two forms of magic were performed: pictorial magic and mimetic dancing. Already we have seen one of the earliest depictions of dance in the so-called 'Sorcerer of Trois-Frères', a shaman who, decked out in various animal attributes, controlled the increase of the hunted game and promoted the hunter's luck. There are approximately thirty-five portrayals of sorcerers disguised in animal skins and masks who can be said to be dancing for the purposes of favouring hunting and fertility. Many paintings of hunted game, including buffalo, aurochs, horses, ibex and stags, if examined carefully, show signs of having been physically attacked. The paintings themselves bear wounds inflicted by a barbed spear, and the wounds stream with blood. Other animals have targets like a dartboard with a bull's eye painted on or near their hearts, or a trap is laid in their path. These are clearly examples of hunting magic preparatory to the actual hunt above ground. Those animals, on the other hand, which are drawn in their free and natural state, may have been regarded as living replacements for slain members.

From earliest times hunting has been a deceitful activity. Disguises and camouflage in the form of animal skins and masks have long been known to beguile and seduce unsuspecting prey. The oldest known animal-hunting masks, dating from approximately 7500 BC, come from Star Carr in England. During excavations led by the archaeologist Grahame Clark no fewer than twenty-five deer frontlets were found. They were made from the skull bones of deer with the antlers still attached, two holes on the sides allowing a cord to be strung through for wearing. Clark thought that the frontlets were worn in dance rituals to promote the hunter's luck. They may in addition have been worn together with deerskins to stalk deer. The oldest known animal masks found among North American Indian tribes are likewise those of deer. Although carved from wood they convey a realism so impressive as to deceive prey of that species; in such a guise a hunter skilled in the observation of the deer's movements could realistically imitate the animal, approach unawares, and seduce the unsuspecting roe; when he had the victim within close shooting range, he let fly his weapon. The nineteenth-century American artist and traveller George Catlin, who was one of the first to record the ways of the

Indians, illustrated how the Plains Indians dressed in wolf-skins to shoot down buffalo. In his painting the figures of two humans carrying bows and arrows can clearly be seen under the wolf disguise.

Hunting is closely allied to warfare. Proven ability to track down animals in the wild is a prerequisite in many cultures for joining the ranks of warriors on the battlefield. Hunting and war require similar weapons, skills and inner qualities. A hunting spear doubles as a warring lance; the hunter's ability to plan the strategy of the hunt, to train and set his dogs on the quarry, to aim and kill the victim, corresponds in war to the plotting of military tactics, the training and arrangement of troops on the battlefield, and the successful capture or routing of enemy forces. And the hunt and warfare are alike in that they require intelligence and sang-froid, courage and fortitude, and a flair for deceit: 'out-foxing' your opponent. In one final way war and the hunt are similar: they accomplish the same end, that of robbing an animate being of its life-force – killing one's brethren.

Predators, in actual fact, are consummate hunters; in mythology, animals of all kinds are proven hunters and warriors. Animals teach men to fight and hunt in the mythologies of ancient Greece, China and India. Cheiron, the wise and beneficent centaur, imparted warring and hunting skills to heroes from Achilles to Aias; in the fourth century BC, Xenophon began his treatise on hunting by naming a score of Greek warriors as pupils and protégés. Achilles, the greatest of them all, took along with him to the Trojan war the ashen spear given to his father Peleus as a wedding gift by the wild horse-man. It is well known historically that the Greek warrior had to be schooled in dance as a martial art before he could ever set foot on the battlefield. Plato briefly describes the martial dance, called the Pyrrhic, as excellent training for attacking an enemy and for eluding missiles by 'bending aside, ducking, leaping and crouching'. The Pyrrhic dance degenerated into an ecstatic dance under the influence of orgiastic rites in honour of Dionysos. The female participants, the maenads, were at once huntresses and warriors; their ivy wands served as spears and their tambourines as shields; clad in panther-skins they tracked down wild animals, later to ingest the inward parts of the beast during orgiastic dances, in the belief that they were consuming the god.

Lucian, the second-century AD author of dialogues, relates an animal fable about apes taught to perform the Pyrrhic dance by an Egyptian king:

'A King of Egypt once taught apes to dance, and the animals learned quickly and gave an exhibition with purple mantles about them and masks on their faces. For a long time the show went well until a facetious spectator, having nuts in his pocket, tossed them into the midst. On catching sight of them, the monkeys forgot their dance, changed from pyrrhicists to the simians that they really were, smashed their masks, tore their costumes, and fought with each other for the nuts, whereby the troop of the pyrrhica was entirely broken up and was laughed at by the spectators.'

In Hindu mythology the monkey-god Hanuman and his followers are frequent allies of gods. The best-known tale about Hanuman, from the *Ramayana*, tells how the monkey and his army helped Rama to retrieve his wife Sita, who had been abducted by Ravana. Thus, dance dramas of the *Ramayana* include choruses of monkey dancers led by Hanuman. According to popular belief, Hanuman and other animals instructed men how to hunt and to fight, and folk-dances of India incorporate the movements of animals known for their fierce attack, such as the tiger. A statue or picture of Hanuman, as the monkey god of strength and speed, is displayed in every Hindu gymnasium as the presiding deity. Certain martial arts of the Orient owe their origins to animals. According to one of the many theories of origin for Chinese *Kung-fu*, the medicine-man Hua To introduced physical movements derived from the movements of animals: bear, tiger, deer, bird, monkey. Another legend tells about a Buddhist monk, Hsuen Tsang, travelling from China to India with his bodyguard, a monkey. The monkey used many methods to defend his master, and from his actions the *Kung-fu* system of Ta Sheng Man, or Monkey style, developed. There is hardly an animal, mythical or real, which does not have a *Kung-fu* style modelled on its particular movements. Crane style, for example, is derived from the powerful beating of the crane's wings and the pecking of its sharp beak. These respectively allow the fighter to break his opponent's limbs or poke out an eye. In Mongolia, wrestlers engage in a preliminary bout in which they imitate the movements of animals such as the lion and eagle, for which the winner is afterwards named.

In a historical context, the overlapping of war and the hunt was dramatized during a visit made by George Catlin to the Mandan Indian tribes living along the Upper Missouri River. Catlin described with a note of sadness a buffalo dance he witnessed which developed into a war dance. For several weeks hunger had been lurking about the Mandan village. As in the Blackfoot myth, the reserves of buffalo meat had been all but exhausted, and the young men sent out to hunt repeatedly returned empty-handed. As was customary in such times of duress, the chief proclaimed a buffalo dance, a charm which never failed to 'make the buffalo come', since it was believed that the dance had the magical power to bend the migration path of the herd by magnetic pull. Within minutes of the chief's appeal, two dozen men appeared in front of the 'Mystery Lodge' with the buffalo masks which they were required to keep hanging at the head of the bed. The hunters performed the dance – which could last several days non-stop until a herd was sighted – in relays, fifteen at a time. They moved in a circle, and imitated various gestures of the buffalo, such as the impetuous pawing of the ground when a bison verges on attack. An exhausted dancer bowed out, bending his frame forward until he sank to all fours. Another hunter raised his bow and shot the falling body, while two men rushed in with knives, dragged the carcass from the ring and made the motions of scalping and cutting up the buffalo for meat.

But the charade was a bitter foreshadowing of the fate of the dancing hunters. On the fourth day, the beating of drums in the camp gave way to galloping hooves as the joyous news arrived that a scout had spotted a herd. Digging into the last of their reserves, the chieftain distributed food and the villagers offered thanksgiving to the Great Spirit for sending the buffalo. A terrible reversal of fortune unexpectedly befell the hunters. They returned wounded and groaning, their horses streaked with blood. Here the hunt was not merely a metaphor for war: a neighbouring Sioux tribe had caught wind of the Mandan buffalo dance. The Sioux in turn disguised themselves as buffalo on a nearby bluff, and imitated the motions of grazing buffalo. Once the Mandan had begun their advance, the herd shifted their pasturing-ground to the blind side of the bluff. But by the time the attackers were close enough to sniff out the stratagem, it was too late. The decoy herd threw off their skins, rose up, charged and attacked the bewildered men, three of whom were killed on the spot.

A sagacious means of attracting game is to appeal first to the guardian spirit of the hunt with songs and dances for help in planning the hunt. Again Catlin recorded beliefs of the Sioux Indians about their bear dance. Before setting out on the hunt, they held a dance in hour of the Bear Spirit seeking the animal's advice and approval. One of the chiefs would wear the entire skin of the bear, while his tribesmen wore only masks made from the skin of the bear's head. The dancers carefully reproduced specific movements of the animal, such as its running motion, or the manner in which it hangs its paws when sitting on the alert for an approaching foe. These flattering imitations of the bear won the spirit over to their side. The chief could then invoke the spirit of the bear for counsel in how best to plot the strategy of the hunt. The ceremony also reminded the Bear Spirit that the hunters did not mean any real harm, but that they were only performing their duties.

Failure to carry out hunting rituals with proper respect to the victims can result in catastrophe. 'The Feast of the Mountain Goats', a myth of the Tsimshian tribes of the North-west Pacific Coast, based on a text recorded by Henry W. Tate, warns what can happen when hunters do not maintain good relations with their prey. The people of Temlaham, the earthly paradise of the Tsimshian people, hunted the mountain goat. This was allowed, so long as the hunters showed due respect and performed hunting rituals. After a time, however, the attitude of the hunters grew slack, and they bullied and harassed their victims, until one day the leader of the goats invited the hunters to a feast on top of the mountain. The goats were skilfully disguised as men; and although the hunters thought it a bit odd when they noticed their hosts eating grass instead of the regular food prepared for the feast, they didn't give it a second thought. During the feast, however, a magical one-horned goat, which the hunters at first imagined to be a cleverly disguised human dancer, rose and began dancing. And his dance was so terrible that an earthquake shook the mountain. All the hunters of Temlaham were swallowed up in the cracks of the earth, except for one hunter who had long ago taken pity on a mistreated kid. Because he nursed the kid back to life, the kid, now grown to a full-sized goat, rescued him from peril.

Hunting songs and poems invoke the animal or guardian spirit. The Eskimos, whose seal mating dance is discussed in 'Courtship and Mating Dances', pray to the guardian spirit:

> You, fatherless and motherless,
> You, dear little orphan,
> Give me kamiks of caribou,
> Bring me a gift
> Of an animal – one of those
> That provide good blood-soup.
> An animal from the sea-depths
> And not from the plains of earth
> You little orphan,
> Bring me a gift.

The hunters show themselves helpless and needful in their appeal by making the guardian spirit, whom they call 'orphan', identify with their own needs. The songs may contain a strain of irony or flattery. In the next song the hunters sing, they beg the guardian to come to them in the form of a beautiful seal, one they may hunt:

> Orphan,
> You little orphan,
> On the other side of the open sea.
> On its beautiful other side,
> Creep there carefully,
> Come out of the water,
> In the shape of a seal!

But in the final analysis, the hunter's real allies are his trusty companions, his weapons. In a hunting chant of the pygmies of Gabon, the archer who is about to fire an arrow calls it 'my lovely, trusty, cousin'. In the actual confrontation between hunter and beast, however, all disguises drop; the hunter does an about-face, shows his true colours, and kills the beast.

The hunters' sentiments of victory are tinged with feelings of guilt and fear that the animal spirit will avenge itself. This ambivalence is clearly expressed in the dialogue held by the pygmies of Gabon when they slay the mighty elephant. Pygmies, though small by our standards, are nonetheless capable of killing an elephant. But they are clearly both proud and embarrassed about hunting down the lord of the forest. The entire hunting ritual takes place over several consecutive days, culminating in a ritual burial at which the chief hunter leads the members of the tribe, including the women, in dances and songs. The leader begins:

I have seen, and we have gone into the forest. . . .
ALL: Bow and lance in hand, we have gone into the forest.
WOMEN: Tidale mo, tidale mo.
LEADER: In the black village, the village far away, the father was there, the father of past times.
WOMEN: Blood, Tears, Death.
            Tidale mo, tidale mo.
LEADER: We made the alliance. We are the master. The sun shines. The moon lightens the night. The sun is dead. The moon is above. We are masters of the dead, masters of the night.
MEN: Masters of the day, masters of the night,
            Death, night shadows, the glow-worms have passed.

In the dialogue, the conflict between the hunters and the old man of the forest is cast as a contest between the sun and moon, light and dark. The forces of night prevail. Man is the master. The ceremony concludes with the leader soaking his spear in the carcass of the hulking beast. Afterwards the pygmies inter the king of the forest. At the grave, they dance and sing:

> Against your children, father elephant,
> Do not be angry!
> We have taken you away, we have given you back life.
> Against your children, father elephant,
> Do not be angry, you begin a better life.
> Honour to you, my lance.
> My lance of sharpened iron, honour to you!

Last of all, the leader places garlands of flowers on the elephant and dances a dance of victory around the corpse.

A humorous poem by a pygmy hunter named Nku describes his various duties and talents, which include elephant-hunting and dancing for the white man's tobacco:

> The forest is great, the wind is good,
> Forward the Beku, your bows and your arms! . . .
> Plomp! an elephant on the ground!
> Who has killed it? It is Nku.
> Who will have the fine tusks? Poor Nku!
> Always strike it down! They will leave you . . . the tail!
> Without a house like the monkeys,
> Who gathers honey? It is Nku!
> Who eats it till his belly aches? Poor Nku!
> Always get it down! They will leave you . . . the wax!
> The Whites are there, good whites!
> Who is it who dances? It is Nku.
> But who will smoke his tobacco? Poor Nku.
> Sit down all the same and reach out your hand.

Finally, a tribe may enact all the stages of a hunt from the luring and capture of the prey to the resurrection of the slain species in a kind of dance drama known as hunting pantomime. The pantomime may work as a hunting charm, or it may have a symbolic significance for the tribe. An example of this is the New Ireland Shark-Hunting Dance, where the third and final episode unfolds as a resurrection, not of the shark, but of dead mariners at sea who were transformed into sharks. Other hunting pantomimes have grown into dance spectacles, as in the case of the Deer Dance of the Yaqui Indians, which has been incorporated in the repertoire of the Ballet Folklórico de México.

The highly realistic Yaqui pantomime was originally a hunting dance of native Yaqui tribes but has now merged with Easter celebrations. Several hunters pursue a deer danced by a beautiful young dancer wearing antlers. The first portion of the dance is an exquisite portrayal of pursuit and elusion down a series of arches. The hunters begin tracking the beast. The deer comes into view, but, growing aware of the hunters' presence, freezes. Alert and erect, the head of the deer twitches nervously, and the animal retreats with rebounding steps. This interplay between hunters and deer is repeated several times until the hunters succeed in luring the deer by means of a decoy. An archer shoots and wounds the deer. The silent anguish of the delicate animal in its death-throes is sustained for several moments. The hunters skin the animal; having slain and skinned it, they strive to appease and revive the deer's spirit in a concluding dance. Appropriately, the resuscitation of the deer's spirit concurs with the resurrection of Christ in a mingling of pagan and Christian traditions.

A hunting pantomime called Gemsbok Play is one of the several dance rituals of Bushman hunting tribes whose ambivalent attitudes towards their principal animal, the antelope, is the focus of the remainder of this chapter and Chapter VI.

Dorothea Bleek, who perhaps knew the Bushmen better than any other outsider, concluded her introduction to a comprehensive collection of Bushman folktales with the words, 'A Bushman is a good lover and a good hater, very loyal and very revengeful. He remains all his life a child, averse to work, fond of play, of painting, singing, dancing, dressing up and acting, and above all things fond of hearing and telling stories.' For over a century and a half the territory of the Bushman hunters has been encroached upon by Europeans and stronger neighbouring Bantu tribes, until nowadays the Bushmen live in sadly diminishing numbers in the poorest areas of South Africa, along the borders of the Kalahari Desert; a few tribes live under more favourable conditions in the Drakensberg Range, which are difficult of access. The poetry, folklore and art of these remarkable people, however, allow us to gain an insight into the mind and eye of the Bushman and his tradition. For, among other things, the Bushman is the inheritor of vast galleries of rock paintings whose most common subject is the antelope.

Bushman hunters work silently in small co-operative groups, relying on bow and arrow and face-hand gestures to chase antelope and other game. Because of the antelope's acute instinct, the animal presents a very difficult challenge to the hunter. But the Bushmen know that the antelope is an inquisitive creature. Hunters exploit this curiosity by making gestures and sounds in imitation of the animal's. A favourite hunting stratagem, for instance, is to appeal to the antelope's maternal instinct by reproducing the cry of the fawn.

Bushman hunters shoot at their prey with poison-tipped arrows which initially may only wound it. The subsequent tracking of the spoor can take the better part of a day and night until the animal is finally paralysed by the poison. During the chase the hunters refuse to speak about the fleeing prey or to eat for fear that either action will give fresh strength to the game.

The Bushmen have an intense craving for antelope flesh, whetted by the anticipation and anxiety of the hunt. The night before setting out to hunt the springbok, a variety of antelope, the hunters pray to a star:

The close relationship between hunter and prey is seen in this Bushman drawing. After Vinnicombe

O star coming there,
Let me see a springbok . . .
Let the dog kill it,
Let me eat it,
Let me eat and fill my body,
That I may lie and sleep at night.

But they are not a little sorry of what they have to do. The hunters pronounce a prayer that identifies them poignantly with the guardian of antelope, in saying:

Please don't kill my antelope,
My darling antelope.
My antelope is so poor,
My antelope is an orphan.

When a Bushman does kill an antelope, he feels guilty and walks around disquieted in a daze for hours: it is believed that the guardian of antelope, Mantis, descends upon the scene of every hunt to inspect the tip of the murderous arrow. When he discovers the owner, the little insect god drives the hunter mad for a time by dancing around him and pinching him! The return home with a hulking carcass, however, is a triumphant occasion marked by dances of thanksgiving. The hunter who first shot the animal then, according to his right, divides the booty among his tribesmen.

As providers of food Bushman hunters are indispensable to the tribe. Their courage and prowess is highly respected: in Bushman

*Rock painting from Ehorongue probably showing the white goddess Ko,
patroness of the hunt, with female attendants*

painting the hunter's virility is often shown through greatly
exaggerated genitalia. The male must display his hunting ability on
two occasions, once at his initiation, and again when he marries. In
the first he demonstrates his courage, sang-froid, and expertise;
when about to take a wife, he confirms his position as provider for
the tribe. Joseph Campbell, an early missionary traveller, reported
in his *Second Journey into South Africa* in 1822 a Bushman mystical
hunting dance. Here Ko, a patroness of the hunt, presided. She
was thought to be a towering, luminescent figure, whose effulgent
whiteness outshone even the fire. She danced with the hunters and
communicated information about the location of game, and who
might or might not eat the victim once slain. It was said that anyone
fortunate enough to be touched by her divinity in the dance could
be assured of improved aim, for the goddess breathed beneficent
vapours onto his arm. The white goddess mingled with the mortal
hunters for only a moment, and then disappeared, to be succeeded
by a choir of attendants. A red, white and black rock painting from
Ehorongue may show such a white goddess superintending her
female attendants, who are pictured in dappled skins with tails.

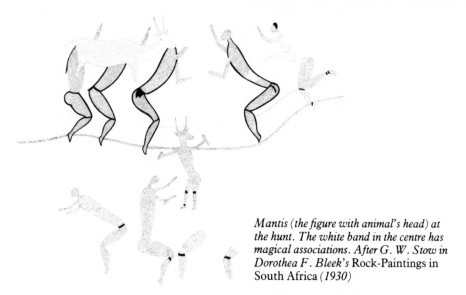

Mantis (the figure with animal's head) at the hunt. The white band in the centre has magical associations. After G. W. Stow in Dorothea F. Bleek's Rock-Paintings in South Africa *(1930)*

In this century the hunting pantomime Gemsbok Play, serving to introduce the young Bushman to the hunt, has a more straight-forward air about it than the mysterious dance allegedly seen by Campbell. In the initiation ceremony an actual gemsbok calf was sometimes used, or, as in the version witnessed by Doke, a Bushman called the *Malxas* took the part of the gemsbok. The hunting mime required several other actors, including four mature hunters and a dozen or more 'hunting dogs' enacted by the young initiates. The role of the *Malxas* was very difficult to perform. To portray this, the main actor, wearing a forked stick attached to his head to simulate horns, positioned himself on the slope of a sand dune, his stage for enacting imitations of the behaviour of the prey; here he depicted the gemsbok at one moment playful, at the next moment alert. He mimicked the animal feeding on tufts of grass, then thrusting his horns in the air, the head twitching and the nostrils flared. Next the *Malxas* scraped at the ground with his feet for roots; after feeding, he lay down. At once the dogs and hunters appeared in hot pursuit and assembled near the dune. The gemsbok sensed trouble and leapt to his feet, tossing the antlers high into the air. The victim managed to keep the dogs at bay, and then courageously charged them single-handed. He butted a few out of the way; however, as he advanced against the men, one of the hunters let fly a dummy arrow. The gemsbok cried out in pain, as the dogs, recovering, viciously surrounded the carcass with a chorus of yelps.

Hunting is, except for notable exceptions, an exclusively male-oriented activity. Where women participate, it is usually in a magical capacity; there are, for example, tribes in which the women remain in the village to dance around an effigy of the hunted species. In the Arunta tribes of Australia, women and children at the encampment dance around pictures of the hunted game drawn in the sand and stick in spears while the men are out in the bush hunting. Their dance transmits telepathically a hunting charm to the hunters in the bush. But the male in hunting societies traditionally provides meat. To carry out his act of provision in an effective way, the hunter relies on weapons and a repertoire of proven techniques. By virtue of his technical skill, man has developed a variety of hunting accessories, such as arrows, spears, boomerangs, nets, traps, etc. He has made the dog and horse serve him by a gradual process of domestication; he has exploited the magic of song, dance and pantomime. A successful hunt requires preparation, mental as well as physical. Preparatory hunting dances warm up the body and condition the hunters to endure lengthy pursuits, and once the victim is in sight, to make a rapid and powerful attack. On a spiritual level, hunting dances give a sense of unity and solidarity to the expedition. Those dances which imitate the hunted species put the hunter in the mind and spirit of the enemy prey. On a magical level, preparatory hunting dances attract the desired species, just as a mating dance attracts and seduces a mate.

Bushman painting of a circle dance in which figures wearing sheepskins crouch with arms upraised in mimetic gesture

V Dances of Courtship and Mating

A Yoruba legend by Ogumefu, called 'The Leopard Man', tells how a handsome stranger one day entered a village and walked about mysteriously and silently. His attractive appearance did not escape the attention of the young women, and each wished within her heart that he would ask her to be his bride; but the stranger soon left as he had come, without saying a word. He reappeared a month later. One of the women fell so madly in love with him that she resolved never to let him out of her sight. When the stranger noticed that the young woman had followed him into the forest, he turned and spoke, begging her to return home. But she would not and exclaimed, 'I will never leave you. I cannot bear to be separated from you.' 'Ah, beautiful woman! You will regret it,' he said sadly and hurried on. But she continued to follow him into the depths of the forest until he came to rest at a tree. Under it lay a leopard-skin. Standing under the tree, the handsome stranger began to move slowly in a dance, his hands placed as if holding an imaginary partner. As he danced he sang a melancholy song in which he confessed to the woman that he was allowed to wander about in the village only once a month in the form of a man: for he was in reality a savage leopard and would tear her to pieces as soon as he assumed his natural form.

At this moment he stopped singing and dancing in this doleful way and flung himself down upon the ground. The leopard-skin leapt up and covered his body; and in his natural form he began pursuing the terrified woman. She ran, and her legs carried her faster than she had ever run. After being chased for a great distance, the woman came to a deep but narrow river. It seemed that the leopard would surely overtake her now, but a tree by the riverbank took pity and fell across the river, allowing the woman to cross. At last, nearly exhausted, she drew near the edge of the forest and took refuge in the village. The leopard, disappointed of his prey, slunk back into the forest, and the handsome stranger was never seen again.

'The Leopard-Man' is related to beliefs in traditional West Africa about 'leopard-men' who, like werewolves, allegedly take on animal form at night and roam about in search of human flesh. The leopard here is a metaphor for sexual potency and the role of aggression in satisfying sensual appetites. The young woman in the village is wildly attracted to the handsome stranger because she senses somewhere deep within him his leopard soul, and this excites her sexually; unconsciously she desires to be possessed and consumed by him. But the stranger, despite himself, cannot allow himself to love the beautiful woman, since he is unable to control his bestial drives. The legend seems to say that if people abandoned themselves totally to their carnal appetites they would devour or be devoured. Although we are human, we resemble wild animals in our mating instincts. In our amorous pursuits, sexual appetites are governed by a predatory urge.

Dance, however, is an activity that can tame excessively brutal impulses while still allowing erotic expression. Once again human and animal meet in the dance, the mating dance, where a tension exists between bestial and amorous forces. Dance in many cultures is an acceptable and effective way for the young to release and express sexual feelings for members of the opposite sex. The tell-tale rhythms travel mysteriously across the dance-floor in defiance of all chaperones. The dances sort out the weak and clumsy and match up those pairs most compatible for matrimony. Courtship dances in the Middle Ages and Renaissance, from the French bourree to the Italian paduana, gave young courtiers the opportunity to display publicly their social graces and to practise the rules of etiquette expected between young men and women in polite, civilized society. At least one of the popular dances was derived from the movement of an animal. The pavane (the French and English form of the paduana) or 'peacock dance' was a proud, showy display in which the male performer swaggered and strutted about with his mantle and dagger outstretched in such a way as to suggest the fan of a peacock's tail. The tune of the pavane was played as a processional for the family of the bride entering the church. The capriole, on the other hand, imitated the thrusting motion of the bawdy goat.

More usually it was the pastoral counterparts of courtship dances that incorporated movements of wild and domesticated animals kept on the farms. Steps imitating the cow, such as the *ru de vache*, a sideward kick of the leg, were widespread, as well as the many horse dances. These dances were not only acceptable forms in which to express attraction for a partner of the opposite sex, but served the additional purpose of promoting the fertility of humans and animals alike. Birds frequently served as models for courtship dances; the *grue* was based on the walk of the crane, a potent fertility animal in both east and west; the mountain cock's mating dance provided the model for a dance surviving today in Bavaria. The *Schuhplattler*, or Shoe-Swatting Dance, includes a section called *Nachsteigen* in which the male woos the female in the manner of a mountain cock mating. Hans Flemming describes the dance in the following way: 'The young man does not simply dance with his maid, but with wooing movements, clicking his tongue, hissing, and clapping the hands, he jumps along behind her or, if space is lacking, next to her, stamps on the floor, take a couple of leaps, or perhaps even turns a somersault. Finally, with his arms outspread or hanging close to the ground, he rushes towards his partner or leaps suddenly in a curve towards her, after he has struck the ground hard with one or both hands.'

Mating dances of birds are carefully observed and scrupulously imitated by certain tribes, in the belief that their reproductive powers can be transferred to humans. The mating rituals of long-necked cranes strikingly resemble courtship dances in their restrained and silent stateliness. During the breeding season these long-legged creatures gather in marshy places and pair off. The wooing ritual consists of the male advancing with outstretched wings towards the female, rubbing his wings against hers, retreating, and then repeating his advances. Their courting dances are imitated in several independent cultures. In Zaire, choirs of young, marriageable girls of the Watusi sing in antiphons the haunting songs of the crane, as pairs of bare-breasted girls repeatedly advance and retreat, rotating with slow, hypnotic repetition their outstretched arms, which serve as wings. With the palm of her hands the girl imitating the male crane gently rubs the cheeks of the other girl to transfer the fertility charm. Anyone who has seen this gentle dance will agree that it is highly erotic.

Among the Bushmen, where virgins were symbolically deflowered by older men disguised as eland in the gemsbok puberty dance, animal dances were openly erotic. Usually the chieftain performed the lascivious dances. He crouched, for instance, on all fours in the manner of a predatory wild animal, in the midst of a circle of wildly gesticulating female dancers, then snatched up one of them and openly performed sexual intercourse with her on the spot. Bushman males excited females in erotic baboon dances

Dance of baboons and elands. Animal mimicry in a Bushman painting. After Vinnicombe

during which they mimicked the playful combats of rival baboons running about on all fours, chattering and grimacing with jealousy. And as a sign of love, male and female Bushman couples picked lice off one another in baboon dances. Frog dances resembling the game of leap-frog and swarming bee dances also had as their goal sexual arousal, leading to pleasurable fulfilment. Among the Bambara, when a baboon dancer dives among a crowd of female spectators they scream and flee in mock horror. There are legends about women actually being raped by baboons. The baboon dancer, called Zantegeba (literally 'he with big paws'), manoeuvres himself with the help of two poles held in the hands. He struts about, showing off his colourful mask with large snout and gigantic teeth.

The Australian Aboriginal lives in close spiritual proximity to the animal kingdom. The Aboriginal does not consciously distinguish the biological process of humans from that of animals: the two are interdependent. The Aboriginals time their marriage ceremonies, called corroborees, and consisting mainly of imitative animal dances, to coincide with the animals' mating season. The tribes become, in a sense, a member of the natural wedding. In Australia there are two marked climates during the year: a long, dry, windy season followed by a short, wet season when the entire plant and animal world bursts in upon the previously barren landscape. During this period of exuberance the animals come into rut.

The human animal has also become seasonal in his breeding habits in Aboriginal Australia. Encouraged by the state of luxuriance in the plant world, the Aboriginals reproduce among themselves. The occasion for their activities is the corroboree, during which danced imitations of reproduction among animals in turn encourage the animals by sympathetic magic to breed merrily and in great numbers.

The following adaptation of a story, transmitted by William Ramsay Smith and called the 'Confusion of Tongues', is about a wedding corroboree and makes important statements about the natural pairing of couples, and the premium placed on the ability to imitate dancers, possessed by the hero of the story, the lyre-bird. Long ago the sun shone on sea and land, giving life and energy to animal, bird, reptile and insect. The sun made its journey across the sky to the mysterious West. There was never a cloud of disappointment or sorrow, only eternal sunshine. Animal, bird, reptile and insect were bound together by one common language. The kangaroo and goanna were able to converse and exchange ideas; so were the eagle-hawk and the platypus, and the wombat and the dragonfly.

Once every year they would all congregate and have great feasting and corroborees, and there would be great marriage celebrations. But a time came when they proposed to do something that would change the condition of the whole race. Some proposed that they should join in marriage the kangaroo with the emu, the dingo with the goanna, the koala with the lyre-bird. While some were in favour of such an arrangement, others were strongly opposed to it. Those in favour were represented by the kangaroos, emus, dingoes, goannas, carpet snakes, koalas, pelicans, cockatoos and lyre-birds. Against these were the tortoises, frogs and crows.

While one party was preparing boomerangs, waddies, reed-spears and other weapons, the three confederates, the crow, the tortoise and the frog, whose one weapon was their intelligence, used to meet on the top of a mountain. They would sit and discuss a method of attack. The three were of one mind, that if their opponents could be made to suffer severe hunger and to become angry with one another, they would soon be rid of all their silly ideas.

Now there were three things that the whole of the tribes admired; and in these things their opponents were highly skilled. First, the crow was a great composer of native songs, and a clever dancer and impersonator. Second, the frog was one of the greatest dancers ever known, and his talent excelled even that of the crow. He had a wonderful bass voice; and, what was most remarkable, he was a ventriloquist. Third, the tortoise possessed neither voice nor ability. But, as it turned out, that in itself was a great talent. The three decided to make use of their gifts, so they invited the animals, birds, reptiles and insects to a great performance.

The first act was a dance by the tortoise in imitation of the kangaroo. This aroused intense curiosity and wonder. Every animal, bird, reptile and insect in the place turned out to see the tortoise dance. They were asked to sit in a semicircle, and no one was allowed to cross over, because the crow required the remainder of the circle for his performance. The crow began to sing the song of the kangaroo. Presently a figure approached to the front of the performance area. There was a great burst of shouts as the tortoise came creeping slowly toward the audience and at a sign from the crow commenced leaping and bounding here and there just like a kangaroo. They whispered among themselves how wonderful it was to see the tortoise acting the kangaroo dance. 'Hurrah! Hurrah!' they shouted. The dancer was really the frog, who was wearing a wooden dish on his back and a shield on his chest.

The second dance, the swan dance, was announced, and it was stated that the tortoise would sing the swan song. The tortoise took his stand in front of the audience and apparently commenced to sing, and the crow danced to the song. The animals, birds and reptiles could scarcely understand how the tortoise could be singing. It was really the cunning frog ventriloquist who was singing. But the audience was carried away with enthusiasm by the marvellous performance of the slow-moving, voiceless tortoise. 'Hurrah! Hurrah!' they shouted again.

For three days and three nights the performance lasted. On the fourth morning everyone began to feel hungry, and the kangaroo called out to the pelican, 'Get the net; bring the net and go fishing. The people are famishing with hunger.' The pelican set out and caught a number of fish, and the crow was unanimously appointed by the various tribes to take charge of the distribution of food. 'Come, let us go over there and cook the fish,' the kangaroo said. 'But you know it is against the rules of the tribe to cook fish where they are caught', replied the crow, who then addressed the pelicans, 'there is not enough food to go round; try to get some more in the bay.'

The pelicans dragged with their nets and caught some more fish.

'Come over here! It is unlawful to make a fire and cook there,' the crow repeated, until the whole assembly became impatient.

They began to abuse the crow, but the cunning frog supported the crow, and made it appear that the voice came from the kangaroo. Presently it seemed that the kangaroo was insulting the emu; then that the goanna had begun to insult the laughing jackass, and the wombat the dingo. They all grew angry with one another. The frog saw his opportunity, and called, 'To battle! To battle!'

The tribes were all so hungry and angry that they commenced calling each other ugly names. Each challenged the other to battle, and they hurled spears and boomerangs. Only the lyre-bird stood aloof and took no part in using insulting words, but strove to bring about reconciliation.

Since the time of this great battle the animals, the birds, the reptiles and the insects each adopted a language of their own, but because he took no part in the fight and tried to maintain peace, the lyre-bird is able to imitate them all.

This is really a story about a marriage corroboree that ran amok; and it was lucky it did so. If the kangaroo had married the emu, the dingo the goanna and so on – if the tribes of animals had intermarried – then they could have produced no young, and man himself would have perished.

The myth ends with the lyre-bird as the hero of the battle. Slightly larger than the pigeon, the lyre-bird is named for the three types of feathers making up its tail, which has the appearance of an ancient lyre. Like our cat-bird, which is capable of imitating the songs of other birds, the lyre-bird is something of a mimic. And bower-birds, of which the lyre-bird is a variety, have the most elaborate mating dance rituals of all indigenous animals. When the mating season arrives, the lyre-bird constructs 'bowers', which the Aboriginals call 'dance huts'. To make a bower, the Australian variety of lyre-bird, *menura alberti*, vigorously scratches the ground to clear a space in the forest. Here the male erects a structure consisting of an entrance and performance area with the help of sticks placed upright. The entrance and floor are carpeted with brightly coloured objects, such as berries, feathers and stones. The males and females display their dancing talents within, and the males compete for the females in dance marathons. Afterwards the winner pairs off with a mate and reproduces. A turn-of-the-century traveller in Australia, named Maclaren, witnessed the dances of another variety of bower-bird imitated by the Aboriginal called the stilt-bird, which holds mating rituals in huge numbers. In *My Crowded Solitude* he gave the following lively description of the amazing spectacle: 'The birds . . . were long-legged creatures, tall almost as storks, and white and grey of feather; and the dance took place in the centre of a broad, dry, swamp from the edge of which, in a place of concealment, we watched. There were some hundreds of them, and their dance was in the manner of a quadrille, but in the matter of rhythm and grace excelling any quadrille that ever was. In groups of a score or more they advanced and retreated, lifting high their long legs and standing on their toes, now and then bowing to one another, now and then one pair encircling with prancing daintiness a group whose heads moved upwards and downwards and sidewise in time to the stepping of the lead pair. At times they formed into one great prancing mass, with their long necks thrust upward; and the wide swaying of their backs was like unto the swaying of the sea. Then, suddenly, as in response to an imperative command, they would sway apart, some of them to rise in low, encircling flight, and some to stand as in little gossiping groups; and presently they would form in pairs or sets of pairs, and the prancing and the bowing, and advancing and retreating would begin all over again.'

The Aboriginal, who places such a high premium on the imitative power of dance, identifies himself with the bower-birds. Like the lyre-bird in the 'Confusion of Tongues', the Aboriginal considers himself the luckiest of creatures, since he can speak the language of every species through sounds and gestures alone. In this sense he is an ideal diplomat, capable of interpreting the reproductive signals of all races of animals; and he can, if necessary, dissolve disputes among the breeding animals. Like the lyre-bird, the Aboriginal too keeps nature in order and harmony through his corroboree magic.

A random sampling of the titles of dances accompanied by songs at corroborees shows the range of species represented. In Arnhem Land the names of literally hundreds of dances have been recorded, including 'Stalking the bulowird bird', 'parrot sucking and eating flowers', 'crow picking food', 'green hornet boring hole', 'crab in a hole'. The lyrics of the emu dance from the Ilpara area dictate the steps of the emu dancers, who appear with sharp sticks. 'Raising their heads high,/ They dance proudly.// The small round hut/ Resounds loudly.// With your strong sticks/ Scar the ground!// As you stab and mark the ground,/ Stoop and bow your heads!// As you stab and mark the ground,/ May you travel far!// Once I am gone,/ Others will sing on.'

While some dances represent the animal more or less realis-tically, many sacrifice realism for the express end of attracting a sexual partner. In tribes along the Roper and Victoria Rivers, men and women each have their repertoire of songs and dances known as Djarada love-songs, studied by Ronald Berndt and others. These have the specific purpose of alluring a partner for sexual intercourse. The dancers perform in groups out of sight, though not out of hearing range, of the opposite sex. In Djarada there are several love patrons led by Mungga-Mungga, 'Mother of us all', whose sexual liaisons were legion. The men are especially excited to hear the women sing her conquests, because they imply a relaxation in rules of who can pair off with whom. Dancing, in other words, is allowed to be openly erotic, just as it was in the early, mythological period known as Alcheringa or 'Dreamtime'. Songs and dances are in fact suggested to the performers through dreams and contain sexual allusions veiled though the animal metaphor. The anticipation of physical nourishment in love-making is, for instance, expressed through the metaphor of a bird feeding at the spring associated with Mungga-Mungga. In 'flying fox goes down to water', the men sing to the legs of a woman so that she will come and drink at a man's fountain, just as a flying fox dives down to a pool to quench his thirst. The 'black-nose snake song' expresses a man's fantasy for the woman, 'breast be close to man, dreaming for genitalia'. The 'dingo song' accompanies a fast-moving, frenzied dance of the women. The words of the song describe the woman standing up naked in a surge of excitation in terms of the dingo bitch in heat. A chorus of women repeat with insistence 'djini', 'djini', the word for the only domesticated animal of the Aboriginals. Also in the women's repertoire is 'Garagan', the chicken hawk, which implores the bird to take her message of love to the object of her desire. Before dancing the men rub their bodies with wallaby fat and the women smear their bodies with paint; the sensuous dancing of naked, oiled bodies, and the freeing from inhibition encouraged by wooing each other openly in the manner of animals, naturally increases the physical desire among the men and women performing in the seductive air of night.

Munggeraui, an Aboriginal artist, painted a complicated corroboree scene on bark. The painting narrates the early dances of the Flying Fox People in the mythological Alcheringa. In the middle of the upper zone of the painting two members of the tribe surrounded by an oval formation of dancers inspect the goings on at the corroboree. These two, Garagan and Gulmadja, the Eagle Hawk Men, spot the two prettiest girls from among the dancers (pictured on either side of the oval) and take them off to the bushes, where they make love. After their love-making the girls change into flying foxes, and the men into eagle hawks (square zone). They fly to a new, comfortable home. When the other dancers in the corroboree see what has happened to the pretty girls, they instantly change themselves into the animals they were imitating in the dance, the kangaroo, goanna, emus and dogs. All scatter and settle in special places. The kangaroos go to a place called Bulbula, the goanna to Gurunga, and the two dogs to Cape Arnhem. In these various locales they create features of the physical landscape, the harbour, rocks and trees, and their spirits reside there to this day.

The belief in the correlation between the reproductive activities of humans and those of animals is widespread. Far to the north of Australia the Eskimos of Baffin Island hold a courting dance just at the time when the seals are about to mate. The most widely known of all Eskimo stories tells about Sedna, mistress of the underworld, who created the fish and sea animals. Sedna was the daughter of a wicked king. She refused to marry any of the suitors her father offered her and instead married a bird. The angry father killed the bird and took his daughter away from the bird's island in a boat. A huge storm arose at sea, tipping the boat and casting Sedna overboard. The father, convinced that Sedna was being punished for her unnatural marriage, made no attempt to rescue his beautiful daughter. Sedna clung for dear life on to the edge of the boat, but the cruel father cut off her fingers. The fingers from the princess's hand became the fish and mammals of the sea. After that time Sedna became the goddess of the underworld, and each autumn, when the sea animals mate, the Eskimos hold a dance festival in her honour.

Baffin Island is a long, narrow strip of land north of the Arctic Circle between Greenland and the Canadian mainland. Almost the entire Eskimo population lives along the coast of the island. Because the earth is frozen, agriculture is impossible, and the Eskimos rely entirely on the meat of sea and land animals for food. During the summer months they hunt for seals in kayaks from which they spear the slippery sea mammal. The Eskimos see a spiritual force in every natural phenomenon – stone and snow, wind and birds, sky and water. They believe that these objects possess human characteristics, and they respect the spirits responsible for watching over them. After the seal-hunting season the Eskimos of Baffin Island take measures to ensure that Sedna, patroness of seal life, is in no way offended by the killing of her animals, since she regulates the supply of seals. They hold an elaborate dance ceremony which climaxes in a couple dance to give thanks to the goddess. During this time they allow Sedna to inspect the behaviour of all members of the tribe. She easily recognizes sin, because the stumps remaining from the fingers cut off by her father smart with pain whenever humans err. Sedna herself does not appear but sends her servant Qailertetang. Her role is played by a sorcerer dressed in a seal-skin suit and wearing a seal mask. Qailertetang is deaf and dumb, but has keen-sighted vision. At a glance she spots any signs of misconduct, and has authority from Sedna to punish offenders.

Towards the end of the ceremony Qailertetang begins dancing, enthusiastically flapping her arms like seal flippers. Her dance is taken as an invitation for the men and women to join in. The goddess's servant arranges the men and women in facing rows. In the course of the dance, Qailertetang weaves in and out among the dancers like a seal dashing about in the water. She sidles up to one dancer and leads him to a certain woman in the line. She continues until each dancer is matched up with that dancer whose rhythm is best suited to his partner's. Two by two Qailertetang dances charms about the couples, then sends them off to be man and wife for a twenty-four-hour period. The ceremony accomplishes two related purposes. First, it increases the human population. But it is also believed that the seals need to be liberated sexually; the Eskimos hope that the seals will be moved to imitate their example and pair off in their own sea mating dances.

Cow and Bull

No animal species is so constantly associated with matrimony as the cow and her consort, the bull. In ancient and tribal cultures where cattle are kept, the comparison between young, marriageable women and cattle is a standard practice pleasing to the girl and her parents. Until recently, when a girl was betrothed the bride's family would offer the girl along with a dowry to the groom's family. A girl's endowment could take many forms: money, fabrics, textiles, grain, property, and very often, cattle. This custom is reflected in the names given to girls in ancient Greece in the hope that they would attract good husbands: 'Polyboia', means 'worth many cows', 'Phereboia' means 'bringing in many cows', and 'Euboia' means 'rich in cattle'.

In addition to the monetary importance of cattle in the institution of marriage, the cow and bull have important symbolic values. The symbolic relationship between cow and bull, queen and consort, can be seen in the marriage vows exchanged by the bridal pair at the weddings of the ancient Romans; at the altar the words of the bride were 'where thou art the bull, I am the cow.' The bull is an extremely potent animal sexually, and when it mates with the cow, by extension the activity magically transfers life to the plants growing in the earth, and to the animals feeding on the plants. The cow is the *alma mater*, the nourishing mother. As milk-producer, she supplies the liquid of life and has become the symbol of mother earth in many cultures.

The association is gracefully captured in an anonymous Sanskrit poem (1500 BC–1000 BC) about the dawn; 'She, like a dancer/ Puts her broidered garments on,/ As a cow yields her udder so bares she her breast./ In Hindu culture, where the cow is still held sacred, cattle accompany the bride and groom to the bride's village in the colourful marriage processions of the Santals. Two to three weeks after the wedding ceremony the bride returns to visit her family. The return visit, called the Sohrae festival, helps to ease the pangs of separation between the departed girl and her friends and family in the village. The climax of the Sohrae festivities consists of a ritual where the bride's cows dance. They are lined up and encouraged by the beating of drums to dance before an egg. Eventually they break it, and this symbolizes the girl's break with her home village.

According to ancient Hindu custom, a youth's manhood was tested before he could take a bride, in a ritual contest called 'Embracing the Bull'. The best bulls were driven into an enclosure similar to a rodeo stockade. The youths danced before the ferocious beasts, and if they had sufficient skill and courage, would leap on the backs of the bulls, embrace their necks, and then, in a virtuoso display of bravery, dance on the back. The successful participants were awarded a bride. A similar custom for girls about to marry is preserved in a dance song from Southern India called 'The Dance of the Cow Girls'. The lyrics of the song tell how a young maiden had to tend a bull for a year to prove that she could take on the task of tending a husband.

An Indian myth about the god Krishna, the Lord of the Cowherds, relates how the god's attendants, the milkmaids, first learned to dance. As a young god Krishna happened upon the milkmaids while they were bathing in the River Jumna. Watching them from a distance, he decided that he liked their nakedness. So he hid their saris which they had left by the riverbank. When the maidens emerged from the river and could not find their clothes, they were at a loss what to do. Their puzzlement turned to embarrassment when they saw Krishna laughing high up in a tree. They hid themselves in the river and begged him to return their garments. Krishna refused to give them back their saris, until all the milkmaids joined their hands and danced around him in supplication. All fell in love with the god and each wanted to hold his hand. So he multiplied his arms as many times as was necessary, and taught them how to dance in a circle around him, the *Rasalila* dance. The peacocks standing nearby watched the dance of the milkmaids and copied their movements in their own dances. In another version of the same legend, all the milkmaids fled except Radha, who begged for her sari and finally became the wife of the Cowherd Lord. This version forms the basis for the most popular Hindu dance drama performed to this day by the *nautch* dancers. It ends with the maidens dancing around Krishna and Radha.

The economy and culture of certain East African tribes are greatly influenced by their cattle. Formerly in Rwanda the most aristocratic of women imitated the walk of cows, and marriageable girls, in their dances, represented the horns of the cow with uplifted and outstretched arms. Today among the Nilotic Dinka of the Sudan, tending cattle is such a major occupation that the Dinka neglect their crops and produce only a small yield of grain. The preoccupation with cattle affects their customs, games, dances and poetry, recorded by Francis M. Deng, which consists mainly of poems in praise of cattle. The people use the dried dung of the cow as an abrasive and even rub their skin with it. Children in their games imitate the behaviour of adults by making cattlecamps. They use shells as cattle or make cattle figurines out of clay. Around fires made with the dried dung they sing make-believe songs about oxen to billy-goats dressed up to look like oxen. The children themselves rig up costumes out of cat-skins in imitation of the costumes worn by adults in their dances. Older children flirt and perform mock wedding ceremonies in cow dances. A common sight in western Dinkaland is that of a young man with both his arms curved over his head and dancing. This attitude represents the horns of display oxen, who are regarded as the equivalents of young warriors. A dance called the *gar* dance involves several young men and girls who imitate the offspring from the great bull. In the dance the men advance and retreat, directing and pushing their partners backwards or forwards. They shout 'e-yi! e-eyi' in marked rhythms while imitating the lumbering movements of the large beast. The young men think of themselves as the oxen, and the girls as the cows.

When a young Dinka man goes courting he stands outside a girl's house and sings a song, usually an ox-song. These sing praises to the beauty, strength and useful services of cattle. The songs also contain references to the customs and social organization of the herding tribes. A man sees himself as the guardian of his woman and performs duties in her honour: 'For a woman, a man spears an animal/ For a woman, a man keeps his cattle.' Women also compose ox-songs which they address to dancing partners who are about to become husbands.

Divorce, on the other hand, is a much avoided institution among the Dinka. It is an extremely complicated procedure because of the cattle already exchanged: determining how many cows should be returned for a divorce settlement is a sticky proposition. However, one of the grounds for divorce is failure to give the promised cattle-wealth, or failure to replace borrowed cattle. Should a Dinka woman be abandoned by her husband, she may compose an ox-poem to try to get him back. Once, the husband was so moved by the strength of his rejected wife's words, that he reinitiated the proceedings to exchange cattle and vows. The following poem, however, was composed by a woman who was divorced for dubious reasons: supposedly she caused the death of her child, but the woman herself thought that her loss of hearing turned her husband against her. To her, divorce meant more than a personal insult; it spelled the death of her people. The fragment of the poem below refers to several cattle exchanged at the original ceremony. They are called by name. One cow, named Yom, apparently was the offspring of a dancing cow called Dau Dancing Leopard, or Akol. The cow at least will live on: 'He will live on Yom, the Cow of Dau Dancing Leopard Akol, cow of my sister Abul./ Abyei, Crossing Wild Dogs, fetch the cow from Maker, the camp of Abyor,/ The Great Camp of Deng, Reverberating Drums,/ Fetch the cow Yom, from the son of the girl of your clan Pajok;/ Tell the son of Makuany de Deng D'Ayuel/ To give me the cow, Yom./ Our relationship is spoiled with the / Family of Baar Shining-Dark Shade . . . / I have brought death to the Family of Baar;/ But I do not know the wrong I have done/ O Mother, daughter of Ajing, the Spotted Leopard . . . / The great clan of Biong d'Allor has always perished/ We are the ancient victims of death. . . .'

VI The Dancing Animal as Guardian, Healer and Helper

'The son of a great woman/ You big red bull,/ You son of
a red she-bull/ You who didst drink my milk,/ You to
whom I did not give my breast slowly.'

BUSHMAN POEM

The initiate passes from an immature, dependent state, to become a
mature and independent member of the tribe. He is now a
provider. The males provide food for the tribe through hunting,
while the females often take charge of agricultural activities. The
females also bear and nourish their young. When male and female
come of age they join in marriage to establish a self-contained,
self-perpetuating unit. They ensure the continuity of the human
population.

The animal too is a provider. In a practical sense the meat from
the animal carcass provides sustenance and nourishment for the
people, its hide and fur, warmth. In a magical sense the animal is a
benefactor, patron and protector of mankind. For example, he
gives people fire, teaches the art of agriculture, or instructs them in
the steps of the dance. The animal bestows favours on people or
secures charms for them from the gods. In preparatory hunting
rituals, as in the hunting dances of the North American Indians
examined earlier, dancers appealed for counsel and advice to the
guardian spirit of the hunt, since it is the spirit who dispenses and
renews the species of hunted game. The animal spirit may inter-
vene on man's behalf for the growth of the crops, curing illness,
protecting a tribe from war, and so on. Provided that the people
maintain good diplomatic relations with the spirit, he may be
persuaded to act as an ambassador to the gods when drought or
famine strike, or when plague threatens. The tribe's medicine-
man, the virtuoso dancer, is the human incarnation of the animal
ambassador. Through his disguises and shape-shifting he journeys
to far-off lands to confront inimical gods and to interpret and
translate divine will into human needs.

The epigram of this chapter is addressed to a mythical Bushman
hero. The speaker is the mother, who calls herself a she-bull, in
other words, the milk-provider. She calls her son the scion of a
red-bull, that is, the eland, or larger variety of antelope. Animal

blood virtually runs through the veins of the Bushman: throughout Bushman culture an empathy and identification with animals, especially the antelope and its cousins, are felt. Poems such as the hunters' lament ('Please don't kill my antelope . . .'), pantomimes, dances, rituals, and most emphatically, works of art painted with pigment mixed with the animal's blood, are consecrated to the eland, rhebuck, gemsbok, hartebeest and duiker. The horizon of the Bushman is bound by these various species of antelope.

The mother–son relationship intoned in the praise poem to the bull-hero speaks for a prevailing metaphor in Bushman social life. The solidarity of the Bushman community, composed of small bands of nuclear families, is buttressed by the survival and continuity of two varieties of antelope in particular, the eland and the smaller rhebuck. Bushman paintings from the Drakensberg Range, which have been painstakingly studied by Patricia Vinnicombe, repeatedly portray scenes of rhebuck in family groupings of ten to fifteen – the size of the herd being about that of the Bushman band – grazing, gambolling and frolicking. The mother and her young are sensitively expressed. The dam gives suck to her young, or leads them to pasturage. In one petroglyph a fawn can be seen still attached to the mother by the umbilical cord. Affectionate portrayals of adult rhebuck are also frequent, and the only representation of copulation in the art of the Drakensberg region is among rhebuck. The larger antelope, the eland, in turn expresses the stability of the Bushmen as a race. This majestic animal has a gentle and benevolent character with a strong disposition for domestication. It is the most often portrayed animal in Bushman art and has inspired lively poems, folktales and dances.

Although prey to both lion and man, the antelope commands respect for its beauty and swiftness, fine instinct and alertness, natural grace, and affectionate care of its young. Seeing an antelope

Petroglyph showing fawn attached to mother by umbilical cord. After Vinnicombe

on the run one is struck by its bristling energy, especially when it skims the terrain in criss-cross movements, often jumping for no apparent reason four to six feet into the air. The antelope's prodigious leaps naturally make it an animal worthy of emulation in the dance; and, indeed, elands sometimes do seem to dance explosively after a rainfall. The Bushman dancer ties a leather pouch filled with dried berries to his ankles, in order to make his rhythmic stomping more audible; rather ironically, the percussive rattles are made from the ears of the antelope. A piece of Bushman folklore describes the loving manufacture of the rattle and the drum, likewise made from antelope hide: 'Springbok ears they are; we call them dancing rattles. They sound well when we have tied them to our feet. Therefore they dance well on account of it, while they feel that the drum, which the women beat, sounds well. The dancing rattles sound well because a woman who works nicely has made them . . .'

It is in between the toes of the antelope that the Bushman god of creation likes to get a free ride. If the antelope is the spiritual protector of the Bushman, Mantis is the material protector and provider. For he created the antelope that sustains and supports the Bushman. In the folktales of the Bushmen the little insect god will tell you that he is like the antelope, that he made his heart and mind in the manner of the eland. The folktales are filled with talking animals, especially animals that quarrel. They play tricks on one another, lie, steal and cheat; they mourn, rescue and resurrect their animal friends and foes. The strong human tinge in these animal fables stems from a belief that at the beginning all animals were humans.

According to a myth about the origin of the eland, Mantis, who is a Bushman god in the form of an insect, created the stately creature by pouring honey onto a dance shoe. In the beginning of the world the sun always shone; night was unknown. It was during this early period that Mantis came upon the discarded shoe of Kwammang-a, whose wife was Porcupine. Kwammang-a himself was the spirit of the rainbow. The little shoe was made of animal hide. Mantis took the shoe down to the bank of the river and placed it at the water's edge, whereupon he poured honey over the leather. Then he went away. When he returned he looked into the still waters and saw a tiny eland taking shape. But it was still so tiny that he left the creature in the protection of the waters. When he next returned he recognized the spoor of the eland on the riverbank. He looked about him and saw the small eland, who shyly approached his father. Mantis, deeply moved by the delicacy and perfection of his son, wept, and as he wept, he caressed the animal, massaging honey deep into its ribs. Mantis left the eland alone for a time to grow, until finally the creature was big and strong, an eland bull. Mantis was deeply satisfied with his creation and left the eland to his own devices.

Ichneumenon, however, who had been deceived by Mantis, led Kwammang-a to the place where the eland was watering to show him what had become of his shoe. And when he saw, he grew very angry, took out his bow, and shot an arrow at the eland, and he perished. Next Kwammang-a cut the hide and stretched it out in the bullrushes to dry. Then, with the help of the male members of his family, he took the meat and the hide back to his camp. When Mantis, who was wandering in the forest, got wind of the heinous crime he came quickly, but he was too late. He lay down by the stream and wept. All he saw was the gall-bladder of the eland hanging in the tree, for the gall was the only part of the animal Kwammang-a could not put to use. In his bitterness Mantis began arguing with the gall. He threatened to burst it open with a rock. But the gall answered that it would engulf him. Mantis pierced the gall and, as he had been warned, it covered the little insect god. The world grew dark. But Mantis managed somehow to make his way about and stole through the night like a thief until he found the shoe of Kwammang-a. He took the shoe and threw it up high into the sky: there it began to shine; it was the moon. And by the light of the moon Mantis created new eland. And so every night the little leather shoe skips across the sky, then falls away to return to life the next day. At night the hunters cannot see, and the eland, under this mantle of near darkness, takes refuge to reproduce its numbers.

Like Mantis, the shamans of the early period of history had the power to create and revive dead antelope. But this race of shamans died off in a dance so violent that blood spilled from their noses until, finally, there was no blood left in their bodies. Now they live as antelope-headed men underwater where they perform their restorative dances. Shamans of the Bushman tribes were considered the living descendants of the antelope spirits. Whenever illness of any kind struck – famine, war, or sickness – the shaman performed the Dance of Blood in honour of Mantis. Arbousset, a nineteenth-century traveller, witnessed the *Moqoma*, or Dance of Blood, and described it in the following words: 'They gambol together till all are fatigued and covered with perspiration. The thousand cries which they raise, and the exertions which they make, are so violent that it is not unusual to see someone sink to the ground and exhausted and covered with blood, which pours from the nostrils. . . . When a man falls, . . . the women gather around him. . . . They carefully wipe off the perspiration with ostrich feathers, leaping backwards and forwards across his back. Soon the air revives him; he rises, and this in general terminates the strange dance.'

Nowadays the remaining Bushman tribes have medicine songs and dances named after potent elements, such as fire, sun and animals. Among the most effective and dramatic of the dances is the Gemsbok Medicine Dance. Like the Dance of Blood, the outward purpose of the dance is to make the medicine-man pour out as much sweat as possible from his body. Before he begins, the shaman swallows gemsbok medicine made from the animal's blood and entrails. The dance itself is extremely dangerous because the medicine-man must work himself into a deep trance from which it is sometimes difficult to emerge. To get the medicine-man hot, the women clap feverishly while chanting the Gemsbok Medicine Song. They crouch in a circle around a fire, flailing their arms like the flapping of bird's wings. The shaman dances near the fire, and as he dances, the body gyrating around the fire acts like an oven to warm the medicine to full potency. When the sorcerer is about to faint, he places himself with his back to the source of the illness and emits a piercing cry towards the sky: he shrieks away the illness. Often at this critical stage he loses consciousness and his heart stops. The women rush to his side and massage the heart. Others wipe the sweat from his limbs and smear it on the invalid. During the trance state, known as 'half-death', the shaman's soul leaves the body and visits the spirits of the water. It is the most dangerous moment, but the power of the gemsbok medicine protects him. When the soul returns to his body, the sorcerer rises and advances towards the patient. Now with the knowledge imparted to him by the eland water spirits, he snorts out the illness, which comes in the form of an owl or a butterfly, or invisible arrows. He makes the patient bleed and transmits the medicine streaming from his pores into the patient's system.

Illness of any kind, whether a blight on the crops, or a disease weakening the individual, is a threat to the entire community. The malignancy must be understood, and at all costs be kidnapped, dispersed, or eradicated. Until the evil influence has been removed, an imbalance reigns, which reflects disorder between man and his supernatural world, gripping all alike in an anxious hold.

39–41 In many traditional
societies, the attitude towards
animals is ambivalent: they are
both guardians and helpers and
the enemy to be hunted and
killed. The North American
Indians put on and dance in the
skins of animals familiar to
them: *right*, grizzly bear; *below*,
wolf. The animal as friend and
foe is epitomized in the Nigerian
dance-mask (*below right*), where
the hunter embraces both his
hunting dog and his prey, the
antelope.

44–46 *Opposite above*, Australian ▷
Aboriginals dancing with personal totems
on their bodies. *Opposite below*, attributes
of the animal totem are assumed in the
costumes of these Aboriginals: *left*, the
eagle-hawk; *right*, the emu.

42–43 Totems, the guardians of an ethnic
group or an individual member, are sometimes
chosen for their ancestral or fraternal
relationship to the totemist. Totems could either
be worn or danced around, as in these North
American Indian totem poles. The pole on the
right depicts a man with three frequently chosen
totemic subjects.

47–49 Dances have been performed in many regions of the world as part of the hunting ritual. *Below*, the Yaqui Deer Dance (Mexico); *right*, the Masai Lion Dance (Kenya); *bottom*, engraving, after Carl Bodmer, from Maximilian's *Travels* (1843), showing the Mandan bison dance (North American Indian).

50 Drawing from George Catlin's *Illustrations* . . . (1876) of bison hunters disguised as wolves.

51 Indian rock painting from Bhimbetka, Deccan (*c.* 5500 BC), showing a hunting dance.

52 Disguised ostrich hunter in a South African Bushman rock painting.

53–55 Dance has traditionally been regarded as an agent of fertility. Many kinds of rain dances are enacted to help mature the crops and ensure a good harvest. *Left*, an Aboriginal rain dancer quivering. *Right*, a Hopi Indian gathers up snakes in the Snake-Antelope dance ceremony, which is performed over sixteen days to bring on the summer rains. *Below*, the North American Pueblo Indians, renowned for their expertise in agriculture, preparing for a rain dance.

56, 57 The wings on the mask of this Bobo butterfly rain dancer of Upper Volta are spun by the drummer to bring on the rainfall. The success of the harvest depends on warmth as well as water and in agricultural societies one of the purposes of fire dances is to 'warm up' the earth. *Below*, a Baining fire dancer wears a giant, elaborate mask again with propeller-like features.

58 The hobby-horse dance is traditionally associated with the change in season. In Padstow, Cornwall, the 'Obby 'Oss dance is performed annually to chase winter's frost from the countryside. The ritual contest between winter and spring is symbolized by the ceremonial beheading and resurrection of the horse. Here the horse's 'old' and 'new' heads are visible.

59 The Blue Flute Clan, who feature in the legend of the Hopi of Arizona about the quest for the four quadrants of the universe, created the hump-backed flute-player, a locust; the sound of his flute brought warmth to the earth. Bowl from the Hohokam culture of Arizona depicting such a figure.

60 The Hopi Indians enact part of this legend in a flute dance. In the ceremony, alternating annually with the Snake-Antelope Dance, the sound of the flute is intended, as in the legend, to create warmth and thereby encourage fertility.

Medicine dances are of two kinds. The first is directed towards curing an individual who is racked by pain and disease, or possessed by a demonic spirit. Sometimes the invalid himself dances, but more often the cure is performed by the shaman, as in the Bushman Gemsbok Medicine Dance. The second type of curative dance confers a general aura of health and well-being on the community, its plants and flocks. In the Green Corn Dance of the Iroquois Indians the immature stalks of corn are treated as invalids. The dancers disguise themselves as various animals and bless the plants, and the green ears are coaxed to full golden fruition. The role of the animals as doctors in the dance is told in the origin myth of a secret society of the Seneca Iroquois. The founder of the society one day observed animals conducting fertility rites and dances. He learned their steps by heart, and upon returning to his people, he taught them how to perform the dances of the animals. The participants in the secret society would imitate the movements of many species, including the eagle, bear and otter in their dances. The purpose of the pantomimes was to cure illness, and in the widest sense to promote the well-being of the tribe and its crops.

Medicine dances which incorporate animal movements such as the Seneca Secret Society Dances are grounded in the belief that certain animals possess powers to assist the shaman in tracking down the illness, much as hunters are helped by dogs to follow the spoor of their quarry. Large predators, such as the mountain lion, buffalo and bear, were held in particular esteem by the North American Indians. But animals can both cause and cure illness. And the same animal that cures may also have caused the illness, or may alone hold the secret for relief. It is therefore crucial that the dancing shaman identify and communicate with the animal. If he does, the animal may reveal to him the source and cure at the moment when the shaman reaches the peak of his ecstatic dance.

Among the North American Indians, the bear was the great doctor. According to legend, the bear gave mankind a potent form of medicine called aster root, capable of curing all illness. The people of the tribe in return gave presents to the bear shaman at the curing ceremonies: a thread from a blanket and a portion of prayer meal, placed together in a corn husk. Before dancing in imitation of the bear, the shaman chewed the aster root which had hallucino-genic effect. The drug and the rapid dancing induced a trance-like state that enabled the shaman to peer into the witch spirit causing the illness. Having localized and paralysed the spirit, the shaman literally sucked it out of the patient's body. To make the cure seem more convincing he would use sleight-of-hand tricks. For example, he hid a fish-hook in his jaws, and when about to suck out the disease, he cut his gum; he then spat out the harmful poison with a mouthful of blood, leaving the onlookers persuaded that the magic of the bear doctor had worked.

The curative power of the animal is enhanced by terrifying masks. Masks of horned animals are common, partly because a mask surmounted by a horn has a more impressive visual impact, and partly because of the intrinsic power of the horn. Perhaps the most outwardly frightening masks are the devil masks used to exorcise demons in the Sri Lankan devil-dances. The large eyes of the masks and a triad of serpents on the crown are meant to frighten the demon possessing the invalid. Beryl de Zoete, one of the most gifted writers on dance, and an expert in dance in Bali and South-east Asia, described the *Kattadiya* devil dance in Sri Lanka. This was a dramatic ceremony which included sixteen masked figures, led by a devil dancer wearing the devil mask. The ceremony was held before a large group of spectators and centred around the victim of possession who was placed in the middle of the performance area. For several hours before the masked dance, a naked youth danced tirelessly before the body of the patient. The dancing of the youth gradually gave way to a processional display of

Sri Lankan devil mask. After Hambley

the masked dancers led by the devil. The cure involved the use of a real animal, the cock. One of the dancers, wearing a shaggy mane the colour of the cock's wattle, brandished a live cock in the face of the patient. He displayed the bird in a vast number of contorted positions, then, fixing a wing between his teeth, he swung the bird in the face of the sick man. At this point a curtain was drawn to hide the invalid from the spectators. Masks more terrifying than before advanced one by one to the area behind the curtain. Finally a masked dancer dressed in leaves and wearing coal-black feathers around his face approached, holding a torch and sticking out his grotesque scarlet tongue. At this final apparition the curtain was whisked away to reveal the patient now cured and standing upright next to the devil dancer. He stared at the crowd and sank to the ground amidst a burst of flames.

Animals are guardians of moral law and social order. In Africa the use of animals to effect social control is prevalent, as for example in the Ikaki Tortoise Masquerade. Animals punish and correct behaviour in discipline dances, as earlier examined in discipline masks and dances for children. In New Britain, adults and children alike of the Baining tribes used to participate in ritual dances, where errant behaviour was punished by flogging with branches representing snakes. The meaning of these rites is imperfectly known since the tribes, now extinct, were secretive by nature and extremely reluctant to discuss the significance of their art and rituals with anthropologists. The masked ghost and snake dance of a Baining secret society, however, was described by Gregory Bateson and others, and is, by all counts, exotic. The general outlines of the ritual suggest that in the course of it the participants allowed themselves to be frightened by the apparition of ghosts and snakes, called Aios, and then overcame their fear by roasting and eating the snakes.

The ritual took place in the bush. The staging and preparation for the snake-handling ceremony were important and built on an element of suspense. The actual location of the rite was kept secret throughout the period of preparation, and was revealed only in time for the participants to assemble. A party proceeded to the forest in the afternoon before the ceremony to make the stage wet with rain, and to prevent anyone from spying on the chosen territory. The stage consisted of a clearing, a number of lean-to structures sheltering yams, taro, leaves, and other food for the feast, and a huge bonfire which the children kept alight during the proceedings.

At nightfall the men arrived first, whereupon they looked in horror upon a ghost looming in the bushes beyond. This was represented by an elder wearing a huge bark mask. The men urged the women to follow, making sure they kept their heads bowed so as not to see the ghost. Once everyone was gathered around the fire, a drummer struck up a steady, slow rhythm. The drumming maintained an aura of expectation for the next several hours, during which the women danced. At midnight the beat of the drum was answered by a distant echo of drums which seemed to come from along the wide path leading to the performance area. The drum reached a climax and suddenly died away. A dancer leapt onto the scene wearing a billowy white fabric mask painted in blood with insects, tortoise bones, opossums' tails, and floral patterns. The upper part of his body was covered by a framework, known as the *kavat*, made from bamboo and covered with strips of bark. The structure stuck out several feet before and behind, giving him the appearance of an exotic insect. To complete his disguise the dancer wore a penis decoration, white and cylindrical in shape, eighteen inches erect and crowned with a mushroom-shaped head. Small snakes spiralled about his wrist and forearms. In his hands he held the ends of a ten-foot snake which he manoeuvred like a jump-rope. The dancer prowled about the fire and, brandishing the snakes, rushed towards the audience. A few moments later a second man entered. He was known as the *vwunggvwungg*, so called because he concealed a trumpet under his mask which made a sound resembling his name. At intervals of a few minutes, more *kavats* and *vwunggvwunggs* bounded out of the forest. Altogether eight dancers haunted the fire, skipping over writhing snakes. Occasionally, to enormous shouts of applause, a dancer leapt through the flames. The ritual reached its climax when the dancers mingled with the onlookers and distributed the snakes. Everyone handled them fearlessly, men, women and children. They took them and played, lacing them through their bodies and arms. The general uproar and commotion completely drowned out the sounds of the *vwunggvwunggs*. Finally the snakes were entrusted to the women who placed them in bags for roasting and eating. The snakes were of a poisonous variety, but their fangs had been removed.

Animals serve as emblems or personal protectors. Initiates into Andamanese society were seen to be protected by the power they acquired from the turtle in dancing. Among the North American Indians, where there was a tendency to associate each tribesman with a spiritual or natural force (with, for example, names like

'Elk's Heart', 'Twisted Rock', or 'Morning Star'), dances solid-
ified the tie between a person and his emblem. At the initiation
ceremony of the Luiseño Indians of Southern California, the boys
enjoyed an intoxicating infusion made from the flowers of *datura
meteloides*; when they were quite drunk they got down on their
hands and knees and began imitating the sounds of birds and
animals like the weasel, hawk, owl, or raven. The animal which an
initiate impersonated most naturally and convincingly became from
that time onwards his life-long protector.

Animal guardians and helpers must be worshipped in some
manner. In Australia animal dances are an effective and widespread
form of prayer. The Aboriginals give groups within moieties names
which show an affinity with the concrete and visual in the natural
world, and a feeling for the poetic image. For example, linguistic
groups of the *Dua* moiety of Arnhem Land call themselves 'cry of
the pigeon', 'gum-tree', 'blanket lizard after wild honey', 'long
white cloud'; groups from the *Jiritja* moiety are named 'shoal of
young mullet', 'wild honey bee', 'parrot calling out upon seeing
spring water flowing'. As the names suggest, the Aboriginal
chooses and identifies himself with a particular plant or animal
which acts as a protective totem. The origin of the animal totems
goes back to the prehistoric period of mythology. The ancestors of
Alcheringa, similar in their habits to the Aboriginals, were nomads
who emigrated from an unknown country far to the east. During
their wanderings they established the geographical features of the
land – cliffs and promontories, sandhills, valleys, ditches, plateaux
and watering-places – locales where after death they returned to
live in spirit. It is believed that the various animal species can
assume human form and visit the ancestors in these sacred places.

Imitative dances of the animal totems or ancestors in rites called
Intichiuma re-enact simple characteristic actions of the animal,
with notable exceptions. The dances are rounded out with songs
describing the wanderings or habits of the animal. In the Emu
Dance, for example, one of the performers imitates the emu taking
a drink in a pool of water; he bows his head down, and before
drinking takes a quick look to both sides; when he is assured of his
safety he sinks down on his knees and goes through the motions of
sipping; another performer meanwhile whistles to produce the
sound-effects. The Witchetty-grub ceremony enacts the birth of
the insect. A long wurley (hut) represents the chrysalis. From inside
the wurley the performers sing about the pre-natal stages of the
insect's life, and as they wriggle their way out, they sing about the

witchetty-grub's birth. A performer representing a snake ancestor drops to his knees, quivers and writhes, hissing. The pantomimes are short and accurate episodes from the natural life of the species. Each totem dance is performed by members named after that totem: the emu dance by emu totemites, the witchetty-grub by witchetty-grub totemites, and so on. The members' life-long association and identification with the individual species are secured through dance and related ritual forms of worship.

Animals reveal divine will by disclosing the future. Divination through the observation of animal movements is a widespread and enduring practice since earliest antiquity. Today, in the heart of New York City's Chinatown, you can, for a very small amount, have your fortune told by a dancing chicken. The scraggly fowl is penned up on one side of a glass case until the customer's coin releases a trap door, allowing the chicken to enter the other side which contains a plate about the size of a gramophone disc. Pellets of grain drop down onto the plate. As the chicken makes a dash for its meal the plate begins to revolve, forcing the chicken to 'dance'. The dance lasts only a minute or so, at the end of which a slip of paper like those found in Chinese fortune cookies emerges from the bottom of the case. A person's fortune is supposedly predicted according to the vibrations received from the plate on which the chicken dances.

Priests of a fox-divining cult of the Dogon in Mali interpret the future for clients. This they do by reading the traces left by a fox dancing on a special divination table drawn into the sand. It requires talent and devotion to become a member of the Dogon fox-divining cult. A man must be gifted with an excellent memory and have a flair for subtle interpretation. Then only after five to six years' apprenticeship can he qualify to read the dance steps of the fox in order to advise clients on what action they should take. The sheer variety of choices facing a diviner and the implications of these choices are staggering. The six zones of the divining table theoretically offer sixty possible interpretations to any question – sixty being an important number in the Dogon cosmogony, since the primordial world, made of placenta, was divided into sixty parts. The table is believed to represent the placenta in agricultural terms; in other words, the table is the field sown by the seed of the fox when he is well disposed towards humans. The diviner is ultimately dealing with questions whose interpretation depends on an intimate understanding of the cycles of life and death, destruction and creation in the human, animal and vegetable worlds.

In Dogon belief, man and fox have a special affinity. The Dogon identify with the wily animal's subtle powers of communication and insight. Yet, they are better than a man's: the fox, they say, is twenty times more intelligent. Yurugu, the pale fox of Dogon mythology, was so clever that he killed his father just by dancing. A Dogon folktale explains how the Creator recognized the fox's unusual intelligence and rewarded him for it. One day Amma decided to test the intelligence of animals. He would tell the animals that his mother had died, but in reality keep her hidden under a pile of blankets inside the house. He called to his side a bird known for his piercing, mournful cry, and bade him proclaim his mother's death throughout the land. As was expected, each of the animals called on Amma to offer condolences. In the doorway Amma met and talked with them one by one, while just inside the mother, hidden under the blankets, could hear their voices. God and his mother noticed that of all the animals the fox did not come. He summoned the wild dog of the bush and asked, 'Why is it that you alone of all the animals do not comfort me in my hour of need?' To which the fox replied, 'Sir, if your mother had truly died, I surely would have paid my respects, but since she is lying just inside the doorway under many blankets, pray, why should I waste my valuable time?' Amma's plan had worked. He had discovered the animal who was most shrewd and intuitive. For this proof of clairvoyance, Amma rewarded the fox with the power of divination and proclaimed, 'Henceforth you shall reveal the future to mortals, and you shall announce your predictions in the dance.' If you were to watch a Dogon fox diviner at work, you would see just outside the village a hunched figure examining a rectangle roughly the size of a shuffle-board court imprinted in the sand. The rectangle is divided into six zones which represent earth, the heavens and the underworld. In one corner are two simple circles, symbols of a man's mouth and food. Carefully the diviner smoothes the sand with a wooden trowel in the shape of an animal's paw. He distributes various small·objects: leaves and twigs, a bit of shell, strands of twine, a coloured pebble. All over the surface he strews grain. It is hoped that the grain will entice the fox, a pale, herbivorous variety, to steal by in the night and dance on the table. The sun disappears. The night passes. Early the next morning the diviner returns and crouches over the rectangle, sniffing at it like a keen-scented hound. The outlines of the drawing have become blurred and several details have changed. Some objects have shifted ground, while others are covered with sand, and the tracks of the animal are visible. The pellets of grain have been whisked away. The fox has come in the night and danced. The diviner notes the changes, ponders, and pronounces a short prayer: 'Hail, Pale Fox! We salute you! We follow your movements by day and by night!'

The fox diviner represents a client anxious to know answers to questions both large and small. Will he travel? Will his wife have children? If so, will the child be a boy or girl? Will the rain water his crops? Will the harvest be adequate? Why has his cow stopped producing milk this week? Will his rifle kill any game in the forth-coming hunt? One recorded question was put forth by a dancer. The man was to appear the following week masked as an antelope dancer in the public square, but had recently killed an antelope in the bush. Would he be jinxed by a malevolent onlooker while performing the dance?

To pose this or any other question the diviner arranges the small objects in a predetermined order and traces the emblem of the client in the zone designating his personal world. Two parallel horizontal lines, for example, would represent the mask of the antelope dancer. The interpretation of the diviner ultimately hinges upon his reading of the fox's response to the personal world of the consultant, in the middle of which are the two circles, mouth and food, symbols of health and life itself. Ideally the relationship between client and animal is a reciprocal one. The food bribe left for the fox conceals a fundamental question: can man in turn expect to be fed by the forces governing the universe?

Divination by reading the traces of animal movements is not confined to the Dogon. Tribes in the Ivory Coast such as the Baule practise divination with mice and sticks, the beetle is used in the Cameroons, and the Chamba tribes of Nigeria unleash crabs onto a divination table for a sort of race. In each case the animal is a helper, an agent enjoying privileged contacts with the supernatural world. The dance floor is a microcosm of the universe. When the animal dances, his secret choreographic language telegraphs divine information which allows the diviner interpretative leaps of intuition.

Most cultures have myths of origin for fire, and often an animal is the original owner, then donor of fire, that most magical of substances which is put to use in cooking, sacrifice, purification, and simply in keeping warm. Birds most commonly bequeath the gift of fire to mankind; as will be seen below (Chapter X), large felines are often thought to be fire-bringers, because of the association with the sun suggested by their colouration.

In the mythology of the American Indian of the West, it is another variety of wild dog, the coyote, which is believed responsible for providing people with fire. In the following myth of the Thompson River Indians of British Columbia, retold by Joseph Campbell, Coyote, the trickster figure, and his people, including the Fox, Wolf and Antelope, are the guests at a dance held by the Fire People: 'Coyote stood one evening on the top of a mountain, looking south. And far away he thought he saw a light. Not knowing, at first, what it was, by a process of divination he learned that he was seeing fire; and so, making up his mind to procure this wonder for mankind, he gathered a company of companions: Fox, Wolf, Antelope – all the good runners went along. And after travelling a very great way, they all reached the house of the Fire People, to whom they said: "We have come to visit you, to dance, to play and to gamble." And so, in their honour, preparations were made for a dance, to be held that night.

'Coyote prepared a head-dress for himself, made of pitchy yellow-pine shavings, with long fringes of cedar-bark, reaching the ground. The Fire People danced first, and the fire was very low. Then Coyote and his people began to dance around the flame, and they complained that they could not see. The Fire People made a larger fire, and Coyote complained four times, until finally they let it blaze up high. Coyote's people then pretended to be very hot and went out to cool themselves: they took up positions for running and only Coyote was left inside. He capered about wildly until his head-dress caught fire, and then, pretending to be afraid, he asked the Fire People to put it out. They warned him not to dance so close to the blaze. But when he came near the door, he swung the long fringes of his head-dress across the fire and ran out. The Fire People pursued him and he gave his head-dress to Antelope, who ran and passed it on to the next runner; and so it went in relay. One by one, the Fire People caught up with the animals and killed them, until the only one left was Coyote; and they nearly caught him too, but he ran behind a tree and gave the fire to the tree. Since then, men have been able to draw fire with fire-sticks from the wood of trees.'

Dance of the fire stealers.
From E. S. Curtis
Indian Days of Long Ago

VII Choreographers of Earth and Sky: Fertility Dances

Fertility means life in the most basic sense of birth, growth and rebirth. Its opposite, sterility, spells death and decay. All around us the forces of life and death are in a state of perpetual conflict, a necessary contest without which everything would come to a grinding halt. For death conquers only to be vanquished in turn by the allied forces of life that ever renew and regenerate. The struggle between life and death, fertility and sterility, extends in its silent fierceness to the crops and flocks of animals, and to mother earth, from which men must win a living. Dance, as a creator and prime mover, is an agent of fertility that has been employed on man's behalf in every season of human history. Our own May Day dance around the Maypole is itself a survival of the triumph of the May, or Spring, over the dreadful Queen of Winter, enacted by dancers stomping out old grey winter, their tripping feet tickling Mother Earth as a gentle reminder that it is time to awaken from her long sleep and feed the human and animal populations.

In cultures relying wholly or in part on agriculture, Mother Earth is the greatest provider of all, as celebrated by an anonymous Greek poet in one of the so-called Homeric hymns: 'Earth, Mother of All Things'. 'I will sing of well-rooted earth, mother of all things,/ Most venerable being, who nourishes all/ Creatures dwelling in the world, all that/ Go upon the mighty land and sea, and all that/ Fly: all these are fed upon your wealth./ From you men are blessed in their children/ And in their harvests. But it is in your/ Power to give and to take away. Blessed is he/ Who honours you in his heart; to him all comes/ In abundance: his life-giving soil flourishes,/ His pastures are covered with cattle, and/ His home is filled with good things. . .' Earth, as the hymn goes on to say, has it within her jurisdiction to provide, as well as to deprive. When angered or aggrieved, the mother of all things has a way of turning her back on the people, flocks and crops. The soil, divested of her cloak of benignity, grows hard, dry and cold, and all vegetation withers. Drought and famine ensue. The Greek myth of Demeter tells such a story. The earth goddess, in mourning for her daughter Persephone, who had been abducted by Hades, roamed the upper world in complete disregard for the crops and fruit: the land thus forsaken, all growth withered, and the human and animal population suffered.

The myth teaches the lesson that Mother Earth must be kept happy, especially at critical points like the advent of the planting season. Earth must be softened up, stimulated, and kept in a mood of health and exuberance until she has delivered the harvest. For she is a maiden, at best a coy one who can be induced to crack a smile; at worse she is cold, obdurate and unyielding, like a frigid woman.

The most straightforward way of warming up earth is with fire, real or simulated. The dancer, as noted earlier, resembles the flickering fire in his protean movements. And the dancer may himself be conceived of as a kind of oven, as in the Gemsbok Medicine Dance, where the medicine-man, dancing around a blazing fire, warms the medicine sloshing around inside him to full potency in his dance of blood and frenzy. So the dancer radiates warmth to the soil beneath him. If sexual potency is the primary symbolism of fire, the ardour of sexual arousal belongs to the arsenal of the fertility dance. The dancer's feet inflame earth: the friction sets the maiden afire with fervent passion.

As the coyote myth from the Thompson River Indians suggested, fire can lie in the province of animals. The first evidence for fire, other than natural, was found in the cave of *Sinanthropus Pekinensis* in the Chakoutien Cave. This early carnivore apparently used fire to keep his chilly home warm, and for cooking; thousands of animal bones – among them skulls of his cavern inmates that had been pierced to suck out the brains – showed signs of burning. During the course of the Palaeolithic the temperature grew progressively cooler until by the middle Palaeolithic a partial ice age had set in, forcing the animals to adapt to the new climatic condition or take refuge, like Peking man, in the caves beneath the earth. Man further kept himself warm by clothing himself in skins of the animals which competed for places in the cavernous shelters.

Here, as we return to the setting of the first prehistoric dances, their meaning, as reflected in the cave-paintings, acquires further illumination. In the utmost recesses of the caverns the Palaeolithic practitioners of art and dance were no longer on earth: they were inside it. That fire played a crucial role in these archaic rituals cannot be doubted: none of the splendid murals could have been executed, nor the dances performed, as they sometimes were, on or near precarious ledges, without the light of torches. Here the idea of the 'seed of fire' was carried to its most literal end by being transplanted into the cavernous earth. Illuminations of large, stalwart beasts such as bison, horse, reindeer or elk in pigments mixed with the animals' blood brought to life the inner walls of earth; shamans added to the formula of magical impregnation masked dancing; the colours bled and penetrated into the walls, and the life-cycle on earth was ensured. The herbivores found pasturage to feed on, and the carnivores, man included, prospered in turn. For the Palaeolithic rituals were fertility rituals in the broadest sense, of general increment of hunted game, pasture, and the human population. To effect this blessed and fertile union the people acted as matchmakers. On earth as it is in the netherworld: what passions could be unbridled within the caves found expression and release without.

Fire dances for the fertility of the earth occur above ground. After the dry season in Australia the man who has captured the most game during the hunting season assumes the right to set afire a pit in the ground recognized by the Aboriginal as representing the vulva. Dancing in a circle around the pit the Watchandi of Western Australia poke in a spear, singing, 'not the pit, not the pit, but the vulva!' With or without fire the pit becomes the focus for round dances in countless tribes. Clearly the pit is a magical symbol of the bosom and the life-generating womb, the earth's hearth.

Fire dances are universally alike. One lights the fire, dances around it or jumps through and over it; one makes the cattle walk through it and dance around it as well; one carries torches in procession with the livestock through the fields, orchards, pastures and stables. Even if an animal like the cow cannot dance (except, of course, the Dinka cow, Dau Dancing Leopard), it can be made to dance magically by human manipulation.

The concept behind these fire fertility dances is threefold. First, as fire makes nuptial rites sacred, so it forges a link between the common heart of man and the natural world. Second, the light of fire sympathetically induces the life-giving sun to shine down upon man, animals, crops and fruit. This second idea is danced out in a most curious way by the pygmies of equatorial Africa. Five elements figure in the dance: a large lizard, a tree, fire, the sun and earth. To provoke the sun to rise and shine on the world, the pygmies seek out a clearing in the forest, light a fire, and roast the varanus lizard. The chief dances around the fire, his hands lifted toward the sky, which he calls to attention with the clacking of castanets. He dances close to the ground with bent knees. Then he stops. With his stomach towards the earth he performs a balancing act on his haunches, lifting head and feet in the air, in sympathy with the posture and gait of the lizard. Now the dancer rises and imitates the falling of lofty tree in the forest. Lying on the ground he sings softly, plaintively to the sun: 'Oh sun, oh sun,/ Death comes, the end is here,/ The tree falls and dies./ Oh sun, oh sun./ The child is born in the breast of his mother,/ Death lives, man lives, the sun lives./ Oh sun, oh sun, oh sun!' After a melodramatic pause the chief rises and begins slowly to circle the fire again. A chorus of dancers imitates his movements while the chief, now standing by the fire, provides the rhythmic accompaniment with the castanets. When the dance is over, the pygmies plant live embers from the fire in the earth. The varanus lizard is cut up into two parts; one of them is offered as a sacrifice to the sun, the other is devoured by the dancers.

In the dance the pygmy identifies both with the lizard, who lives close to earth, and with the tree, rooted in earth. Neither could exist without the sun beaming down upon them, nor could earth sustain man, lizard, tree, or any other living creature. Sun, man, tree, lizard and earth are all conjoined in the dance ritual. The man takes into his body what he feeds the sun, the lizard; and the life-giving power of the sun, symbolized by the fire roasting the lizard, is transferred through the live embers. These are hidden and cherished in the bosom of earth until they die and the next sun rises.

The third idea associated with fire dances is purification. Thus cattle are made to walk and dance around fire in India and other parts of the world, thereby branding them with a fertility charm when they come into rut. Before the planting season in ancient China, the earth had to be purged of vermin and small pestiferous animals. The spirits of large animals with a favourable disposition towards people were activated in animal dances as a means of driving away evil influences at the onset of the agricultural year. The principal event of the New Year's celebration, known as Ta-No, was the 'Dance of the Twelve Animals'. Throughout the country the dance was performed – in the capital at the imperial palace, and in the provinces in the courtyard of the highest local functionary. As described by Marcel Granet in *Danses et légendes de la Chine ancienne*, twelve boys between the ages of ten and twelve danced around Fian-sian-che, an imposing figure wearing a mask with four yellow, protuberant eyes made of metal, and a bear-skin. The youths wore masks of various animals, skins, feathers and horns. Once costumed and assembled, the leader and chorus approached before the dignitaries in the throne-room of the palace, and hurled menacing gestures at the forces of evil. In the ensuing dance Fian-sian-che and the twelve animals whirled themselves in incessant circular motion. After a time they disappeared from the performance area, suddenly to reappear brandishing torches. Thus armed, Fian-sian-che and the twelve animals ran through the countryside. The combination of animal masks and the purifying fire sniffed out the animals causing pestilence and banished them from the land.

Once the earth has been warmed or opened, cleansed and purified, how can she be made pregnant? She can, oddly enough, be fed. Many peoples bake loaves of bread or cakes in the shape of phalluses or breasts; cakes are also baked in the shape of animals known to possess the powers of fertility. The ancient Greeks celebrated the Eleusinian mysteries in honour of the annual return, in the Spring season, of Demeter. An agreement between Demeter and the Lord of the Underworld permitted Persephone to spend one-third of the year under the earth with Hades and two-thirds of the year on earth. Initiates of the Eleusinian cult witnessed a re-enactment of the mysterious rape and return of Persephone in the silent language of dance mime. Part of the admission fee to the ceremony was an offering of fertility cakes shaped like pigs, the animal sacred to Demeter.

In Western European culture there is the strange custom at Easter of dyeing chicken eggs, a faint echo of fertility rituals practised by the Egyptians and Persians, who coloured and ate eggs during agricultural festivals. We have the tradition of hiding them in the grass for the children to find. What is especially curious about the custom is the belief about how they got there: children are told not that a hen laid them, but rather that a rabbit brought them in a basket. The reason for this belief is simple enough. It is well known that rabbits and hares copulate frequently and produce large litters. Rabbit and hare are fertility animals, and their reproductive powers are recognized in the expression 'pregnant as a hare'.

The Easter celebration, which marks the rebirth and resurrection of Christ, concurs with Spring when the flowers hatch their blossoms after the still winter months. It is interesting that, according to an old superstition, the warm sun rising on Easter

*Detail from
a medieval
masquerade
with mummer
in animal
disguise*

morning danced in the heavens, a belief derived from an earlier, pagan festival when worshippers danced in honour of the sun's ascent. The English Renaissance poet Sir John Suckling refers to the dancing of the Easter sun in a humorous wedding ballad: 'Feet beneath her petticoat/ Like little mice, stole in and out,/ As if they fear the light!/ But oh, she dances such a way!/ No sun upon an Easter-day/ Is half so fine a sight.'*

Another pagan belief which has survived in England is the power of the hobby-horse to rid the farmlands of winter's frost. The process of stomping out the old and bringing in the new is acted out in an amusing play featuring the horse. Here then is a third way of bringing earth to life: by entertaining her in a humorous way, making her burst open with laughter, that the seeds can be sown. In Padstow in Cornwall the village inhabitants perform a two-day play featuring the hobby-horse at the beginning of spring. The performance is a mummers play, 'mummer' being a word for a masquerade, especially in animal disguise. The practice was widespread in Europe throughout the Middle Ages and survives in festivals in England, Germany and Bulgaria, among other places.

In the Padstow play the dramatis personae are fixed: an old man, a policeman and the hobby-horse. These three give a performance consisting of dialogue, insults, pranks and wrestling in the local pub on the night of the first day of the festival. The costume of the hobby-horse consists of an oversized hoop dress with a bobbing horse's head at the front. The dancer stands upright inside the hoop skirt and wears another mask to cover his emerging head. To act out the ritual contest between winter and spring, the horse kneels to the ground and is ceremonially beheaded. This represents the triumph of spring over winter. But suddenly the horse comes to life again, and, shifting identities, enacts spring in full exuberance. He takes off with a snort and a gallop, running through the fields and the village to spread waves of fertility. Along the way he catches women under the hoop of his skirt and dances a fertility jig with them. The hobby-animal is a universal character in traditional rites. Already we have seen a hobby-ox-antelope in Nasolo, the preceptor of Senufo boys, and in Chapter XI, 'Horses Dance', other examples of the hobby-horse from France to the South Seas are described.

Phallic animal processions also entertain earth in the spring season. Instead of wearing masks, the people carry huge phalluses

* 'A Ballad Upon a Wedding', stanza 8, composed in 1641 by Sir John Suckling, 1609–1642.

or sculptures of animals propped up on poles. The sculptures may simply represent animals endowed with an extra-large dose of fertilizing power, or the animals may themselves be shown with enormous erections. In ancient Greece phallic animals in honour of Dionysos, such as the bull, goat and cock, were paraded through the farmlands by people dressed as satyrs. The men wore artificial breasts and strapped phalluses around their waists.* According to the Greek historian Herodotus, the Greek phallic procession resembled the Egyptian version of the ritual. But he says that instead of phallic animals the Egyptians carried puppets about eighteen inches high, the genitals of which were reputedly as big as the rest of their bodies, and which could be made to stand erect by pulling on a string!

In the already hot lands of the Yoruba in western Nigeria and eastern Dahomey, the object of dance festivals is to keep the earth 'cool' and temperate. A Yoruba creation story tells about the first rulers of the world, birds who perched in lofty trees. Some were good, others evil. The evil birds had crooked talons and long, thirsty beaks with which they sucked men's blood. An ancestor named Orunmila, however, taught humans how to fend off the wicked birds by wearing masks in their dances. The masks, made of special materials like quills, feathers and shells, kept away the great needling beaks of the birds who were allergic to these substances. Nowadays the Yoruba believe that the birds appear in the form of witches of the night, evil spirits sent by the Great Mother Earth to punish corrupt behaviour: for the actions of humans can adversely influence the crops. At the end of the dry period, when cultivators are looking for the first signs of rain, the Efe and Gelede dance festivals are staged in honour of the mother and her attendants, who are attracted and flattered by seeing their image reflected in the costumes, masks and gestures of the dancers. During the daytime performances of the Gelede festival (Efe is nocturnal), pairs of masked dancers perform dances that keep the witches cool, since the worst thing is for a witch to lose her temper. They imitate animals which are believed to transport the witches, like brooms, through the sky. For instance, two dancers may appear disguised as the ugly wart-hog. They imitate the wart-hog scouring the earth for food, digging, rooting, swallowing and wallowing. At the peak of the humorous performance, the dancers fall to the earth and burrow with their big snouts along the ground

* The word satyr was believed by the Greeks to derive from σαθή [sathé], *membrum virile*; the related word *satyrion* means testicle in ancient Greek.

in search of food. Praise poems composed by the oral poets accompany the performance: 'Oh Great Wart Hog, corpulent beast,/ Whose mouth is a veritable hoe . . ./ Who digs up the soil right down to the roots,/ And whose face is blemished by huge knobs . . ./ O Wart Hog, earth digger in the dense forest bounds.'

In nearby Mali the Bambara have a myth about the origin of agriculture. *Tyiwara* was both man and wild animal. In the beginning of the world he taught the people how to transform the bush into fields of millet. The Bambara became cultivators, and through their efforts grew rich and prosperous. But the people soon grew lazy and forgetful of their debt to *Tyiwara*. In response to this ingratitude, *Tyiwara* buried himself deep into the soil and awaited the time when the people would pay him his due respects. Later the Bambara paid homage to the patron of agriculture by sculpting antelope effigies. Today these are worn as head-masks at the beginning of the planting season in the *Tyiwara* initiation society, the last but one of six phases of instruction a Bambara undergoes from childhood to middle age. The female antelope, representing earth, bears two erect horns on her head suggesting the growth of seeds in the soil. On her back she carries her offspring, the fawn, for she is in addition believed to be mother of mankind. Also along for the ride is the hippotrague perched on the back of the fawn.

The Bambara critically judge animal dancers for their fidelity to the species. Since the antelope is still present in large numbers near their settlements, the choreography of *Tyiwara* tends towards accuracy. Unlike most dances which take place in the plaza of the settlement, *Tyiwara* is performed on a field when the villagers are tilling the soil. Though the word means 'wild animals' it is commonly understood to mean 'excellent farmer'. The dancers, two in number, concentrate on reproducing the high jump of the antelope: the higher the better, since the height attained by the dancers represents the height to which the millet will grow. The dance also represents a wedding dance. Although both dancers are male, one dances the male antelope, the other the female to exalt the marriage of sun and the life-giving earth.

The Bobo of Upper Volta use three types of masks to propitiate Wuro, the Creator who established a balanced order among sun, earth and rain. But human nature, being what it is, upset the balance. In particular, the practice of agriculture was seen as a violation of the virgin soil; Wuro and Saxo, the divinity of the bush, were offended. Dwo intervened as a mediator in the dispute between people and their divinities.

At the end of the dry season between the first rainfall and the resumption of cultivation, purification rites involving the three types of masks cleanse the land and the people of stain and corruption. The first type of mask is made of leaves, the second with fibre, and the third, and most substantially crafted, of wood. These sculpted masks are invariably in the form of animals. Anthropomorphic masks, in fact, are rare, since, according to Bobo belief, man must resist human arrogance and worship Dwo. One of the masks has already been mentioned as an example of the dance mask in motion. This is the propeller-like butterfly mask which is twirled about in excitation after the first rains have appeared. Other animal masks include the male and female buffalo, the wart-hog, the cock, the toucan, fish and antelope, and the snake, which reaches ten feet in length. This or other tall 'plank' masks appear at ceremonies in the dry season. It is said that the towering masks 'scratch the bellies of the clouds' to force a tear of laughter.

A last way of making earth happy and fertile is roughly the match-maker technique. This occurs in Palaeolithic ritual where the big animals parade about as the privileged consorts of earth. The sun, too, is commonly paired off with earth, as in the pygmies' Lizard Dance. In courtship and mating dances, it could be shown that in an area like Australia the biological cycles of man and animals are interdependent; this interdependence can be extended now to include the plant world.

Fertility rituals scheme to arrange a wedding between sky and earth in cultures where the annual rainfall is precariously low. The ultimate goal of these rites is to consummate the marriage by having the sky rain down its seed upon earth. Rain charms of all varieties are, of course, widespread. The Tasmanians, now extinct, hurled themselves down on the ground, rolled over and over, and pounded the ground with their hands and feet. They were simply imitating in their rolling and beating the thunder that means the beginning of a good storm. The Thunderbird Dance of the Pueblo Indians was much more indirect but no less amusing than the Tasmanian tantrum. It was, in fact, a rather roundabout way of making rain fall. The Pueblo believed that if they could make thunder, the rain would follow and water the crops. But what caused the thunder? Pueblo belief held that when the eagle or thunderbird flew behind the clouds it farted. And it passed wind with such a loud and violent explosion that thunder joined in chorus. When the Pueblo needed to produce this effect, they staged a Thunderbird Dance. Two dancers, male and female, carried feathers from the wings of an eagle and wore head-dresses with huge golden beaks. In the dance the male and female circled around one another, weaving in and out with swirling movements. The drummer in the background beat his drum as loudly as possible to imitate the appropriate farting sounds.

Perhaps the most elaborate rain charm found among tribal peoples is the Snake–Antelope Dance of the Hopi. In the course of the sixteen-day Snake–Antelope Dance ceremony, marriage vows between the Antelope Youth and the Snake Maiden are consecrated in a divine wedding. The beliefs associated with the Snake–Antelope Dance, involving a tension between hot and cold, frigid and yielding, fire and water, wet and cold, and the power of music, animals and dance to melt the earth and move the sky to tears, conveniently summarize the principal elements of fertility dance rituals.

The Hopi Indians, like the Dogon who form the central example of the next chapter, have an extremely complex set of beliefs about the beginnings of the world, some of which reveal a startling consistency with scientific and geographical fact. A cycle of Hopi legends called the Road to Life, collected and adapted by Frank Waters, tells about the wanderings of the clans and the migration of the spirits of creation, and how finally they established the cardinal points of the universe. The journey, as the Hopi draw it, took place along meandering paths, as in a labyrinth: the ultimate quest was to find the centre, since there they would establish a settlement. Hopi ceremonies likewise are directed towards ordering the world by seeking out the four chief points of it, in an effort to determine the middle of the universe. Once found, harmony is restored in the land of the Hopi.

As examined above in children's dances in 'The Waters of Birth', Hopi spirits are represented by wooden figures clothed and disguised with masks, often of animals, as the names indicate. The Kachina dolls are placed in the earth next to an altar in a man-made cave or shelter, called a *kiva*. When the adults dance, they perform before the statues, wearing masks and costumes mirroring those worn by the figurines. The dancing brings to life the spirits who actively rescue the Hopi from evil spirits and restore health and order to the people and their crops. The ceremonies are in general purification rites that weed out the evils which have infiltrated through previous generations. The specific purpose of many Kachina dances, accompanied by prayers, is to bring rain. Here is a Hopi prayer sung to the Butterfly Kachina: 'Now for corn-blossoms we wrestle/ Now for bean-blossoms we wrestle// We are Youths, in the corn/ Chasing each other in sport,/ Playing with butterfly-Maidens// Come here!/ Thunder will move here,/ We shall summon the thunder here,/ That the maiden plants/ May help one another grow up.'

From the Road to Life comes a legend about a migration northward to the Back Door of the world. The journey was led by Spider Woman, who created man and animals, and also taught man the difference between man and his animal brethren. Five clans made up the expedition: the Spider Clan, named after the leader, the Blue Flute Clan, the Fire Clan, the Snake Clan and the Sun Clan. At first the going was easy. They travelled through tropical lands, and there was plenty of fruit and vegetables to eat. As they moved north the clans had to stop to plant and harvest crops of corn. But after a time the land became drier and colder, until finally they came to a land of perpetual ice and snow. At night they dug their way into the snowbanks for warmth. For water they placed on the ground a little jug which they always carried with them, and a spring gushed forth. They also had brought a little bowl of earth in which they planted seeds of corn and melon. As they sang and danced over it, the plants yielded their crops. At long last they reached the Arctic Circle. They could go no further. The way was blocked by a mountain of snow and a sea of ice. 'Clearly this is the Back Door of the Fourth World,' they said. 'We can go no further.' Spider Woman, however, urged them to go on. 'Use your magic powers. You can melt this mountain of snow, this sea of ice,' she said. The Spider Clan agreed at once and persuaded the other clans to pool their magical powers. The Blue Flute clan made the humpbacked flute-player, a locust, bring tropical warmth with the sounds of his flute. The Fire Clan summoned the fire inside the earth; the Sun Clan made the sun shine more brightly than ever, and the Snake Clan used the snake, which had the power to send vibrations along the world's axis because it lived in the depths of the underworld. Four times they tried to break through the Back Door by melting it, and four times they failed.

Sotuknang, the nephew of the Creator, appeared and told Spider Woman that if the clans had succeeded, disaster would have come. For had they melted the mountain of snow and the sea of ice, the whole world would have been flooded. Sotuknang admonished Spider Woman: 'Because you helped create these people, we gave you eternal life and beauty. Now because you have disobeyed us, we are going to let your thread run out.' And they did just that.

The thread of Spider Woman ran out until she was no more than an ugly old woman. Sotuknang then ordained that the Spider Clan return to the South where they would breed wickedness and evil. The other clans turned eastward to the Atlantic. When they reached the coast, they turned back and began their westward migration to their homeland.

Hopi Indian snake ceremony. From E. S. Curtis, Indian Days of Long Ago *(1914)*

Once every two years the Hopi hold the Flute Ceremony. It occurs at the summer solstice when the crops of corn, squash, melons and beans are hardening. It alternates with the mystical wedding rite, dance and race of the Snake–Antelope Dance. Both rituals help mature the crops during this critical dry period by bringing on summer rains. They hope that, as in the myth, the music of the humpbacked flute-player and the slithering of snakes will warm the icy reservoirs of water in the sky enough to bring rain and that they may be able to plant a second crop of corn.

The United States Bureau of Indian Affairs once tried to prevent the Hopi from holding the Snake–Antelope Dance because of what they considered to be a disgusting aspect: the dancers perform one of the dances with live snakes in their mouths. On the twelfth day of the sixteen-day ceremony, after the Snake and Antelope altars have been erected, the most important preparation takes place: the gathering of the snakes. The snake-hunt lasts for four days. Then men go in the four directions: first to the west, then to the south, to the east, and finally northwards. Each hunter carries a water-jar, a sack of corn-meal and two buzzard feathers. When waved over the snake's head the wing feathers have the effect of quelling the anger of the dangerous reptiles. A Hopi named Hoahwyma, who was once cured of a lingering illness through snake medicine, describes the effect of the men's singing on the snakes. 'There were all kinds of snakes: rattlesnakes, big bull snakes, racers, sidewinders, gopher snakes – about sixty all tangled on the floor. The men started singing, and the singing stirred them. They moved in one direction, then another, looking over all the men in the circle. The men never moved. They just kept singing with a kind expression on their faces. The snakes began to roll on the sand, taking their bath. Then a big yellow rattler moved slowly toward an old man singing with his eyes closed, and climbed up his crossed leg, coiled in front of his breechcloth and went to sleep. Pretty soon this old man had five or six snakes crawling over his body, raising their heads to look at his closed eyes and peaceful face, then going to sleep. It showed they had found their friend, looking within the heart of this one upon whose body they chose to rest.'

Once the snakes have been gathered, they are placed on the altar of the Snake *kiva*, an enclosure built into an earthen wall. Meanwhile preparations for the mystical union of the Snake Maiden and the Antelope Priest have already begun. Before midnight of the eleventh day of the ceremony the Snake chief brings in a young girl dressed in a dancer's skirt and a red and white cape. She is the Snake Maiden – a curious blending of female with a traditionally male animal symbol. The Antelope Chief then introduces into the *kiva* the Antelope Youth, who carries a snake. The Youth and Maiden are seated on either side of the altar. Before the altar sits an earthen bowl containing soapy water made from the roots of the yucca plant. This is used to sanctify the marriage, according to the Hopi custom of washing the hair of man and woman, then twisting it together in a knot. Here, however, the union is mystical and symbolic of the desire for the unification of forces in man and nature. Snake and antelope each in their own way present fertility to the Hopi – the snake of earth, from which it and all living things issue, the antelope of multiplication and reproduction, since the female generally bears two offspring. The marriage of the Antelope Youth and the Snake Maiden is, like any marriage, a blending of the sexual and the spiritual. According to the Hopi colleague and informant of Frank Waters, Oswald White Bear Fredericks, the snake and antelope correspond to the sexual and spiritual centres of a man. As the snake has access to the vibratory centres of the world axis, so in a man the snake by analogy represents the generative powers in the lower part of the body, that is, the genitals. By contrast, the antelope represents the highest centre in human consciousness through the animal's main physical attribute, the horns crowning the head. Transposed onto a cosmic level, the snake and antelope represent, respectively, the generative function of the earth and the collective world spirit.

The marriage rite of the Antelope Youth to the Snake Maiden is bridged to the Snake and Antelope Dances by the intervening snake and antelope races. Like the migration paths of the legend, these races link the individual to the cardinal points of the universe.

The culminating sequence of the ritual is the Antelope Dance and the Snake Dance. The two dances are similar, except that beans, melons and squash are used as dance accoutrements in the Antelope Dance, whereas the live snakes gathered in the *kiva* come into play in the concluding Snake Dance. The Antelope Dance, called a 'practice dance', is a warm-up to the Snake Dance, the last hope of squeezing any moisture from the sky. In the Antelope

Dance, running antelope dancers simply imitate the sound of thunder to set in motion the vibrations that call forth the clouds from their heavenly shrines.

The Snake Dance focuses on the plaza in front of the Snake *kiva*. In the *kiva* are stored the snakes; in the middle of the enclosure is the *sipapuni*, a small opening in the earth which represents the place of emergence from the underworld. It is also the orifice through which the snake awakens the vibrations of the world axis. This vital region is covered with a wooden plank which resonates when the snake dancers pass over it.

Frank Waters, an eye-witness of one Snake–Antelope Ceremony where rain appeared at the conclusion, describes in *The Book of the Hopi* the emergence of both Snake and Antelope dancers in the plaza for the final crescendo:

'Then suddenly they file into the plaza – two rows of twelve men each, the Antelopes ash-gray and white, the Snakes reddish-brown and black. . . . Silently they encircle the plaza four times – a strange silence accentuated by the slight rattle of gourds and seashells. As each passes in front of the *kisi* [shelter housing the snakes] he bends forwards and with the right foot stomps powerfully upon the *pochta*, the sounding board over the *sipapuni*. In the thick, somber silence the dull, resonant stamp sounds like a faint rumble from underground, echoed a moment later, like thunder from the distant storm clouds.

'This is the supreme moment of mystery in the Snake Dance, the thaumaturgical climax of the Snake–Antelope ceremony. Never elsewhere does one hear such a sound, so deep and powerful it is. It assures those below that those above are dutifully carrying on the ceremony. It awakens the vibratory centers deep within the earth to resound along the world axis the same vibration. . . . There is no mistaking its esoteric summons. For this is the mandatory call to the creative life force known elsewhere as Kundalini, latently coiled like a serpent in the lowest centers of the dual bodies of earth and man, to awaken and ascend to the throne of her Lord for the final consummation of their mystic marriage.

'The power does come up. You can see it in the Antelopes standing now in one long line extending from the *kisi*. They are swaying slightly to the left and right like snakes, singing softly and shaking their antelope-testicle-skin-covered gourds as the power makes its slow ascent. Then their bodies straighten, their voices rise.

'The Snake chief stoops in front of the *kisi*, then straightens up with a snake in his mouth. He holds it gently but firmly between his teeth, just below the head. With his left hand he holds up the upper part of the snake's body level with his chest, and with the right hand the lower length of the snake level with his waist. This is said to be the proper manner of handling a snake during the dance. Immediately a second Snake priest steps up with a feathered snake whip in his right hand, with which to stroke the snake . . . . As they move away from the *kisi* another dancer and his guide pause to pick out a snake, and so on, until even the small boy at the end is dancing with a snake in his mouth for the first time. It is a large rattlesnake, its flat bird-like head flattened against his cheek. All show the same easy familiarity with the snakes as they had with the squash vines the day before.

'After dancing around the plaza the dancer removes the snake from his mouth and places it gently on the ground. Then he and his guide stop at the *kisi* for another snake. A third man, the snake-gatherer, now approaches the loose snake. It has coiled and is ready to strike. The gatherer watches it carefully, making no move until it uncoils and begins to wriggle quickly across the plaza. Then he dexterously picks it up, holds it aloft to show that it has not escaped into the crowd, and hands it to one of the Antelopes singing. . . . The Antelope, smoothing its undulating body with his right hand, continues singing. . . .'

Throughout the history of mankind the most ingenious means have been devised to arouse earth, thereby allowing for impregnation by the grain. She can be humoured by entertainment and food; she can be warmed by fire; man can play match-maker by arranging a marriage between earth and a consort, usually a potent animal – a bull or snake; or a divine union may be contracted between earth and sky, the latter being persuaded to consummate the union by raining down upon earth to germinate the seed; and earth can be aroused in dances during which disrobing, kissing and caressing take place. In the Hopi Bean-Planting Dance related to the Snake–Antelope Ceremony, performers dressed as animal Kachinas dance to make their children, the bean plants, grow. The extent to which the gesture and atmosphere of the fertility dance resemble the prelude to the sexual act is obvious, but it is, above all, an act of pragmatic eroticism.

VIII   The Final Season:
the Dance of Death

'On old one-armed, black scaffolding/ The hanged men
dance;/ The devil's skinny advocates,/ Dead soldiers'
bones . . .// And there in the midst of the danse
macabre/ One wild skeleton leaps in the scarlet clouds,/
Stung with madness like a rearing horse/ With the rope
pulled stiff above his head.'

ARTHUR RIMBAUD*

Rimbaud's gruesome portrayal of the hanged soldiers, the Devil's
skinny advocates, powerfully evokes the *danse macabre* of the
Middle Ages. Although related to dance manias, the Dance of
Death was not a dance but rather a widespread literary and
iconographical tradition, inspired by the effects of the great plagues
which periodically swept across Europe, decimating the
population. Mass hysteria brought on by the plague was vividly
reflected in the oxymoronic depiction of death, that ordinarily
listless and sleepy state, as an orgiastic dance. Death itself was
variously portrayed, often as a dancing skeleton whose intestines
spewed forth in the form of snakes. Absolutely no class distinctions
dictated who could and could not join in the choral dance: before
the Grim Reaper all came as equals. 'His cruell daunce no man
mortall can stent/ Nor lede his cruell cours after his intent/ The
pope nor Emperor, if they be in his hande/ Hath no manner might
his sore cours withstande . . ./ The bishop, lorde, the Pore man,
like a state/ Death in his daunce ledyth by the sleve.' (Sebastian
Brant, *The Ship of Fools*)

Danse macabre *depicted in a*
medieval illustration

*'The Hanged Men Dance', from *Complete Works*, tr. P. Schmidt, Harper and Row, 1967.

All around him a man saw how Death swooped down and snatched up his victims from among the dancers. Mercifully, the 'dance' lasted only three or four days. After the initial symptoms – the appearance of pustules on the thigh or arm and the spitting of blood – involuntary convulsions, which in part gave rise to the dance comparison, wrestled down the victim in a spasmic hold.

In the West, where dancing is hardly encouraged at funerals, the expression 'Dance of Death' has only a faded meaning in the bitter-sweet metaphor for the process of dying in the plague-ridden Middle Ages. Dances of death, however, play an integral and meaningful role in the mourning rituals of tribal peoples, who may see in the vitality of dance a safeguard against sterility in the natural world, as well as an assurance of continuity in the deceased's spiritual life.

Perhaps dance, too, makes death less hard to bear. But the mood cannot be too gay. An Australian Aboriginal myth tells about an owl who had to put the snake dancers in line. A story from Goulburn Island, to the north of Arnhem Land, included by A. Elkin in *Art in Arnhem Land*, recounts how the big-eyed owl taught the Dijalmung Snake Spirits to dance to her song, so as to encourage the other spirits to participate in mortuary rites. At first when the owl sang, the spirits danced with suggestive, sensuous movements. This was wholly inappropriate to death, thought the owl, who stopped singing and looked at them sternly. When he started up again, the spirits now danced gaily and with wild abandon. Again the owl stopped singing. This time he reproached them with words, saying, 'Dance properly so that all the other spirits will come out to dance!' Now when the owl sang their song, the Snake Spirit Song, he sang it so beautifully that all the Snake Spirits broke down and wept. According to the story, they actually felt sorry for the song. Then they began dancing very slowly. Other spirits came from far away places and admired the slow and graceful movements of the snake dancers and the haunting beauty of the owl's singing. And when the other spirits saw the Snake Spirits lifting their long dancing wands to the sky, they too joined in the dance, and this was the beginning of the funeral dance.

As recorded by W. Lloyd Warner in *A Black Civilization*, when an Aboriginal is very near to death, his people gather around him and lament. Some of the relatives sing cycles of songs about the clan totems, while others dance. During this last rite, the dying man is meant to listen to the songs and follow their advice, which is directed at his soul. At the time of death the corpse is painted with the design of the clan emblem, for example a duck. Another cycle of songs and dances is performed. In a typical ceremony, two lines of snake dancers stand on one side of the fire; opposite them are two lines of caterpillar dancers. While the two groups dance, iguana dancers interrupt them by putting out the fire. The snake and caterpillars are meant to be preparing for battle, but the extinction of fire by the iguanas signals a truce. Like the owl's injunction against sensuous dancing, arms shall be laid down to observe a man's passing.

Above the deceased's grave a mast is erected. Two months later the corpse is exhumed. The bones are cleaned and wrapped in paper bark, and the mast removed and burned. The clan again performs dances of the totem. Warumeri clans dance the whale; the Djirin dance the turtle; the Liaalaomir, the snake. These totem animal dances remove the man's soul from the land of the living and help send it back to 'the other land'. The purified bones are then placed in a hollow log coffin and deposited in a well.

Among the Murngin tribe this is followed by a ceremony performed by dancers painted as cockatoos. One of the dancers climbs a tree and hangs from a limb; he calls out in imitation of the sulphur-crested bird. Another dancer, representing the wandering soul of the dead man, meanwhile dances in front of the mourners. When he tries to climb up into the tree next to the cockatoo bird, the bird utters a shrill cry to keep him away. Later, both dancers descend. One picks up the bones in the log coffin from the well and dances with them, while the other follows and watches his movements very carefully. The dancer holding the bones then delivers them to a female relative, who keeps them until another log coffin can be hollowed out for the final burial.

Dances of death honour the dead with tokens of last love. The Batak of Sumatra dance with a puppet representing their departed leader. The Yoruba fashion a striking likeness of the dead man's head out of wood, and a relative wearing this portrait mask animates a last time the character of the deceased for the survivors. Mortuary figures of the Australian Aboriginals represent not the deceased but a likeness of the deceased's animal totem. Dances of death, both propitiatory and tributary, have a mutual effect on the living and the dead: the Batak and Yoruba dances, which honour the fallen man with a danced likeness, allow the mourners to envisage their lost tribesman one last time; the Aboriginal dance, which refracts the deceased's spirit back to its totemic origins, strengthens the tribe's ties with its ancestral totem. Something familiar can be secured through the intermediary of dance: there is yet possible a relationship between the living and the dead in dance. For the dead, of course, continue dancing. The belief is poignantly reflected in the burial practice of the Andamanese, who ensure continuity by dressing the corpse in the white costume of the dancer and then having the tribe dance around him.

Paradoxically, dance is a form of movement peculiar to the dead, since it belongs to their province, as suggested by the title of the fourteenth-century Old Dutch hymn, 'In Heaven There is a Dance'. The idea originates in the universal belief that all extraterrestrial motion is dance motion. The moon, sun, stars and planets dance in their orbits; and somewhere among them dance the gods, spirits and souls of the dead projected from the world below by dancing human feet. At the initial moment of pause, it is therefore vital that the living set in motion the rhythms of the dance for the corpse; only in this way may the spirit be reassimilated and taken back into the midst of the cosmic choral dance, the Harmony of the Spheres.

But all death dances are not so sweet. Death has its practical sides. The Pomo Indians of California saw death as a painful experience, but also as a necessary sacrifice to the living. In the Pomo myth of the origin of death, Coyote, the great trickster-figure of South-western Indian mythology, is responsible both for creating people and for bringing death. One day Coyote saw a rattlesnake go into a hole. Dancing around the hole Coyote called all of the people to come and observe.

'A beautiful bird is hiding in this hole,' Coyote said. 'If you want to see for yourself, come dance as I do.' The chief's daughter came forward, and as she danced around the hole, the rattlesnake bit her on the ankle. She cried out in pain, but Coyote only snapped, 'Your dancing is all wrong!'

Within a few hours the chief's daughter died from the wound. 'Coyote,' said the stricken chief, 'my daughter must live again.'

But this is how Coyote had planned to bring Death to people, and he replied, 'No, if people live forever, there will be too many people and not enough food to go around.' The dead maiden was carefully dressed in her finest clothes, laid on the pyre and cremated, according to custom. In secret the chief plotted his revenge.

Several days later Coyote woke to find his daughter had died. The chief had had her poisoned. All through the night Coyote mourned.

The next morning he approached the chief and said, 'My daughter must live again. Let it be so.'

'No,' said the angry chief. 'When my daughter died you said that it was wise to let people die to prevent the world from having too many people.'

'Yes, you are right,' conceded the Coyote. 'We must dress my daughter and cremate her according to custom.'

The people built another funeral pyre and placed Coyote's daughter on it. Coyote mourned again that night and every night thereafter. Thus it is that Death came to the world and that the coyote always howls.

Not even Coyote, author of life and death, could spare his daughter from dying. Death comes to all alike as a matter of necessity to the living who would otherwise suffer from food shortage and over-population.

The inexplicable phenomenon of death arouses responses that are far from rational. Irrational attitudes are heightened by two main things: loss of the loved one, and fear that the disembodied spirit will return. Fear of the rotting corpse and its spirit is virtually universal. Until the corpse is properly disposed of, the vagabond spirit runs wild, confused and lost; or worse, it may return to wreak vengeance on the living, like the unappeased spirit of the hunted game. To avoid these disastrous consequences, the soul must be captured or driven away and directed towards the land of the dead, as distinct from the land of the living. Pueblo Te'en dancers armed with whips treated the souls of the dead as battle enemies. When a man died, the dancers cracked yucca whips and shrieked aggressively at the spirit. Another effective means of keeping the ghost at bay is the masked dance, where the most potent and visually horrific masks come into play. Masks of demons and animals with long snouts, protuberant eyes, curving horns, shaggy manes, and so on repel the dead. Banda masks of the Nalu of Guinea, used for a variety of functions including mortuary rites, combine elements of human physiognomy with awe-inspiring parts of animal anatomy, such as antelope horns, serpent heads and crocodile jaws. The dancers cover their bodies completely with grass skirts to protect themselves from harm. Alternatively, spirits of the deceased may be lured and trapped inside a mask. Here the mask attracts the wandering spirit by presenting a familiar face; an accompanying chant serenades and beckons to the spirit. Masks of animals are often used for this purpose, since animals are thought to be less vulnerable to contamination by the dead than humans.

Mask used in the dama,
or funerary pageant,
of the Awa mask society.
After Griaule,
Masques Dogon *(1938)*

Nevertheless the masks are burned afterwards to avoid possible pollution to people. Once captured, the spirit is led to its final resting-place, the animal again serving as psychopomp.

Fertility purification rites and dances are intimately wed to funeral rites in certain cultures, and the concurrence is especially widespread in sub-Saharan Africa which is largely made up of agricultural societies where farming the land is looked upon as an offence to Earth. This sin must be paid for by human life, sometimes directly, sometimes coincidentally. Consider the fascinating complex of myths and dances relating to original sin among the Dogon, whose Awa mask society stages a highly moving funerary pageant, known as the *dama*. This panoramic tableau consists of hundreds of masked dancers; together they represent the re-creation and re-ordering of the Dogon universe, from animal and vegetable species to artists, craftsmen, hunters, to the sun, moon and stars. More than any tribe the Dogon prove rewarding for analysis in a funerary context because of the rich set of beliefs associated with a veritable bestiary of animal dance masks, whose significance has been painstakingly researched and presented by Marcel Griaule and his team of French anthropologists in *Masques Dogon, Le pâle renard, Conversations with Ogotemmêli,* and other publications.

The dwellings of the Dogon stand close to the steep cliffs of the Bandiagara range of Mali. Tribal organization among the Dogon centres around the chief or 'Hogon' of the group. He is the guardian of all sacred objects, many of them almost unrecognizable after being fed with daily blood sacrifices in the shrine adjoining his living-quarters. Among the votive statues are the sandals worn by the first Hogon which recall the myth of the ancestor who descended to earth with scorching feet that had to be shod. Story-tellers, like the famed blind Ogotemmêli, recount such myths and interpret Dogon beliefs.

Materially, the Dogon are among the poorest people in the world. Their economy is based on what onions and millet can be coaxed to grow in the sandy soil. A few people own a cow or two. Animals pass by the habitations of the Dogon, but there is no organized hunting. Spiritually, the Dogon, from among those tribes that have been studied, excel in the richness and complexity of religious beliefs, exuberantly expressed in dances. The Dogon are the finest and most avid exponents of the masked dance. Dogon production of wooden masks is truly prolific; up to four hundred different types may be deployed in a dance ceremony. The origins of many individual masks are explained in myths collectively generated by the Awa mask society. The story of original sin and the institution of masked funeral dances by the Awa mask society is told in a series of myths from the Dogon creation story, the first of which may be recognized as an alternative version of how Yurugu the fox acquired the gift of divination.

Yurugu the pale fox was the *enfant terrible* of the first gods. In the beginning there was Amma, creator of the universe. After Amma had sewn the stars in the sky he created Earth, hurling from his body a lump of wet clay. It landed in the form of a body, hands and legs in a sprawl. In the centre lay its vagina, an anthill, and its clitoris, a termite hill. Lonely and desirous of intercourse Amma mounted the anthill, but the termite hill rose up, preventing penetration. In his frustration God severed the offending clitoris and copulated with the excised Earth. From this defective union sprang, not the twin Nummo couple as intended, but Yurugu, the lone fox, symbol of God's difficulties. When the solitary fox desired a partner he turned to the only existing female, his mother, Earth, who was in the form of an ant. He stole from his mother the 'fibre skirt' (i.e. his mother's pubic hair) thus committing the first act of incest and causing the flow of menstrual blood.

The story-teller Ogotemmêli recounted the origin of the first dance performed by Yurugu clothed in the fibre skirt. The story is better appreciated by understanding that in Dogon belief the moist fibre skirt is analogous to the mixed metaphor, the 'loom/womb of language'; creative words, that is, prophetic utterances, emanate from the pubic hairs moist from sexual arousal.

The theft of the fibre skirt angered Amma and made Yurugu the enemy of God. One evening the fox saw God asleep and thought him dead. He ascended stealthily in the fibres to the rock terrace overlooking his father's house and there mourned his father mockingly in a dance that shaped all subsequent funerary rites. Like a cyclone the sheer force and vitality of Yurugu's skilled dance threw the world into disorder and displaced Amma. As he danced more furiously the fibre skirt grew moist and warm, and out of it emanated the first Word revealed to the fox by the Seventh Nummo of the Water, the twin serpent spirit who taught men to dance from the liquid bowels of the earth. 'In his dance,' said Ogotemmêli, 'he left three tracks lengthwise and three crosswise, representing God's roof, the inside of his house, and the recess where the altar of the dead is placed. He planted millet seeds, little pieces of wood, placed stones and traced designs', as the fox diviners later were to do. Yurugu laid bare the secret of the world and in his anger he let out the secrets of God. He had taken his mother's fibres, which were full of the word that contained the designs of the celestial powers. So the first dance had been a divination dance; it was also a dance of death, for it was to flout his father that the fox had invented it. For his theft the fox had to pay a price. He had revealed the first Word, but beyond that he could not go. Amma, who was the Creator, awoke from the dead and decreed that Yurugu could speak no word to mortals, but only impart his knowledge in the dance of divination.

When the fox danced on the roof of his father's house he wore the fibre skirt stolen from his mother the ant. Since the fox had committed incest the fibre skirt was drenched with menstrual blood, and had to be placed over an anthill to dry. The fibres emitted a strange and fearful glow. A passer-by, seeing the terrible redness, exclaimed, 'Is it the sun? Is it fire?' But it was neither fire nor sun, but something entirely new and forbidding. After a time a mortal woman took the fibres and adorned her person with them. Her costume so impressed other women that she reigned as queen in her radiant robes. The men greatly envied the red fibre skirt. 'What a terrific costume it would make for our dances!' they said among themselves, for this was still in the days before they used masks. The men decided to steal the fibres just as Yurugu had once done, and made from them enough skirts for all the dancers. There was a sudden burst of dance activity. The men danced night and day to flaunt their conquest, while the women looked on admiringly. The men thought they could justify the theft by the positive effect it had on the women; for the skirts aroused the women sexually. As the men danced, the sweat pouring from their bodies moistened the fibre skirt, the mere sight of which in turn moistened the genitalia of the women and helped them to conceive children.

The theft, like the original sin of Yurugu, cost the men dearly: they paid with their immortality. Here lay the origin of death. The group of dancers had disregarded an important rule of protocol. For it had been decreed that the men should announce any change or innovation in their dances to the chief, who was the oldest and most venerable of all – so old, in fact, that long ago at the end of his human existence he had changed into a serpent. As the first ancestor he supervised men's activities with a sharp eye. And so when the men neglected to inform him of their intention to dance in the new fibre skirts, the serpent waxed wroth at this disregard for seniority. One day he stopped them on their way to the dancing-place from the cave where they kept the fibres hidden. He reproached them vociferously, using the Dogon language so that there could be no misunderstanding about the gravity of their sin. But this was his downfall. Since the chief no longer possessed human form, he ought to have used the secret language appropriate for spirits; by speaking in the language familiar to men he had transgressed a prohibition. He cut himself off both from the superhuman world and the human world. He died, and his death was a grim prelude to man's.

The men were horrified by the spectacle of the limp serpent ancestor. They decided to act quickly and took the carcass to the cave where they wrapped him in the very fibres that had caused his wrath. Then a most unexpected thing happened. The spirit of the serpent emerged and sought refuge in the body of a pregnant woman wearing a red fibre skirt who appeared for an unknown reason in the cave. She bore a child, but the child in no way resembled a human child, since it was red and spotted, like the serpent. Only after the men had hewn a serpent out of the trunk of a towering tree did the child become normal. The spirit of the serpent was transferred from the child to the serpent mask. Now the mask offered refuge to the serpent. The world of the living dead had been inaugurated. From that time the dead inhabited wooden masks representing at first dead persons and later animals.

The men of the Awa dance society repeated the fox's sin. Like the fox they were alone and incomplete: as yet they had neither mask nor fibre costume. When the men of the Awa dance society stole the fibre skirt covered with the menstrual blood from Yurugu's original sin, they too were punished. They lost their chief, the serpent ancestor, but recaptured him by fashioning a serpent mask. They learned to attract the vagrant spirits of other ancestors with animal masks. The masks are repositories, or wombs. As the dance provides the Nummo with the thrust to emerge from the placental womb, so the masked dance lures and entices the spirits of the dead back to the womb. The dancers masked as animals imitate the animal, but in an essential way they are also imitating the woman with a womb whenever they wear a mask. For the dancers always wear red fibre skirts in imitation of the pubic hair of the woman. The costume of the dancer, mask and skirt, makes the dancer male and female, that is, bisexual and complete, like the Nummo.

The story goes on to tell how a much older serpent died and regenerated himself along with the serpent ancestor through the swimming dance. The first Dogon serpent is the mysterious Seventh Nummo who taught men to dance. After Yurugu was born, Amma copulated for a second time with his wife, the Ant, or Earth. Wishing to avoid the disastrous consequences of Yurugu's birth, he brought in a third party, the rain, or divine seed. Together they fertilized Earth, who gave birth to twins, called Nummo, representing the ideal couple. The Seventh Nummo was the ideal organic unit because it combined in one body the couple – the number seven representing the sum of the three sexual parts of the male and four parts of the woman. Nummo is a composite of snake and man. His head is a serpent's with a great forked tongue; from neck to waist he is man; below a long sinuous serpent. His eyes, though red, are like a man's – wide open and piercing in their gaze. Nummo is the God of the Waters.

But the Seventh Nummo died. Many ages passed. At the time when men and women inhabited the earth, the Seventh Nummo was reborn in an extraordinary dance of resurrection. To the clanging of a smith beating and blowing anvil and bellows, Nummo stood erect on his serpent's tail. he stretched out his arms and flung them over his head, then brought them in close by his body; and again he flung them in such a way as to resemble the butterfly stroke of a swimmer, for the movements of the dance in the underworld were swimming motions. The Seventh Nummo swam in dance to the tomb of the serpent ancestor. His last action was a swallowing followed by a rhythmic vomiting. The Nummo snaked his way to the north of the body of the ancestor, where the skull was, and swallowed it, ingesting it deep into his womb. He infused new life in it. Then in time to the beating of the anvils the Nummo danced out his pains of labour. He expelled into the tomb a torrent of water and the transfigured serpent ancestor. With the serpent came the Third Word, the new order of the world.

Gradually men learned to reproduce the swimming dance and the vomiting action of the Seventh Nummo. Ogotemmêli describes the men's efforts: 'It was the Seventh Nummo who taught men to dance. He had begun by repeating his first rhythmic movement in the underworld. He danced with the top half of his body, standing upright on his serpent's tail. At first men danced on one spot, rotating on themselves or imitating swimming motions, but these movements were exhausting. Gradually they began to move their legs, imitating the slow walk of the chameleon, who has all the Nummo's colours, that is to say, the colours of the rainbow. Then the movements became more rapid. The *gona* figure recalls the Nummo's vomiting in the tomb; dancing is a relief, like vomiting. Later men took to leaping, raising one leg and then the other. The leg stretched out, while the body was lifted in the air, represented the tail of the serpent on which the Nummo stood erect. To get to the dance-floor, the dancers run in Indian file forming a serpentine line with broken segments. The zig-zag line represents the line of the Nummo, that is to say, the line of a river flowing full.' The dance took place in the field before the smithy. And once they had learned the dance of the serpent the smith beat out rhythms suggestive of other dance-figures: the monkey, the antelope, rabbit, hyena, ostrich, duck, crocodile. For all these dances the men wore masks of the animal carved in wood.

Why does the serpent swim into the first dance movements? And why do men imitate his swim dance? Because the Seventh Nummo is god of the waters. Imagine that the serpent inhabits the ground under the divination table representing the primal field. The area beneath is the placenta, the waters of birth. For many ages he lies dormant under the earth. He embodies, however, the ideal couple; like the man and woman who store, sow and grow grain as in an act of love, the ideal couple regenerate the Nummo in the medium of the placenta. He floats like an embryo in the womb. The smith beats the anvil, and this insistent rhythm, like that of dancers pounding the earth, induces the Nummo to give birth, as it were, to himself. The swimming movement recalls the foetus in and emerging out of the womb through the waters of birth. Once resurrected the Nummo in turns swallows the serpent ancestor into his womb, and the rhythmic vomiting is the labour pains of the Nummo giving birth to the ancestor, again as in a dance. The serpent ancestor was later buried as a seed. When the rain falls it inseminates the grain. Dance is like water. It is a vital, activating element.

As for the men who first imitated the serpent swimming, why did they dance on one spot and feel constricted? They were, so to speak, still unborn and moving within the confines of the embryo. And when Ogotemmêli says that the dancers moved their legs in imitation of the walk of a chameleon, he is describing the baby learning to crawl on all fours. The pace picks up: the men leap like children, and finally they run. The serpent dance describes the stages of life in terms of human mobility.

A Dogon continues dancing throughout his life; in death he hungers. The expression 'dead drunk' has a very literal meaning for the Dogon. When a man dies his appetite does not die with him. The dead are thirsty, and they thirst for beer. To help them slake their thirst, the living drink millet beer. Drinking, then, has its positive social values. The old especially are expected to drink beer in large quantities. It is their duty to spend large amounts of time consuming beer, thereby nursing the dead. Sharing drink with the dead has a distinct advantage for the living. The dead are impure from the fact of their death. If left uncared for, their impurity will adversely affect the millet grain. Rather than run the risk of endangering the crops, the first of the harvest is continually divided with the dead as an ongoing process of purification.

Death is a highly critical moment, and the need for purification at a funeral is intense. At this transitional point great quantities of millet beer are consumed amidst the celebration of masked dance, prayers and songs. Dead foxes too thirst for beer. It should come as little surprise, in the light of Yurugu's original sin against Earth, that provisions for purification and burial rites exist for the fox as well as humans among the Dogon. A dead fox is an enemy: he may make the other foxes rob the soil of its seed, that is, throw disorder into the world as Yurugu once did.

The pale fox is a wild and rare animal. Except for diviners and initiates of the bush few people have seen a live species. Should a hunter spot a dead fox lying in the bush, he immediately returns to the village to warn the fox diviners about what he has seen. There is tremendous concern, not only that the fox will destroy the seed, but also that his divining charm will be lost. Having notified the priests of the cult of the fox's death, the hunter leads back four priests to where the animal lies, its head rolled to one side, the sharply pointed muzzle agape. If the fox is female, and her coat a very light colour, this spells a great loss, since both traits are believed important assets in procuring accurate and detailed predictions. The four men take care to swathe the animal with sheets of cotton as they would a dead man, and lift the fox into the cleft of a rock. Outside the village the four men are joined by the other diviners, who prepare huge quantities of beer and boiled millet for a memorial dance to be staged around the shape of a fox drawn in the sand. They pour some of the millet onto a rock nestled in a pile of leaves alongside the fox silhouette as a libation offering, and leave more in a jug for the foxes of the night. A tambourine-player beats out a quick, frenetic rhythm. First he alone encircles the drawing. His steps are fast and intricate, leaving behind herring-bone and hatch-mark patterns; at every fifth beat he throws his head back convulsively. Eight dancers join the circle. As they dance they chant a song of mourning appropriate to the male or female fox. The dancers sow the figure of the fox with millet. For at the beginning of the planting season the fox appeals to the spirit of the millet. The planting of the objects, like the intricate steps of the dance, re-enacts the planting of the bait which lures the fox to sneak by in the night and dance. The pantomime ensures the continuation of the animal's indispensable role as ambassador to the gods and prevents the fox's spirit from harming the grain.

Like the spirit of a fox the spirit of a man is a potential risk to the well-being of the grain and the community at large; but if captured it may be put to good use. The more powerful a man, the more potent his spirit. A man who has held an important religious or social position will be lavishly honoured, as will a man who was present at the great Sigui festival occurring only once every sixty years. For such people there are two funerary rituals. Brief ceremonial respect is paid at the moment of death. This initial rite institutes the period of mourning which may last up to two years. The more elaborate *dama* ceremony performed by the Awa mask society marks the end of that period. It is essentially a memorial service. Preparations for the *dama* are lengthy and costly. While in mourning the family of the deceased undergo strict taboos. They must sacrifice and trade goods that will enable them to organize a large masked dance. Several months before the *dama* the voice of the first serpent ancestor announces the festival through the droning rhombe. The male members of the tribe gather the dance masks that are still in good condition. These are taken to rock shelters and repainted. New masks are carved here as well. The *dama* itself consists of songs, recitations, dances, and abundant consumption of millet beer. The memorial dance takes place on the flat stone roof of the deceased's house, a reminder of the dance of Yurugu that shaped all funerary rites. Wearing their masks and the red fibre skirts, the dancers crowd into this area to portray the whole world in motion: all crafts, all ages, all animals, all birds and reptiles, all types of men, both the Dogon and their neighbours. This moving picture of the world draws into its rhythmic vortex the wandering spirit of the dead man.

Olubarene, 'The One of the Bush', was a man of great religious importance. The *dama* ceremony of such a man typically begins with the vibrating tones of the bull-roarer biting into the hollow air and staking out the four quadrants of the universe. The men address their funeral chant for Olubarene to 'the low-toned instrument with the beautiful voice': 'One of the Bush has departed/ The eye of the Awa goes red;/ The eye of Awa is large./ The turtle-dove returns to the bush;/ The sea-crow flies back to water;/ The crocodile glides back into water./ The lion returns to the bush;/ The vulture flies back to the bush;/ The spirit returns to the bush;/ All are your friends./ The red mask is your mask./ It is the mask of Amma./ It is the mask of Ant./ It is the mask of the pale fox./ The woman comes back to the village./ The man takes the mask./ How beautiful is your voice./ Misery, misfortune, misery./ Pardon; Peace!' In his lifetime Olubarene was keeper of masks. Since he was an initiate of the bush and more conversant with animals than with men, the care of the animal masks was delegated to him. It was Olubarene's duty to burn some of the masks after ceremonies and to store others in the annex to the house of the chief Hogon where he kept them alive with blood offerings from a sacrificial chicken.

Now the members of the Awa society of masked dancers commemorate the passing of the custodian of masks; and the animals, who are his friends, join in sympathetic mourning. Each animal species returns to his haunts, and their return encourages the spirit of the departed man to find its natural haven in the red mask. For at the time of death the spirits of the dead as well as the animals' spirits become anxious and dislodge from their customary seats. They roam at large, lost like children. The dances lure and offer refuge to the orphaned spirits. The rhythm of the dance ensnares the lonely, marauding, or fractious spirits, while the masks restore and regenerate them to a beneficial status, redistributing their power to mankind; and the force too revitalizes the crops and makes the cattle fecund. Towards the end of the ceremony the mourners direct Olubarene to his mask, which a woman had procured from the animals and entrusted to the chief dancer. Because he was an important man, the mask of Olubarene combines the attributes of the first parents of the world, Amma and the Ant, and their offspring, the pale fox, whose dance of death prefigured the dances of the Awa society.

Dogon cosmology investigates the depths of human existence by endeavouring to come to terms with the fundamental contradiction between life and death in a land where survival is difficult. The framework for this exploration is biological. The universe is a unity, yet also conceived like a body articulated into members and internal organs. Earlier the Dogon universe was seen through the divination table on which the fox performed. That table equally represented the placenta of the womb in agricultural terms; in other words the table is the field impregnated by seed when the dancing fox is well disposed towards humans. The cardinal importance of dance in Dogon society is confirmed above all in their mythology which features two dance animals. The Serpent Nummo is related to birth – both the germination of the seed and the regeneration of mankind; it was Nummo who taught men to dance. Yurugu the fox also taught men to dance: the dance of death. Yurugu the diviner perpetrated the original sin. He is both sinner and saint. He sows seeds of growth and seeds of destruction. He fertilizes and destroys. Together Yurugu and Nummo represent the conflict between Eros and Thanatos seen in Satan and the satyr.

Hence dance has dual forces, creative and destructive. Sometimes one or the other may predominate, but almost always both the life-preserving and life-destroying powers are conjoined in dance. In the Tsimshian hunting myth the thunderous dance of a magical one-horned goat caused an earthquake to swallow up the hunters of Temlaham; but a Tsimshian shaman, wearing the crown of goats' horns, danced with their magic power to positive effect. Similarly in the Kalabari creation myth the sole survivors of the Tortoise's dance of destruction banded together and imitated his dance in order to create a masquerade society. In New Ireland the birth of man is re-enacted through the dance of the man-eating shark, in the belief that dance and all life flow from the sea. The snake, another symbol of birth, is appeased in dance by the Australian Aboriginals, who fear that the python will flood the earth. Every initiation ceremony includes a symbolic death followed by rebirth: masked dances to the sound of the bull-roarer mortify the initiate, while the initiate uses dance to revitalize himself and establish personal autonomy. Ritual dance combats between Spring and Winter chase out the hoary old man and usher in the dewy maiden. And the dual function of dance stands out dramatically in hunting cults where dance is first a rhythmic lure for killing game and second a magical means of replenishing those slain. No one learned more clearly the importance of restoring the spirit of the fallen animal victims through magical dance than the Blackfoot maiden to whom Buffalo Bull gave a chance to revive her trampled father – with the provision that the Blackfoot in turn promise to revive the game in the buffalo dance.

The dual forces of dance are present even in death. The dance of death does not differ fundamentally from other dances; in fact, elements of funerary dances are interchangeable with elements of birth, fertility, and especially hunting and initiation dances. Like hunting dances – those magical animations for apprehending and resurrecting the game – the funeral dance captures the deceased's spirit, then restores it to its own territory. Dances of death too resemble initiation rites, characterized as they are by a stage of symbolic death followed by a reunion with the tribe. So in the final season the dance of death is but another rite which rejoins the departed with the first ancestors of the tribe.

The human cycle is complete, and we have come full circle in the animal dance.

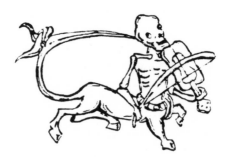

Death dances as a horse. Illustration from Amiens Missal (1323)

IX   Dances of Dogs
and their
wild Cousins

*Singing dog plays dance drum
at a new year's rite. Aztec
drawing from Madrid Codex*

Mankind has used dances imitative of animals to describe, and even push forward, the human cycles and earthly seasons from birth to death, and from year to year. The practical and magical advantages of imitating the animal in dance are many – from the punishment and education of children, to the impregnation of earth and the chasing away of souls. The function of a given animal species need not remain static or unchanged within a tribe. The ways in which particular animals are characterized often appear arbitrary to the outsider, even in terms of the tribe's own beliefs. The variation of function of an animal species is even greater when one goes outside a tribe. The dance of a bird may spell death in one tribe and bring joy in another. The multifarious roles in which animals are cast can be demonstrated by taking four major figures and showing the diversity of interpretation from culture to culture. Animals who are most familiar to the Westerner – dog, cat, horse, bird (and their wild counterparts) – will serve.

★   ★   ★

Of all creatures cats and dogs live most closely and harmoniously with human beings. In the confines of our homes these four-legged friends allow themselves to be kept and fed. We gladly take care of them in return for what pleasure, amusement and companionship they bring. Our inmates soon grow adept at reading and mirroring human mood and gesture with their own postures and expressions. Colette, who wrote extensively about animals, including her own pets, cited the example of a Pekinese which unfailingly leapt up from his station the moment she capped her pen, signalling the end of the day's writing and the beginning of their walk.

The essential differences between cat and dog can be traced through the process of domestication back to their forbears, and it is these wild ancestors which the survey of cat and dog dances

concentrates on. The cat has changed remarkably little through
mutation. There is a wildness lurking beneath the surface that
rises in the stiffly arched back when the creature is about to attack.
It is really a little tiger. The dog, by contrast, has been altered
greatly through a process of domestication that started when Stone
Age hunters first recognized the useful scavenging and hunting
services of wild dogs, the jackal and wolf. Since this early
co-operative venture a deep friendship has grown, making of the
dog an animal capable of both expressing and eliciting great
sympathy.

But dogs have a wild or demonic side that reverts to their wolf
and jackal origins. In Europe, during the Middle Ages, dogs were
sacrificed to the devil near graveyards, under full moon. And the
face of the man in the moon was explained as being the first
murderer, Cain, and his dog, who were turned into the devil and a
thorn bush. People in many parts of the world pronounce curses
and incantations against enemies over the body of a dead dog, and
the Dog Dance of the Eastern Sioux described below is a danced
variation of this practice. The dog is believed furthermore to have
psychic powers, serving as a clairvoyant or interpreter of omens. In
the ancient Greek healing cult of Aesculapius, it was a sign of
imminent recovery if a patient dreamed about a dog. And in the
same cult the dog had the power to lick invalids back to health!

The associations between the dog and death are strong. The
rabid dog is, of course, a real threat. In Greece and Rome, the
plague-bearing dog was associated with Sirius, the Dog Star,
appearing in late summer. During this hot, dry period, called the
Dog Days, dogs in general were believed to go rabid, causing
humans to contract fever and have convulsions, the ancient dance
of death. In the mythology of many independent cultures the origin
of death is attributed to the dogs' wild cousins (Dogon and Pomo,
for example), while in others the dog serves as guide to the dead in
their journey to the underworld.

In keeping with the belief that the dog has close ties with death,
danced imitations of the dog are performed in funeral and war
dances. In the mourning rituals of the ancient Aztecs a virtuoso
dancer impersonated the great old coyote Huehuecoytl presiding
over the ceremonies. Sioux warriors boasted of their man-hunts in a
bloody dance during which they actually ate the heart and liver of
the dog, believed to contain the strength of their victim – an
example of symbolic anthropophagy. The artist George Catlin
memorably described and illustrated the exotic dance:

'General Patterson, of Philadelphia, and his family arrived about this time . . . and a dance was got up for their amusement; and it proved to be one of an unusual kind and interesting to all. Considerable preparation was made for the occasion, and the Indians informed me, that if they could get a couple of dogs that were of no use to the garrison, they would give us their favorite dance, the "dog dance". The two dogs were soon produced by the officers, and in the presence of the whole assemblage of spectators, they butchered them and placed their two hearts and livers entire and uncooked on a couple of crotches about as high as a man's face. These were then cut into strips, about an inch in width, and left hanging in this condition, with the blood and smoke upon them. A spirited dance then ensued, and in a confused manner, every one sung forth his own deeds of bravery in ejaculating gutturals, which were almost deafening; and they danced up, two at a time to the stakes, and after spitting several times upon the liver and hearts, catched [sic] a piece in their mouths, bit it off, and swallowed it. This was all done without losing step (which was in time to their music), or interrupting the times of their voices.

'Each and every one of them in this wise bit off and swallowed a piece of the livers, until they were demolished; with the exception of the last two pieces hanging on the stakes, which a couple of them carried in their mouths, and communicated to the mouths of the two musicians who swallowed them. This is one of the most valued dances amongst the Sioux, though by no means the most beautiful or pleasing . . . The dog dance is one of distinction, inasmuch as it can only be danced by those who have taken scalps from the enemy's heads and come forward boasting that they killed their enemy in battle, and swallowed a piece of his heart in the same manner.'

In the folklore of the American Indian of the West, Coyote is a major trickster figure. He can bestow gifts on mankind, like the gift of fire in the Thompson River Indian myth; but he also brings evil to people, and incidentally does himself in as well. In the Pomo origin myth for death, Coyote makes the chief's daughter dance around the hole of the deadly rattlesnake, but in retaliation the chief poisons the trickster's daughter. Many Zuñi folktales, collected by Frank Hamilton Cushing, feature Coyote as a negative example of human vanity, weakness and excess. Like the Aesop fable about the grasshopper who danced irresponsibly all summer long while the ant dutifully stockpiled provisions for the long winter, two of the Coyote tales end with morals which reflect upon how the wild dog imperilled himself by trying to dance with birds.

One of these fables, entitled 'How Coyote Joined the Dance of the Burrowing-owls', contains a vicious warning to people not to meddle in other people's affairs and imitate their actions. The fable begins by describing how long ago the animals lived in peaceful co-existence. The Prairie-dogs got on fairly well with the Grasshoppers, Rattlesnakes, Horned Toads and Burrowing-owls; the Dogs were especially friendly towards the Owls, who were sacred and venerable beings. For this reason, the Prairie-dogs never intruded upon the Owls' councils and ceremonies; and when they held dances, the Dogs kept their distance.

But Coyote, who was always nosing into everyone's business, was on a certain day prying into the goings-on of the Grasshoppers and Prairie-dogs, when he came upon the dance of the Burrowing-owls. The dance they were performing was held especially sacred by them, and it required great talent and concentration. For on their heads each carried a bowl of foam; but they danced with such dexterity that never a drop spilled onto their sleek black feather head-dresses. And though their legs were crooked and disjointed, they danced gracefully to the whistling of some and the clapping beaks of others. The dance so intrigued the nosy Coyote that he could no longer contain his curiosity. Picking up his ears, and lifting his tail, he approached the leader of the dance and said, 'My father, how are you and your children these days?'

The trickster Coyote
paddles up the river.
From E. S. Curtis,
Indian Days of Long Ago
(1914)

'Well and happy,' replied the Owl, turning his attention back to the dance.

'Yes, but I see that you are dancing. A very fine dance indeed! Utterly charming! And why should you not be dancing so if you were not well and happy?'

'We are dancing,' replied the Owl, 'for our pleasure and for the good of the town.'

When Coyote persisted in asking about the bowl of foam on the dancers' heads and the limping movements in their dance, the Owl said to Coyote, 'You see, my friend, we hold this to be a very sacred dance. And to become dancers my children must be initiated into the mysteries of this society, which can work great and strange miracles. You inquire about what is on the Owls' heads. Look a bit closer, my friend. Can you not see that it is their grandmothers' heads they have on, the feathers turned white with age?'

'So it seems,' said the Coyote, twitching his nose as he examined the heads of the dancers more carefully.

'And you ask why they limp when they dance,' said the Owl. 'The limp is indispensable to a proper performance. You see, to dance this way, my children go through great pain by having their legs broken. Instead of becoming clumsier, they gain by it. Good luck follows them everywhere. And they earn the distinction of dancing as no other creature may dance.'

By this time Coyote was quite entranced by the joyful dance of the Burrowing-owl, and his bristly tail kept time to the music. Without further ado he inquired, 'Do you think that I too could learn to dance in this way?'

'Well,' replied the Owl. 'It is very difficult to learn, and you haven't undergone initiation. But if you are still bent on learning the dance – incidentally, you do have a grandmother?'

'Oh yes! And a fine old woman is she,' Coyote said, looking towards the hole where his grandmother was preparing his breakfast.

'All right then,' said the Owl, 'if you want to join in our dance, you must meet the prerequisites, and then I think we can take you into our order.' And then aside, 'The silly fool! The stinking wretch! I will teach him to stick that sharp nose of his into people's affairs.'

'All right. I will do it then,' said Coyote. He hurried home to where his grandmother sat on the roof, which was a rock beside his hole, preparing breakfast.

'My dear grandmother!' exclaimed Coyote. 'What a fine thing

you will enable me to do.' The Coyote scrambled up onto the roof. Taking in his hands a leg-bone he whacked her again and again until she was dead and sawed off her head with the teeth of a deer. And the head, all soft and streaming with blood, Coyote placed on top of his own. Then he got up on his hind legs and tried to imitate the way the Owls drooped their wings when they danced. It worked admirably well, so Coyote found a rock, and laying his legs across it, smashed them with a stone.

The Coyote howled, 'If the dance be a fine thing, the initiation is anything but!'

However, still determined, he tried to get up to walk. But he could only drag himself by the paws, as his hind legs trailed miserably in the dust. In great pain he hurried along as fast as he could to the dancing-ground of the owls with his grandmother's grisly head bobbing up and down along the ground.

When he reached the dancers, they pretended to be pleased with their convert, and greeted him, in spite of his sorry appearance, with an overwhelming welcome. The Coyote looked dreadfully ill, and he kept looking at his hind legs as if he wanted to lick them. But the Owl would not let him and invited the initiate to join now in their dance. The Coyote tried to bow in a dignified manner, but when he got up on his stumps he fell over, and his grandmother's head rolled in the dust. He picked it up off the ground and slapped it back on his head, and again raised himself, whimpering, and pranced around. Soon, however, he toppled over again. The Burrowing-owls were so delighted at the pathetic sight that they laughed until the foam on their heads dripped onto their shining feathers. And then, with a rude parting gesture, they dismissed Coyote, who limped home, realizing that he had been made an utter fool.

The moral of the story is that readiness to busy oneself in the affairs of others, to make a general nuisance of oneself, and to try to imitate everything one sees, is an instinct that will be punished, as the Burrowing-owls had done to Coyote.

It is perhaps ironic that this fable was related to Frank Hamilton Cushing, who is described by William Webb in *Dwellers at the Source*, containing A. C. Vroman's original photographs of Zuñi and other South-western tribes, as 'an outrageously arrogant and condescending busybody who felt no reservations about prying into the most secret and private parts of Zuñi life'. But more universally the fable makes important statements about the exclusivity and the sanctity of dance ceremonies in tribal cultures. And the tale can be fitted into the folk beliefs of several cultures, where the birds in myths are the rightful owners of dance. As a symbol of the joyous levity of spirit that comes through dance, the flight of birds, and not earth-bound creatures, is on balance more fitting.

In Indian tales of the American West, Wolf frequently appears as the steadfast companion of Coyote. Both share guile and deceit, qualities possessed by another of the dog's wild cousins, the sly fox. As wily, sly fellows, they are made out to be allies of death and, by extension, of the warrior's art. In European fairy-tales too, the wolf figures prominently as a deceptive creature posing a threat to helpless flocks of sheep and innocent children. Little Red Riding Hood and Peter and the Wolf are the best-known examples. These myths and fairy-tales show that the wolf behaves badly whenever he crosses over into the habitations of men. But the wolf has another side. In the wild, the wolf can have a benign character, nursing abandoned infants like Romulus and Remus, the mythical founders of Rome.

This second, more positive portrayal of the wolf reflects more accurately the true disposition of this animal, an essentially shy creature sharing a strong bond with other members of the pack, and capable of extreme devotion to humans. Myths about man-devouring wolves are resoundingly invalidated by fact: apart from a handful of cases where the attacking wolf could be shown to be rabid, there are few documented cases of a wolf killing a human being. There is, after all, only a small degree of difference between the wolf and the dog. The wolf is a creodont, the dog a cynodont, but both have forty-two teeth. Anatomically, the shoulders of a wolf are narrower than a dog's, firmly set, and turned inwards. The wolf's breast is shallower, and keel-like in shape. Whereas the dog carries its tail in the air, a wolf's hangs.

The social organization of wolves is elaborate, resembling military or hunting hierarchy. The pack is led by a dominant male or female, known to mammalogists as the 'alpha' male or female of the pack. Although a dominance order is established in an early stage of each wolf's life, the order can change. Individual animals must maintain their status by continually reasserting self-confidence. Those who show initiative rise in rank; weaker specimens become extremely submissive and a pack will eventually pounce on the lowest member. Wolves hunt collectively and share their food. A division of labour exists between hunters and patrol scouts. Packs, numbering between four and thirty-six, have a keen sense of hunting territory which must be continually staked out. To maintain territorial rights, while at the same time finding food for survival, a pack has a complex system of communication. There are no fewer than five distinct cries, for announcing alarm, the sighting of prey, territorial encroachment by another pack, and so forth. Up close, wolves are known for their uncanny ability to communicate among themselves through posture and expression. It is said that a wolf can even convey mood to other members of the pack through facial expressions.

It is this social aspect of the wolf that emerges in myths of the North-west Coast Indians, who have a scientific understanding of this animal species. Among these tribes the wolf is recognized as the symbolic guardian of warriors, and this is supported by myths which repeatedly tell how wolves created and educated warriors.

The North-west Coast Indians inhabit the strip of coast between Juan de Fuca Strait and Yakutat Bay. Although composed of many individual tribes with linguistic differences, the customs, beliefs, arts and industries of the tribes constitute one culture more distinct than any other on the North American continent. Along the coast, as in other areas inhabited by tribal hunting societies, the animal largely dominated everyday life. The mythology of the North-west Coast Indian is permeated with animal myths, and splendid animal motifs crop up everywhere in wood carvings and dance masks. Masked animal dances are legion among these people and form the predominant type of dance. This may reflect the Indians' belief that animals taught the tribes to dance. The refrain from a dance song from Cape Flattery goes, 'The animals taught the dancers, the dancers, the dancers.' No species of the indigenous fauna is excluded from portrayal. Insects, birds, fish, sea-mammals – all inspire dances. The dances are sometimes sad, like the dance of the mournful white owl which portrays the returning spirit of a drowned person seeking out a favourite haunt; sometimes they are gay and entertaining, like the racoon dance, which ends with the dancer climbing the rafters!

An early traveller to the North-west Coast, Captain James Cook, who entered the Nootka Sound in 1778, was received by the chiefs who were casting eagle's down on the waters and delivering orations to the accompaniment of bird-shaped rattles; on their heads the people wore great ceremonial masks. Cook later wrote in his journal, 'If travellers or voyagers in an ignorant or credulous age, when many unnatural and marvellous things were supposed to exist, had seen a number of people decorated in this manner, they would readily have believed that there existed a race of beings partaking of the nature of man and beast.' The dual nature, man and animal, of the North-west Coast Indian tribes is compellingly rendered in transformation face masks. The exterior of the mask, for example, may show the head of a wolf; but when swung open on its hinges by an invisible string, reveals the face of a man. Among the many legends of the North-west Coast Indians, transformation myths are most popular and people never tire of seeing them acted out during the Winter Dances with the help of such transformation masks. The myths ultimately revert to beliefs about the creation of the world, a time which the Indians say they cannot remember, since this was before animals were transformed into people. Creation stories describe how the first ancestors descended to the world as animals, later to take off their masks and skins. The mythical conception is embodied in the Kwakiutl tribes' word for 'lineages', *numayms*, referring to the links in the chain back to the earliest animal ancestors. A typical myth begins: 'The first man of the Tsawatenok was Kawatilikalla, but before he was a wolf, and his wife was a wolf. . . . One day a heavy rain was falling and Kawatilikalla said, "I do not see why we should remain animals. We had better leave off these skins and use them only in dancing."'

The major ceremony of the Nootka tribes, which share Vancouver Island with the Southern Kwakiutl, was the Wolf Dance. Known to the Nootka as the Shaman's Dance, the ceremony commemorated an ancestor who played dead in order to find his way to the hideout of the wolves which taught him the dances necessary to ensure their assistance in war and the hunt. Warfare amounted to little more than skirmishes with neighbouring Kwakiutl clans, and more sporadically, buccaneering and other sea adventures connected with the slave trade along the coast. The Nootka were bold seafarers and hunters of the great killer whale. On the prow of their canoes the warriors would paint the wolf; like a hound going ahead of the hunters, the 'wolf' would sniff out and track down the quarry.

Essentially the Wolf Dance was a tribal initiation into a secret society. Boys and girls aged seven and eight were most frequently candidates, but in principle anyone could take part in the mysteries. Occasionally even infant heirs to powerful chiefs joined in the rite. Although an individual became a full initiate only after participating in the Wolf Dance, he could repeat the experience as many times as he wished to better the standing of his family. The import of the Wolf Dance was social, not religious. It was held by a wealthy chief wishing to affirm and strengthen the hereditary rights of himself and his heirs. The chief who sponsored the ceremony was known as the Wolf Owner.

Edward S. Curtis, the pioneer photographer and mythographer of the North American Indians, carefully recorded a Nootka dance origin myth which explains something about the beliefs behind the Wolf Dance. 'How Dance Was Obtained from Wolves' tells of a young chief named Yanamhum, who washed himself ceremonially every day in a stream by scrubbing his naked body with painful hemlock branches. From time to time two wolves would appear to scrutinize the young man's ritual. One day, after rubbing very hard, Yanamhum lay down in the stream, closed his eyes, and pretended to be dead. The two wolves, taking notice, came out of the forest and dragged the body away. 'Now the Wolves turned into a trail through the woods, and after a time entered the mouth of a great cave. . . . The man was thrown to the ground, and the Wolves crept through.

'After a time Yanamhum heard . . . people saying to one another, "Here is the person we have been hunting". This was the Wolf village, where the Wolves, removing their fur coats, lived in the form of human beings.

'"Do not let him lie too long", said a voice. A plank was laid with one end raised, and under the lower end was placed a wooden dish to catch the blood. For they were going to cut him up and eat him. One of the Wolves with a knife kneeled beside Yanamhum. "Why," he said, "this animal has fine fur!" For the animal people regarded humans as animals with fur. He placed the point of the knife on the body. Then suddenly Yanamhum grasped the knife, tore it away from the Wolf and leaped up. Instantly all the Wolf people dashed for their skins and tried to scramble into them. For the animal people were ashamed to be seen without their skins, and had no power without them.

'The chief begged, "Will you give us our knife?" But the man refused to give it up. . . . He kept his eyes fixed on an object hanging on the wall, wrapped in balsam boughs.

'Then the Wolf chief pondered. At length he turned to his people: "We had better give him what he is looking at, and get our knife." So one of the Wolves took the bundle down from the wall and revealed a stone club as long as a man's forearm. "For our knife," said the chief, "you shall have *mukwanhl*. If you are hunting sea-otters or seals, or anything else, show this, and when the animal sees *mukwanhl*, it will die . . ."

'Now the family of Yanamhum became anxious about him, and

when he was not found by those who were sent to look for him at the place where he had been washing, the people began to mourn him as dead. . . . The parents went away from the other people to be alone at Chektlis, while they mourned.

'After a year they set out to return to the village. The woman sat in the bow crying, while the man paddled in the stern. As they went they became aware of the howling of a great number of Wolves, . . . and mingled with the howling was a faint sound like a human voice crying. But so far away was it that they could not be sure it was not a crow. . . . "Stop crying and listen! It is not a crow; it is singing!" . . . They hastened homeward.

'On a point of land ahead they saw a Wolf, and when they came closer they beheld a great man, hundreds of them. To the midst of them stood a man, their son! . . .

'When they reached the village, the man hurriedly told the people what he had seen, and advised them to prepare their spears for a fight. . . .

'The people [came] in canoes [and] approached them, and a man with harpoon . . . struck Yanamhum in the arm. . . .

'The Wolves dashed away to the village and began to tear down the houses . . . And the falling timbers crushed some of the people but others quickly made fires . . . out of their old clothing, and the human odor drove off the Wolves.

'Now when other tribes heard about these things many of them doubted, and from every direction they came to see for themselves.

'When Yanamhum knew that they were coming, he made a wooden club in the likeness of *mukwanhl*. Then one day the beach was black with canoes, and Yanamhum let it be known that he would dance twice on the housetop with the wooden club, but the third time he would dance with the *mukwanhl* itself and those who continued to doubt would pay for their unbelief. So while the visitors sat in their canoes, he danced on the roof, holding the wooden club above his head. Then dropping the wooden club he raised the stone one and tore off the wrappings. Immediately the people fell dead, and the canoes were overturned.

'Now Yanamhum covered his weapon and went to the beach. He dragged out of the water the bodies of those who had not scoffed at him . . . those on whose faces he sprinkled water sat up as if awakening from a long sleep; but all the nonbelievers he left dead in the water. . . .'

Many such myths are told by North-west Coast tribes. Typically they concern a boy like Yanamhum, who has been scolded by his father for not being man enough. The boy goes to commit suicide but stops short. Instead he purifies himself and begins to make a man of himself by inflicting bodily harm. He further develops his virility by feigning death before the wolves, and finally by acquiring the death-dealing instrument, the most powerful weapon in the wolves' arsenal. Recognizing him as a heroic leader, the wolves teach the boy how to dance when he needs to summon their power. The dance is really a gesture dance, and one of heroic gesture to match the newly acquired stature of the boy. Dance here is a metaphor for self-mastery and the manipulation of power within the tribe.

The Wolf Dance is now obsolete, but a member of each Nootkan tribe could take you to the exact spot in his territory where the wolves abducted the ancestor. When it was current, individual Nootkan tribes naturally performed the Wolf Dance with local variations. Accounts from various informants which were recorded by Curtis, Boas and others nevertheless concur on the overall programme of the ceremony. It comprised three parts: the abduction of the initiates by the wolves; their seclusion, during which the spectators enjoyed a sort of saturnalian feast; and finally the return of the initiates, who were expected to display what privileges the wolves had given them.

The dramatis personae of the Dance were the initiates and their relatives, the Wolf Spirits and the many extras needed to perform the animal dances in the middle phase of the Dance. Each initiate had a wolf attendant known as a Sa'ishsi, meaning 'Crawler'. This was an inherited position originally designated by Yanamhum, who had obtained dance from the wolves. The Wolf Spirits did not wear masks: these were reserved for the initiates' display dances at the end. Originally the 'Crawlers' wore real wolf pelts, but blankets were subsequently used. They were tied over their backs with one corner projecting over the heads to represent snouts. Their faces, arms and legs were painted jet black.

The cry of the wolf announced the beginning of the ceremony. From afar in the woods the Sa'ishsi imitated the various calls of the wolf on cedar whistles bound together by cherry bark. The ubiquitous bull-roarer, here said to be the wolf's lashing tail, added to the air of expectancy. Now the wolf spirits, fully covered in blankets, rushed out of the forest on all fours. General pandemonium broke out as the wolves went from house to house knocking ominously on doors, entering, and dragging people out of bed, in case anyone thought he might escape the call of the wolves. The first time the wolves entered a house they would pretend to be looking for a missing person; the second time they entered, they threatened the inhabitants with bodily harm; the third time they knocked over furniture and broke kitchen utensils. According to pre-arranged plan, the initiate-to-be would blow a tiny whistle, pretend to drop dead, and, amidst the feigned cries of relatives, allow himself to be carried off on the wolves' backs. Initiates were thus borne away in canoes to the Dance lodge and held hostage for several days. It was here that they earned privileges and learned the Wolf Dance.

Back in the village a debauched festival took place. Dances of all the animals were performed. The women traditionally performed bird dances: the snipe, bufflehead (butterball) duck, sawbill duck, mallard, and the hilarious woodpecker dancer. The men on the other hand performed dances of game including the deer, the killer whale and the hair-seal. The performances were given at the Wolf Owner's request by clubs named after the animal. To the animal's name was appended an 'iniq' suffix, meaning 'imitation'. The first and last dances were the War Chief's Imitating Club, which dramatized war by mimicking mean animals. Some dances had quite a practical purpose, like the Devil-fish Dance. The dancers acted like policemen, enforcing the observation of taboos. Anyone who broke a taboo would be 'harpooned' by the devil-fish. Since the Wolf Dance in general was intended to strengthen hereditary rights, the Wolf Owner sometimes specifically hired clubs of dancers to represent his material possessions. On one occasion, for instance, it is known that a chief paid a group of dancers a great deal of money to dance like frogs, in allusion to a nearby lake he owned that teemed with frogs! As part of the system of ceremonial giving or 'potlatch', some dances were designed to distribute gifts from the Wolf Owner to the spectators. In one Wolf Dance the distributors of largesse were several women imitating butterflies. They wore strips of white cloth painted with multicoloured stripes; on their heads antennae were represented by two supple boughs that nodded gently during the dance. Afterwards the Butterfly Dancers dispensed brightly coloured gifts to all the women present. Many dances were purely entertaining, such as the Periwinkle Dance, or the Dance of the Sea Cucumber – dances which did not make great acrobatic demands of the performers. The favourite dance was the Woodpecker Imitation. The dancers wore masquettes with long beaks. In their mouths they concealed whistles reproducing the bird's call. The dance was energetic, staccato and highly percussive. Some dancers climbed upon house posts which they pecked at with their 'beaks'. Others jostled the audience about as they chattered and pecked people at random. Sometimes small children entertained adults, as in the Moth Dance, where they were asked to mimic the small moth that brings sleep.

At the conclusion of this saturnalian festival the relatives began to feign great indignation at the absence of their kin, and like the parents of Yanamhum, set out in canoes. Once they located the place where the wolves were hiding the initiates, the relatives disembarked and declared war against the wolves. A mock battle ensued. An informant described the battles: 'Each time the Wolves appeared, some of the people made ludicrous attempts to capture them. Some of these men, and some women, had brought such armaments as outsized halibut hooks baited with sea biscuit, sea urchin poles, duck nets, or lassos representing the loop snares for ducks. These people annoyed the Wolves into chasing them down the beach. They fled in mock terror, screaming for their lives, into the water to their canoes. If a man could manage to tip a couple of canoes over while scrambling for his own he counted the day a success.' The relatives gradually gained the upper hand, and the wolves retreated back into the forest. The initiates, who had grown to like their home away from home, protested vehemently when the relatives tried to make them return to the village. All the way back they stomped and stormed, knocking down people and breaking things.

On the final day the initiates were revived by songs and dances and themselves were asked to show the songs and dances they had learned. Standard among these was the Wolf Imitation, for which the initiate wore a wolf mask. To perform the dance the initiate held his arms straight out in front of him, fists clenched; he hopped on both feet at once in a step called the 'tuhtuh'. A few ostentatious Northern Nootkan chiefs furnished hobby-wolves made of poles covered with canvas for the initiates to ride on. After the Wolf Imitation, initiates sang wolf songs and announced the names the Wolves had conferred upon them. If the Wolves had bequeathed him an object, the initiate proudly produced it from a fold in his costume where he had hidden it. To receive the Supernatural Quartz Crystal meant that the initiate would himself some day be a Wolf Owner.

X The Royal Sun: Feline Dances

Dog meets cat in the dog-lion sacred to Buddha, who was believed to be so powerful that even the mighty king of the forest trembled before his step. The dog-lion is a humorous example of human laziness and the force of tradition. A Chinese artist, asked to represent an animal he had never, or at least, rarely, seen, modelled the lion after the Emperor's Pekinese, and all artists afterwards followed his example. Lion dances first appeared during the T'ang Dynasty (AD 619–907), perhaps introduced by Indian jugglers and travelling animal trainers. As the emblem of Buddha and protector of his religion, the lion, when animated in the dance, drove evil out of the world. The dances took place at Chinese New Year. Today lion dances are performed in China and in cities with large Chinese populations, such as San Francisco. In China, companies of trained acrobats, dressed in yellow and blue costumes, manoeuvre the large cloth lion supported on a wooden frame to simulate leaps and attacks directed against imaginary prey, the spectators. In San Francisco, instead of two performers, one dancer, wearing a huge mask, acts out the part of the lion.

In the Western world, dogs fight jaguars in zany Mexican dance dramas called Tecuanes, or the Dance of Wild Beasts. In one of the dances surviving from the State of Guerrero the old men make a double line, followed by one or two ranch owners, two dogs, a deer in a grey suit, two vultures, a doctor called the 'bone-buster', an archer, and a man dressed as an old woman. The jaguar is played by a man disguised in a spotted skin and wearing a mask with great jaws, tusks and whiskers. The jaguar goes around annoying the dancers with its detachable tail, as they try to keep on dancing to a kind of one-man band. After a nonsensical dialogue, the jaguar is hunted down by the dogs and killed, then eaten by the vultures. The doctor lamely suggests that they resurrect him.

Cats appeared early on in a musical context. The Egyptian sistrum, a plucked instrument similar to the lyre, was the emblem of the cat-goddess, Sekhmet; a cat shape usually formed a part of the instrument. An Egyptian amulet shows a cat playing a lyre and is inscribed to Bast-Re, Lord of Happiness. In Athens, female participants in the Sabazian mysteries danced carrying lyres which featured cat ornaments. The association between the cat and music was suggested by their distinctive voices. According to medieval legend, the meow of the cat contained sixty-three notes. A cruel device from the Renaissance, called the cat organ, confined a live cat in a cage; by pulling a string attached to its tail, the performer could make the cat meow. The *saron*, a Javanese dance instrument, is shaped like a cat sitting with outstretched paws and open mouth. The two parallel bars on the back can be played like a xylophone and the impression is given that the cat is singing.

Cats also dance. A relief from Rome shows a woman playing a lyre and trying to teach a cat to dance. Above the cat's head she has hung two dead birds from a tree so that the cat will 'pirouette' on its hind legs. French caricaturists of the nineteenth century, like Grandville, portrayed choruses of cats dancing to orchestras composed of musical cats and other animals. The movements of cats have been incorporated into Tchaikowsky's ballets and several modern ballets, including *Pas de Chat*, *Kikimora*, or Balanchine's *La Chatte*, choreographed in 1927 when he was still with Diaghilev. The cat is one of the four animals portrayed in Balanchine's later work, *Renard*.

In the survey of the cat in myth and dance in the non-Western tradition, we shall be looking at its wild forbears (lions and leopards, tigers and jaguars) and focusing on the complex of mythological associations centring around the sun. Feline cults figure in three principal geographic areas: the Far East, Africa, and Central and South America. The first has been touched on briefly in connection with Buddha and his lion dancers. The second area, comprising the Saharan, eastern and southern regions of Africa, may rightfully lay claim to the most ancient feline cults, involving rituals that stretch back to Palaeolithic times; and in a modified form these cults persist today. In Central and South America a consistent portrayal emerges for the man-slaying jaguar, a werebeast whose identity is confused with man, god, spirit and shaman.

A fundamental concern among tribal populations is that of ensuring, magically, the continued alternation of night and day. This theme has already appeared in the Andaman origin myth, as well as in the Bushman origin myth for antelope. In the Andamanese tale, when Da Tengat the Spider crushed the cicada in his hand, the world became shrouded in darkness which persisted until the little spider taught the ancestors how to restore daylight with fire, song and dance. Another insect god, Mantis, caused the world to grow dark by piercing the gall-bladders of the antelopes hanging up in a tree with a sharp stone. The myth goes on to tell how Keggan stole the shoe of the murderous Kwammang-a and hurled it high into the sky, where it lodged and became the moon. Whereas the Andamanese tale is a charming and simple episode about conquering the fear of the dark, the Bushman myth alludes to a complex set of beliefs about the sun characteristic of African hunting cultures; and, whereas night embodies evil in the eyes of the Andamanese, it seems benign to the Bushmen, since night protects the hunted game. The cloak of darkness allows them to hide, and in this refuge, to regenerate. The creation of the moon is believed to have a restorative effect on the antelope population. The obscure half-light of the moon prevents hunters from accomplishing what the sun enables them to do by day. The all-seeing, omnivorous eye of the sun, on the other hand, is the hunters' greatest ally: it helps them sight, pursue and shoot unerringly at their animal victims. The sun *is* the great hunter in the mythologies of hunting peoples. The keen-sighted vision it imparts to hunters is translated into the image of a hunting weapon: the rays of the sun pierce like an arrow. At dawn the rays of the sun scatter the night-time herds of the sky, the stars; then too the herds on earth stampede, becoming easy prey to the winged barbs of archers.

Ocelotl the jaguar bearing a standard and crowned with flowers, in an allusion to the legend of the creation of sun and moon. Codex Borbonicus

In the wild, lions – or, more precisely, lionesses – are keen-sighted hunters. While the lioness stands by to spring on the flocks of sheep, the males of the pride mysteriously project their muffled roar like ventriloquists. The herds panic, and the chosen victim easily falls prey to the vicious, acrobatic leap of the chief huntress. Unlike men, however, lions have the uncanny ability of hunting at night with 'cat's eyes'. The familiar sight of a cat's eyes flashing brilliantly in the headlamps of an oncoming car can be explained by the fact that the lens behind the cat's retina is extremely dense and highly reflective. The eyes of all felines are constructed in this manner; and the phenomenon has haunted shepherd and hunter alike when, suddenly, out of nowhere, eyes illumined by the campfire signal the presence of the murderous intruder. In many parts of the world, myths and legends demonstrate the folkloric belief that the eye of the feline actively emits light, or even fire. The eye of the feline then becomes, by extension, the sun.

In Middle Kingdom Egypt a cycle of legends related how the eye of the sun was returned in the form of a lioness's eye. In a late version of the myth, the sun's eye had retired from Egypt to Nubia, where it resided in the shape of a wild lioness. The sun god, desirous that his daughter should return, sent her brother, Shu, the lion-shaped baboon, on a mission to retrieve her. After scouring Nubia, Shu finally discovered his sister in the eastern mountain of sunrise called Ba-gemet, and with great difficulty, he persuaded her to return to Egypt. She consented, and upon returning was greeted with a great festival of music and dancing; and the sacred baboons, who salute the sun each morning, were led in the processional welcome by Shu. Afterwards the Sun was reunited with his daughter in Heliopolis.

The coloration and markings of felines also encourage an association with fire and the sun. This is especially true in the case of the male lion, whose head, encircled by a tawny mane, suggests the sun's golden disc. In South American Indian mythology the jaguar's colours have marked him out as the original master of fire. He alone of all the animals did not burn to a crisp when he leapt into the conflagration, but was merely scorched, leaving him with his distinctively mottled hide. A story goes that the jaguar in the beginning of the world was the sole owner of fire. At that time he ate only cooked meat; but when, owing to his negligence, a rabbit stole fire from him, the jaguar was forced to eat his meat raw. In the cosmologies of the ancient Aztecs and the Incas, the jaguar creates and destroys the sun, and causes the eclipse of the sun or moon.

This he does by viciously attacking and devouring a portion of the heavenly body. In a spectacular Aztec dance ritual described below, knights of the Jaguar Order superintended the feeding of the sun through human sacrifice.

The mythological association between the lion and the fiery sources of light led to the adoption of the lion as the emblems of the king and hero. Louis XIV, the Sun King, had among his emblems the tawny-maned lion. His predecessor Richard Coeur-de-Lion, was, of course, the namesake of the greatest of Greek heroes, Herakles, the Lion-hearted (Leontokardios). His first labour, in which he slew the Nemean lion, earned him the right to wear its skin. The hide disguised and protected him in all his exploits, including his wrestling match with Periklymenos, Triton, the Old Man of the Sea, and other shape-shifters. Possessing the lion in some manner or form implies splendour, mastery, brute strength, and heroic stature. In every part of the world the king of beasts is the king's beast. The lion was Judah's emblem and today adorns the crest of the British monarch.

The king of beasts in Palaeolithic Africa was the Master of the Animals, whose position was worshipped and in turn appropriated by shamans in Stone Age hunting cults through masked dance rituals. Already the feline master had been seen in the polymorphous Sorcerer of Trois-Frères, who presides over the multitudinous painted herds. The phallus is that of a feline. A dancing sorcerer disguised as a lion reigns over herds in a rock drawing in the Sahara-Atlas range in North Africa. Contrary to the practice of drawing figures in profile, the shaman, like the Sorcerer, is shown in full frontal view; and again like the Sorcerer, he shifts step in the manner of the cakewalk. The feline eyes gaze piercingly straight ahead, positioned in such a way as to be hit head-on by the first rays of the sun to reach the rock enclosure. The exchange of rays and arrows between lion and sun kindles looks that kill. Here is early evidence of the lion symbolizing the human hunter, and empowered by the great hunter of the sky, the sun. In this part of Africa, the eye of the feline is to this day feared. A propitiatory hunting ritual in Morocco prescribes that when a panther is killed, the slayer must quickly run up behind the carcass and blindfold the beast so that it will never again recognize its murderer.

Stone Age man desired the hunting mastery and physical strength of the lion to be his, and went to great lengths to acquire them. The ritual, however, took on a religious significance and the lion was, in effect, slain and resurrected. First the beast was killed and flayed; then the teeth were extracted, the eye-sockets driven through with bones, and the head erected on a stake as a trophy to be worshipped. Lastly, a shaman – dressed like the lion-sorcerer of the Sahara-Atlas rock painting – danced the lion's spirit back to his own kind, thus resurrecting it in the way the Blackfoot tribes learned to do for the buffalo.

Happily the meanings of these actions can be reconstructed by means of archaeology and contemporary ethnographic parallels. In the Palaeolithic there were two Masters of the Animals, the bear for the northern hemisphere, and the feline for the southern. Both species are cave animals; and sacrificial remains, which show clear evidence of post mortem operations on the head, have been excavated by archaeologists at cave sites.

A well-documented bear-cult survives today among the hairy Ainus of the northern islands of Japan. As described by Joseph Campbell in *The Masks of God*, a bear cub is captured from its mother at an early age, suckled by an Ainu woman and looked after by an Ainu man. When the hugs of the little bear begin to hurt, it is put away in a cage where it is kept until its second birthday. One day the decision is made to send the little guest back home to its parents. This decision provides the occasion for great rejoicing, singing and dancing. The bear, as the centre of attraction, is supposed to be extremely pleased by the goings-on – even though the little guest is baited, strangled, shot through the heart with an arrow and, finally, decapitated. Left in this speechless state, the bear is prayed to and asked to repeat to its parents, 'I have been nourished for a long time by an Ainu father and mother and have been kept from trouble and harm. Since I am now grown up, I have returned. Please rejoice!' This plea is intended to make the bear's parents very happy. And with this lighthearted farewell, the bear is ceremonially danced away to its ancestral home by the hairy Ainu who trips lightly around a pole bearing the head and hide of the bear.

In the Gold Coast such a pole has been found as a trophy stand for a leopard. In the Sudan the shape of a leopard which has slain a man is re-created in an earthwork. But the feline's head is conspicuously absent. The earthwork becomes the maypole around which dancers perform. A circular barrier of thorns is erected about the leopard effigy; outside the barrier, warriors gather in a circle, while the hunter responsible for slaying the beast enters the enclosure to dance around his tribesman's murderer.

Clearly the avenging spirit of the feline, especially the man-slaying leopard, must be propitiated. But in so doing the warrior-hunter acquires the beast's strength and cruelty, and that is good for the hunt. The Hausa Lion Initiation Dance prepares one to become a Mahalbi, or hunter. A candidate who has already shown extraordinary skill by tracking down predators must furthermore be endowed magically by touching a lion or leopard effigy. Before the dance he must engage in sexual pleasures, then hunt down a respectably large animal. When he returns with his booty, he dances next to it, spurred on by whirring bull-roarers, until he achieves a state of ecstasy. At the climax of this exhilarating dance, he stops abruptly. Now in a blind trance, he is led to what he believes to be a lion or leopard, and is made to touch the animal. According to certain accounts, the feeling of sudden terror he experiences is forever branded on him when at this moment one of his testicles is cut off.

The greatest virtue of the dancer is his ability to leap high. A virtuoso dancer is distinguished from a member of the corps de ballet by his pre-eminent and electrifying leaps; he is not merely a dancer but an acrobatic dancer. The lioness is, in a sense, an acrobatic dancer with a limited dance vocabulary. But what is a vigorous leap in the dancer is vicious in a feline. The lioness leaps incredible distances with infinite precision, the aggressive leap being her most powerful weapon. She in effect turns herself into an arrow as her sharp claws tear at the neck of the victim. The method of attack is quite ingenious: the overpowering weight and momentum of the spring cause the prey to lose balance, fall, and in so doing, break its neck. This is a common artistic motif in Palaeolithic art. The lioness prepares to pounce on the neck of an antelope, whose head is frozen by the artist at the moment it smells alarm, a posture reminiscent of the bison lured by Palaeolithic 'Orpheus'. The motif is mythological in import, taking us back to the Bushman myth of the creation of antelope, where the lion, Master of the Animals, represents the great celestial hunter, the sun.

This Palaeolithic motif is repeated millennia later in West Africa in the gold weights of the Ashanti and in the dance masks of the Epa cult among the Yoruba of Nigeria, described by Robert Farris Thompson in *African Art in Motion*. The Yoruba Oloko mask, portraying a feline leaping upon an antelope, is worn in a dance contest among youths who must leap – just as their masks dictate – from a mound to a flat area before a council of elders. Here the meaning of the motif is no longer connected with hunting but rather with the regulation of government, and specifically with equilibrium: justice and the balance of power. The ruler must hold sway over his subjects and, if necessary, crush insurrection. The ruler's emblem is the royal feline, Oloko, the leopard, invoked by women at the beginning of the festival as 'Oloko, master of the beasts about the farm; terror to all animals within the bush'. The challenge of the contest is to see which youth can dance longest without faltering, while still supporting the Oloko masks. Huge and cumbersome, the masks weigh at least fifty pounds. The winner of the dance marathon earns the right to dance with the chief of the Epa cult, whose authority is refreshed and stabilized by the energy of the youthful leopard dancer.

On the lighter side of things are feline clown masks from the Yoruba Gelede festival, already seen in connection with nocturnal dances to assuage the witches of Mother Earth. Towards the conclusion of the all-night ceremony, pairs of dancers on stilts entertain the children and adults. One dancer is a sort of puppet operated by the other dancer. The feline has a special association with the earth goddess. The Mother Earth is a feline and therefore a huntress, but she is also a nursemaid tending her children, the way lionesses will gather in a sorority to care for a new-born cub.

In the Cameroons, the pre-eminent status conferred upon the ruler through the symbol of the leopard is paired up with the indomitable might of the elephant, the lord of the forest. The Bamileke chieftain, known as the *fon*, must periodically assert his position of power by demonstrating the ability to transform himself at will into the twin lords of the forest. In a spectacular dance display he wears a sort of reversible coat with leopard fur on one side, and, on the other, fabric embroidered with tiny glass beads. A stylized elephant mask emphasizing the ears and trunk crowns the ensemble. Materially, the leopard fur and the thousands of beads exhibit the chieftain's wealth; spiritually the identification with the mighty beasts of the forest reinforces the *fon*'s sovereignty.

The most haunting of shape-shifters is the man who assumes animal form at night by donning the animal's pelt. In the European tradition this Dr Jekyll and Mr Hyde is best known in the guise of the werewolf, who by night roams about the habitations of men in quest of human flesh; by day his skin is transformed and he returns unnoticed to his normal activities.

The prefix 'were' from the Old English *wer*, meaning 'man', can theoretically be combined with any animal. In cultures where there are no wolves, the fiercest animal takes its place: this often means a feline. Thus the 'were-tiger' is found in Borneo and parts of Asia, the 'were-leopard' in Africa, and the 'were-jaguar' in Central and South America. The were-beast is a vicious man-slayer and the enemy of the shaman. But the shaman can himself assume animal form and use the power of the were-animal. In certain pockets of West Africa superstitious beliefs about the existence of were-leopards are played upon by individuals who hire self-styled shamans or magicians called 'leopard-men' to put away an enemy. A leopard-man, in short, is a professional murderer. This form of witchcraft is occasionally practised today within a few tribes in West Africa, although governmental sanctions have severely curtailed the activity. The leopard-men operate in the following way. A fee is paid to the leopard-man by a member of a tribe who wishes to murder a personal enemy, for example an in-law, without being held responsible for the action. The leopard-man performs his job stealthily at night, dressed in the feline's pelt and wearing a leopard mask. Carrying with him special tools, an iron claw, and a club shaped like the leopard's paw, he sneaks up to the sleeping victim and attacks swiftly. He mauls the victim with the claw, leaving the impression that an actual leopard has attacked. And he further covers up his crime by making the tracks of a leopard with the club in the dirt about the scene of the crime.

In Central and South America, where the wolf is not part of the indigenous fauna, the jaguar is the were-beast. In the pantheons of ancient Central and South America, were-jaguars were transformations of gods, not men. The Incas did, on a cosmic scale, something similar to the African witchcraft practice of hiring leopard-men, in employing the celestial jaguar-god to pounce viciously at the moon; simply by making as much noise as possible, they induced the feline to leap at and devour the moon, thus causing a lunar eclipse. The Aztecs, according to an Aztec creation myth, believed that the sun was knocked out of orbit during a cosmic dance combat between two gods who took on the shape of jaguars. These were Tezcatlipoca and his adversary, Quetzalcoatl, the Plumed Serpent.

The Aztecs did not believe that there were natural phenomena, *per se*, but rather divine forces that guided the stars, winds and waters. Tezcatlipoca, meaning 'Smoking Mirror', was a wind god and shape-shifter, and of all the divinities in the Aztec pantheon, the most awesome. He was invisible, yet he saw all; in his wanderings as the night wind, he sought out evil-doers and penetrated to their inner being. He could take human shape. In the guise of lord of banquets and festivities, Tezcatlipoca affected people through drink and the contagious rhythms of dance. A colourful myth tells of Tezcatlipoca's arrival in the form of an old medicine-man at the city of Tollan, ruled over by his chief adversary Quetzalcoatl. The story goes that Quetzalcoatl complained of an ailment for which Tezcatlipoca prescribed a strong liquor as a cure. But the drink was so strong that it incapacitated the god. Tezcatlipoca then transformed himself into a naked Indian from a foreign tribe and posed as a seller of green peppers. When the daughter of the temporal ruler of Tollan saw the handsome naked man she fell in love. The chief, noting his daughter's sudden infatuation, angrily asked the stranger why he went around with no clothes on, whereupon Tezcatlipoca indignantly replied that it was the custom of his tribe to do so. The exasperated chief, unable to change his daughter's love-struck condition, ordered Tezcatlipoca to cure her. His remedy was to marry the girl, thus making him a chieftain in Quetzalcoatl's city. Having won this victory over his opponent, he immediately proclaimed a festival to take place in the city of Tollan. He caused all the people to drink and dance until they grew dizzy and demented; as they danced they plunged to the depths of an abyss where they were transformed into rocks. And so gradually Tezcatlipoca brought the reign of Quetzalcoatl to an end.

Although a wind god, Tezcatlipoca was frequently represented as a jaguar, the were-beast, and patron of magicians, in commemoration of his act of creation. According to one version of the Aztec creation myth of the Four Suns, Tezcatlipoca made the first sun, and it was called *nahui ocelotl*, from which the French naturalist Buffon derived the word 'ocelot'. In fiery splendour Tezcatlipoca reigned 676 years until his adversary, Quetzalcoatl, changed into the man-devouring jaguar of the night. Seizing a club, Quetzalcoatl engaged Tezcatlipoca in a ball game which is akin to a dance combat and thereby succeeded in dislodging him from his orbit. As Tezcatlipoca soared through the vault of the heavens he changed into the shape of a jaguar and lodged in the sky as the Jaguar constellation, which we call Ursa Major.

Meanwhile on earth the jaguars wheeled on men and devoured them. This was at the beginning of the reign of Quetzalcoatl. The second sun ruled for another 676 years, at the end of which Quetzalcoatl's brothers deposed him. For seven times fifty-two years Tlaloc was Sun. And so the sun continued to be destroyed and replaced, until finally Tlaloc threw his own beloved son into the fires of the sun and the moon was born. Ever after the sun rose following the daily setting of the moon. This sun, by decree of the gods, had to be fed on human hearts and human blood to stay alive;

and the Aztec people made a covenant with the gods to ensure the sun's nourishment. The Aztecs, called the 'people of the sun', believed that they were a race specially elected to control and perpetuate the course of the sun until the apocalypse came. That it would come was certain, since the four preceding suns had all been destroyed. The fifth sun, the sun of the Aztec people, was called 'four earthquake', a name aptly reflecting the precarious state of cosmic affairs. Daily the jaguar monster Tepeyollotl leapt out of the earth's cavern in the west to seize the setting sun, and its roars could be heard in the echoing hills.

To ensure the nourishment of the sun, warfare was instituted. Captives were served up in sacrificial ceremonies to the sun, Ton Aiuh, under the supervision of the valiant Knights of the Eagle, Jaguar and Arrow Orders. One such ceremony took place on the day of Four Earthquakes, marking the passage of the sun through the heavens. At daybreak a war captive dressed as the Sun God ascended to the platform in front of the temple. Four priests laid out the victim, and a fifth prized open his breast to tear out the heart as an offering to the god. The people then feasted until noon, gashing their ears and bodies with obsidian blades. In the afternoon the Eagle and Jaguar Knights, followers of the Sun God, took part in a dance enacting the sacred war, during which the sun was slain, to be reborn the following day. The dance ended in a gladiatorial sacrifice. Specially chosen Eagle and Jaguar Knights slew another captive tethered to a circular stone representing the sun's disc.

Moving southward to the equatorial zone of South America, one enters the spirit world populated by demons, ghosts, wandering souls, spirits of the forest, and again the were-jaguar. Men encountering spirits in one form or the other is the substance of much of the folklore of South America. The spirits will adopt a man or a woman and transform them into spirits, reflecting a widespread religious belief in metempsychosis; or spirits may be disembodied souls, or else human beings restored after death to their original animal or vegetable form. Beast-embodied souls are generally to be avoided, and the were-jaguar is the form of reincarnation most to be shunned.

The were-jaguar is the patron of magicians and shamans in South America. It is commonly believed that shamans wander at night as jaguars attacking victims at random. There is real confusion about whether the shaman actually goes in jaguar disguise or merely sends forth his spirit in the form of a jaguar. Even experienced hunters are unsure. A jaguar which exhibits extraordinary fierceness undermines the confidence of the hunter, who reasons, 'if the jaguar is an ordinary wild beast, I may kill it with a bullet or arrow, but what will be my fate if I attack the man-destroyer, the terrible Kenaima?' For when a hunter slays a jaguar his spirit is in great peril of becoming possessed by the soul of the animal which has entered into his body. The man who has murdered a jaguar afterwards must clothe himself in a jaguar skin thrown over his body like a cape. About his neck dangles a necklace strung with the most dangerous parts of the jaguar's body, the teeth and claws. To shake out the jaguar's soul he dances, repeatedly making furious leaps in imitation of a springing jaguar in the midst of a circle of women lamenting the feline's death. But their wailing is nearly drowned out by the dancer, who accompanies himself with vociferous roars that help to shriek away the intrusive soul.

Gnawing fears about were-jaguars may reflect the practice of cannibalism in certain areas of South America in the last century. A nineteenth-century German ethnologist, Hans Staden, held prisoner by the Taupinambi tribe of the Brazilian coast, describes an embassy he made to the chief, who reportedly 'had before him a great basket of human flesh and was busy gnawing a bone. He put it to my mouth and asked if I did not wish to eat. I said to him: "there is hardly a wild animal that will eat its kind; how then shall I eat human flesh?" Then he, resuming his meal, replied: "I am a jaguar and I find it good." '

Eating the flesh of one's own species is a common motif in jaguar myths. A myth from the Eastern Bororo tells of a jaguar who marries the chief's daughter. The jaguar warns his bride about his evil mother, a caterpillar, who has a reputation for her killing sense of humour. The husband instructs his bride never to laugh at her mother-in-law's jokes. At first the girl succeeds. Time and again the mother tries to make the girl laugh, but her jokes fall on deaf ears. But later when the jaguar husband is away, the mother makes her daughter-in-law laugh at her wicked jokes – so hard, in fact, that she explodes and dies! The jaguar arrives home to find his wife lying dead and his mother being pecked to death by a falcon. The jaguar rushes and cuts open his wife's abdomen and out come twins. One of them, Bakororo, orders the animal species henceforth to desist from eating human flesh.

Bakororo gives his name to the spirited Bororo animal pantomimes which are representative of the spontaneous love for mime throughout tropical South America. The forte of the Bororo is animal mimicry. The night before the men set out for the hunt, the most talented mime artists imitate the animal to be hunted, usually the tapir. The tapir's form is modelled out of ashes and around the effigy the waddling movements of the swine are reproduced with an eerie realism enhanced by the effects of cocaine. Afterwards mimic dances of other animals are performed while a member of the tribes tells jokes and invents riddles and conundrums about their animal being represented.

As a trickster-figure the jaguar is humorously portrayed as a kind of acrobatic dancer, the juggler. One mythological motif describes the jaguar juggling with his shining eyes. He is endowed with the unusual talent of being able to take out his shining eyes, juggle with them, then replace them in their sockets. But he must not juggle with the eyes beyond a certain number of times, otherwise he will lose them. The Taulipant tribes tell about a crab who persuaded the jaguar to perform his juggling act. The jaguar, much flattered and wanting to show off, lifted out his eyes and began his act. He juggled with them one time too many, however, and the beautiful shining eyes slipped through his fingers into a nearby river where a fish swallowed them.

Myths such as this that reveal the jaguar's vulnerability are attempts to make the keen-sighted predator and shape-shifting were-beast seem less awesome. The full mystery and terror of the jaguar are preserved in the following haunting story brilliantly recounted by Father van Coll. The myth, 'The Source of Evils', is the Carib Indian version of the tales of Pandora. Like its Greek counterpart, the Carib myth contains many disparate elements and unresolved threads that give it a strangely powerful impact.

The main characters in the myth are a handsome lad Maconaura, his mother, his young bride Anuanaitu, and her father, named Jaguar. He is a *peaiman*, or sorcerer, who conceals his identity by wearing a calabash over his head. But the true vehicle for transformation is the animal dance. Here it is a kind of dance of vengeance in which the avenger allows his soul to be possessed by the spirit of a predator, such as the jaguar. There are several short dances in the myth, including the *Kenaima*, the word encountered above for the man-destroying were-jaguar.

The long myth opens with a description of the world in a golden age. The wild beasts live in perfect harmony, and the rivers flow smoothly and evenly without drought or flood. Maconaura and his mother live peacefully with the tribe of handsome people. One day, however, Maconaura discovers that his fishing net is broken and that his fish have been devoured. With the help of a cuckoo he

learns that a cayman is responsible and shoots the ugly reptile
between the eyes with an arrow. The very same day Maconaura
meets Anuanaitu, a beautiful young girl of mysterious origins. She
lives for a time with Maconaura and his mother and grows more
beautiful by the day; once of age, she becomes his wife.

When the young woman desires to return home to see her own
mother, Maconaura wishes to accompany her in order to formalize
their marriage with her folk. Much to his surprise, Anuanaitu
warns that this would mean sure death for both of them and
Maconaura's mother as well. But he prevails on his wife and
together they go to her home. There Maconaura discovers that his
father-in-law is an evil *peaiman* named Kaikoutji, meaning
'Jaguar', who keeps his true identity concealed by a calabash worn
over the head. Disdainful of Maconaura's suit, he challenges the
young man to make several things for him, including a *halla*
(sorcerer's stool) with the head of a jaguar on one side and
Kaikoutji's true portrait on the other. This is difficult, because of
the calabash; but with the help of a ruse Maconaura manages to see
the whole horrible head of Kaikoutji at night and so succeeds in the
test. Having won the hand of Anuanaitu, Maconaura wishes to
return home to visit his mother. This he must do alone, since
Kaikoutji will not allow his daughter to accompany him.

Maconaura and his mother spend several happy days together.
When he indicates his intention to return to the home of his bride
and her family, the mother protests, and a local *peaiman* predicts
that evil will come to him. Firm in his resolve, Maconaura departs.
Upon his arrival he is met by his bride and mother-in-law. Both
women are in tears and warn him to turn back immediately, since
Kaikoutji is furious with him. Despite their strong pleas, he
proceeds to the lodge of the evil sorcerer, who shoots him between
the eyes with an arrow the moment he crosses the threshold.

An owl singing *popopo!* has the task of announcing Maconaura's
death to his mother; with the help of the bird, she finds her son's
canoe and body, and returns home sadly to her own people . . .

'All assembled to hear the funeral chant, the last farewell of
mother to son. She recounted the tragic tale of his love and death,
and then, raising the cup of *tapana* to her lips, she cried: "Who has
extinguished the light of my son? Who has sent him into the valley
of shades? Woe! woe to him! . . . Alas! you see in me, O friends and
brothers, only a poor, weak old woman. I can do nothing. Who of
you will avenge me?" Forthwith two men sprang forward, seized
the cup, and emptied it; beside the corpse they intoned the

Kenaima Jaguar song, dancing the dance of vengeance; and into one of them the soul of a boa constrictor entered, into the other that of a jaguar. . . .

'Then two men came, one in the hide of a jaguar, the other in the mottled scales of a boa constrictor; and in an instant Jaguar and all about him were struck down, some crushed by the jaguar's blows, others strangled in snaky folds. Nevertheless fear had rescued some from their drunkenness; and they seized their bows, threatening the assailants with hundreds of arrows, whereupon the two Kenaima ceased their attack, while one of them cried: "Hold, friends! we are in your hands, but let us first speak!" Then he recounted the tale of Maconaura, and when he had ceased an old *peaiman* advanced, saying: "Young men, you have spoken well. We receive you as friends."

'The feast was renewed more heartily than ever, but though Anuanaitu, in her grief, had remained away, now she advanced, searching among the corpses. She examined them, one by one, with dry eyes; but at last she paused beside a body, her eyes filled with tears, and seating herself, long, long she chanted plaintively the praises of the dead. Suddenly she leaped up, with hair bristling and with face of fire, in vibrant voice intoning the terrible Kenaima and as she danced, the soul of a rattlesnake entered into her.

'Meantime, in the other village, the people were celebrating the *tapan*, delirious with joy for the vengeance taken, while the mother of Maconaura, overcome by drink, lay in her hammock, dreaming of her son. Anuanaitu entered, possessed, but she drew back moved when she heard her name pronounced by the dreaming woman. Throwing herself upon the old woman, she drew her tongue from her mouth, striking it with venomous poison; and leaning over her agonized victim she spoke: "The cayman which your son killed beside the basket-net was my brother. Like my father, he had a cayman's head. I would pardon that. My father avenged his son's death in inflicting on yours the same doom that he had dealt – an arrow between the eyes. Your kindred have slain my father and all mine. I would have pardoned that, too, had they but spared my mother. Maconaura is the cause that what is most dear to me in the world is perished; and robbing him in my turn, I immolate what he held most precious!"

'Uttering a terrible cry, she fled into the forest; and at the sound a change unprecedented occurred throughout all nature. The winds responded with a tempest which struck down the trees and uprooted the very oaks; thick clouds veiled the face of Adahelikl while sinister lightnings and the roar of thunders filled the tenebrous world with a deluge of rain mingled with the floods of rivers. The animals, until then peaceable, fell upon and devoured one another: the serpent struck with his venom, the cayman made his terrible jaws to crash, the jaguar tore the flesh of the harmless agouti. Anuanaitu, followed by the savage hosts of the forest, pursued her insensate course until she arrived at the summit of an enormous rock, whence she gushed a cascade; and there, on the brink of the precipice, she stretched forth her arms, leaned forward, and plunged into the depths. The waters received her and closed over her; nought was to be seen but a terrifying whirlpool.'

The world is turned upside down. It passes from a peaceful, innocent state to a state of dread conflict, symbolized by the animals devouring one another for the first time. The sinister ending is foreshadowed by the bestial thirst for revenge arising after the deaths of Anuanaitu's brother and Maconaura himself. At his funeral the avengers of Maconaura's mother intone the song of *Kenaima*, the man-destroying were-jaguar, whom a hunter must shake out of his body in a dance of frenzy in order to avoid soul possession. But to be possessed, to incorporate the evil and vicious aspects of the predator is precisely the goal of the dance of vengeance. The spirit of the feline dreaded by hunters in South America and Africa alike, is summoned by the avenger and directed against his enemies. The act of dancing bares the soul, allowing the animal to enter. When man and beast are thus allied, the venom of revenge rises in the fangs of the would-be avenger. Anuanaitu becomes a rattlesnake, the avengers of Maconaura a boa constrictor and jaguar. Like the early shape-shifter Proteus, these two wrestle their victims in the manner of animals – the one crushing his opponents with blows, the other strangling with snaky folds.

The various transformations and concealed identities in the Carib myth rest on beliefs about metempsychosis in South America, where the were-jaguar is the prominent symbol for a man incarnate in bestial form. In Africa this finds a parallel in the Leopard-men, expressed in the Yoruba tale told at the beginning of Chapter V about the leopard who is allowed to take on human shape only once a month. As that tale recognizes the predatory urge in human sexual conquest, so the Carib myth deals with the bestial urge to seek revenge for murder of one's kin. Here, then, is a new function of the animal dance, as a vehicle for wreaking vengeance for blood guilt.

Horse being taught to dance in a medieval manuscript. BL MS Roy 20 D IV, f. 137

The horse, called man's most noble conquest by the French natural historian Buffon, has a long and varied role in the history of mankind as a source of food, as a helper in war, hunt, and the ploughing-field, and as an entertainer. There were two types of horse, from which all modern horses descend: the Tarpan, originally from Mongolia, which bears a close resemblance to the ass; and the Przewalski, discovered as a wild breed still inhabiting the Steppes of Central Asia in 1871 by the Polish commander for whom it was named. The creature which we know to stand taller than a man began life as the quadruped Eohippus, measuring a mere fifteen inches, roughly the size of a small dog. Judging from Stone Age cave paintings, the horse had by that epoch nearly attained the impressive stature by which we know him. Even so it was a much less dangerous animal to hunt than the buffalo and other wild species in spite of its size, and therefore provided an easy and abundant source of nourishment. Owing to its central position in the diet of Stone Age people, the horse is the most commonly represented species in Stone Age art. The thousand-foot-long corridor in the cave of Les Combarelles in France also contains engravings of some 300 horses. The domestication of the horse did not occur for several thousand years after the Stone Age horse-hunters, when semi-nomadic tribes began keeping horses in corrals like herds of cattle as a ready food supply. The horse escaped being used as a beast of burden or as a means of transport until approximately 500 BC.

In warfare the horse became a powerful weapon. Harnessed to a wicker chariot, pairs of warriors dashed across the battlefield behind teams of horses – the one warrior manoeuvring the vehicle while the other cast his spear. In the Bronze Age, the Hittites and Egyptians first employed the war-chariot on a wide scale. The use of mounted cavalry troops came later, around the eighth century BC. It is recorded in the Second Book of Kings that Rab-shakeh, ambassador of Shalmaneser, King of Assyria, offered Hezekiah, the King of Judah, two thousand horse 'if thou be able on thy part to set riders on them'. (2 Kings xviii)

In mythology, the horse is a noble animal with fine instincts, inexhaustible strength and energy, and above all speed. Many cultures believe that the horse is born from the winds. It is also the servant of sky and weather gods. Thor drives a chariot drawn by steeds. In Greek mythology Helios every day brought across the sky the sun and a chariot drawn by four horses. The rhythmic beat of the galloping horses' hooves and the rattling chariot were the thunder, and the lightning the scourge that whipped them on.

The beauty, energy and streamlined movement of horses caught the attention of poets. Homer tells the story of the amphibious steeds of King Erichthonios, legendary King of Troy. Said to be the richest man, Erichthonios had among his holdings 3000 horses. When Boreas, the North Wind, desired to mate with the mares, he changed into a stallion with a black mane. From the union sprang twelve fillies. Homer describes the swift and delicate prancing of the fillies on land and sea in terms of acrobats: 'When they would leap over the fields of grain/ They skimmed the tops of the cornstalks without breaking them./ And when they would leap over the broad back of the sea,/ They skimmed the crest of the waves of the hoary sea.'

The horse not only 'dances' but provides a platform for dancing. Again Homer compares in a simile in the Iliad the deft movements of the warrior Aias in the fight at the ships to an acrobatic dancer performing on the backs of four horses: 'As when a man that knows how to ride/ Harnesses up four chosen horses, and/ Springing from the ground dashes to the great city/ Along the public highway, and the crowds/ Of men and women look on in wonder/ While he with all confidence, as his steeds/ Fly on, keeps leaping from one to another/ So Aias leapt with great strides upon the decks/ Of many ships, as his battlecry reached the firmament.'

The close association between horse and rider has engendered a mythological breed of horse-men, or centaurs. In fact, when the Spanish Conquistadors arrived on horseback in the New World, the native Indians, who had never before seen the strange creatures, believed the horse and rider to be one ghostly being. The ancient Greeks, too, were greatly impressed by the sight of horseback riding and invented many stories about the centaur, a creature who was half man, half beast – how they were born from river gods, how they fought brandishing branches of trees, how they got drunk and raped women. The Greek satyr, an imaginary creature half man, half horse or goat, is really a centaur who has taken on a man's body. The most distinguishable characteristic of a satyr is his flowing horse-tail; sometimes he has horses' hooves. The satyrs were the constant companions of Dionysos, god of wine, dance and drama. In early Greek drama, actors dressed up as satyrs by putting on masks with goats' ears and strapping around their waists horses' tails that waved about behind them when they danced. An amusing pot, now in Berlin, shows riders with whips and rabbit-like helmets on the backs of hunched-over dancing satyrs wearing horses' masks. On the pot is written EOCHEIE! ('Giddy up!')

From an early date the horse has played an important role in entertainment and military ceremonial. After the death of the warrior-king in ancient Greece honorary funeral games were held to decide a successor. The games were tests of skill and endurance. The central event was the chariot race, a dangerous but exhilarating affair which required the utmost courage and presence of mind. At the end of the course stood a post around which the charioteer had to manoeuvre his team, making a hairpin turn. If the driver lost control, and the nervous thoroughbred bolted, havoc could result from a massive pile-up.

Chorus of horse-dancers on a Greek black-figure vase in the Staatliche Museum, Berlin

Horses dance; or rather the horse can be taught to dance. According to an anecdote by the second-century AD compiler Aelian, the Crotoniates defeated the Sybarites in war through a ruse. The Sybarites were a luxury-loving people living in the ancient land of Magna Graecia. They indulged in an excessive display of gold and passed a great deal of their time attending sumptuous feasts in richly embroidered garments. Banqueters were entertained by flute-players and dancing girls, and according to legend the Sybarites trained even their horses to dance in rhythm to the sound of the flute. Their neighbours, the Crotoniates, getting wind of this strange custom, decided to use it to their advantage. In 510 BC, the Crotoniates declared war on the Sybarites, who for once dropped their lazy ways and responded to the call to battle. The Crotoniates meanwhile equipped their foot-soldiers with flutes instead of the usual trumpets. As soon as the Sybaritic cavalry approached the enemy, the Crotonian foot-soldiers began playing dance tunes on the flutes. This made the horses of the Sybarites rear up and throw their riders; the horses, believing themselves in the midst of a feast, began skipping, leaping and dancing! The Crotoniates had no trouble defeating the enemy and succeeded in killing a great many men and horses in the short encounter.

In the Renaissance, kings and nobles took great delight in staging elaborate tournaments as well as spectacles which treated Graeco-Roman mythological subjects. These extravaganzas often included horse ballets in which scores of trained horses paraded in formation and executed acrobatic stunts. At a carnival in 1616, the 'Guerra d'Amore' or War of Love, Cupid was portrayed with his followers in an amphitheatre. A mock battle involving forty-two horsemen and foot-soldiers took place. When the fight reached a feverish pitch, a white cloud was released from the back of the amphitheatre to unveil Cupid, the three Graces, Laughter, Play and Pleasure. Cupid then rose and sang several songs, the last of which introduced the horse ballet. When the musicians struck up their tune, the riders guided their horses through a series of intricate manoeuvres and leaps.

The Florentine artist Stefano della Bella (1610–1664) made detailed records of theatrical amusements and civic pageantry. One of his etchings commemorates the marriage of Ferdinand II, Grand Duke of Tuscany, to Vittoria della Rovere, Princess of Urbino, on 15 July 1637. The union was celebrated by a horse ballet designed for twenty-five riders, possibly by the equestrian choreographer Agniolo Ricci.

Louis XIV and his noblemen indulged in lavish equestrian displays enshrined in a sumptuous engraved volume entitled *Courses de testes et de bague* (1670). Great attention is given to describing the fantastical costumes of the participants. The caption given for 'Escuyer et Page Turcs' in translation reads: 'The head-dress was in part bonnet and in part turban. The bonnet was of blue satin embroidered with silver, and the turban was of silver linen stripped with blue. In addition to the usual feathers, there were feathers fashioned into wings, both on the bonnet and on the rider's shoulders of the colour of the Quadrille . . . The trappings of the horse of the Escuyer were a lion's skin whose mane was of gold.'

Whoever has seen the famous Lippizaner horses of the Spanish Riding School of Vienna can appreciate the precision with which a horse can be trained to move. The School was started by Maximilian II, emperor of the Holy Roman Empire, who decided after visiting Spain that his knights needed a riding-school. Unlike ordinary dancing horses in circuses which are taught to perform tricks, the trainers at the Spanish Riding School developed the inbred talent of the Lippizaner stallions, which are specially conditioned for war. The most impressive step, for example, the *cabriole*, or the kicking out of the hooves, was first used in battle when a warrior wished to clear the field of men around him.

The North American Indians were deeply impressed by the arrival of the white man's horse. Soon the Indians began breeding their own stock, and the horse became a part of Indian life, lore and warfare. This accounted for the origins of the horse in myths. The Dakota Indians, for example, saw the horse somehow as a cousin of the dog and called it 'that mysterious dog'. Horses were believed by other tribes to have emerged from the floor of the other world, which was covered with a layer of fire, water, winds and waves.

Horse dances were rather common with the Indian. To rouse courage in fighters before war, the Blackfoot Indians staged a horse ballet with specially ornamented steeds. Their tails were tied, as they were in battle, with hawk or owl feathers. A human scalp hung from the lower jaw. The horses were painted with wounds on the body; on the neck were painted the handprints of an imaginary enemy who had been trampled to death.

The Omaha Indians had a horse society whose members were believed capable of attaining supernatural communication through the exact imitation of their steeds. In their ceremonies participants covered their bodies in white paint and smeared their shoulders with mud in imitation of the markings of a piebald horse. They

wore necklaces made of horses' manes, and around their waist-belts
they strapped a horse tail dried stiff so that it stuck out from the
body. In a dance they imitated the neighing and whinnying of the
horse as it throws its head back in alarm, the nervous sniffing of the
horses' flared nostrils, and the pawing of a horse which senses that
danger is afoot.

The Shoshone Indians took on the identity of their ponies in an
imitative horse dance called the *pooke*. The display dance under-
lined the importance and prestige which the animal conferred on
the owner in war and in the hunt.

Above, in Chapter II, the Chiapas Indians of Mexico were seen
to punish naughty children in a horse dance, called Parachicos,
meaning the dance 'for children'. During the winter festival, older
men on horseback wore masks; they sought out the naughty
children one by one and made the horse ogre stand pawing
impatiently before them. The Oglala Sioux had a Horse Owner's
Society composed of mounted archers. The warriors, arrayed in
costumes and masks, conducted equestrian ballets.

The Creek Indians had a kind of mating dance in which they
imitated horses kicking. Called the *Tcolako obanga*, the dance took
place at night around the fire to the accompaniment of two
drummers. Two lines of dancers entered from north and south and
as they neared the fire, they circled in opposite directions. When a
man in one line passed a man in the other line, he kicked at him like

North American Indians on horseback.
After H. B. Alexander, Indian Painting

a horse that has been startled from behind. Around the outside of the circling dancers stood women waving handkerchiefs. When a man had kicked another 'horse' twice he had the right to seize a handkerchief and to lead the women into the circle for a dance.

The descendant of the Greek centaur and satyr is the hobby-horse or horse seen in connection with fertility rites in the Padstow mummers play. The dance may simply be performed by a dancer holding a stake mounted with a horse's head or skull. The usual costume, however, consists of the body of the horse, in the form of either a round or oblong wooden tub or skirt draped around a wooden frame in which the dancer stands upright. Sometimes his upper body will stick out above the tub, in which case he may wear a wood horse mask or hood; or sometimes the dancer or dancers are completely concealed within and must be led around by a squire.

The dance of the hobby-horse traditionally coincided with change in the vegetation cycle. Where it is still performed, in Europe, the hobby-horse is danced at the end of winter when the people are anxious about the arrival of spring; the conflict between winter and spring is enacted through the ritual killing of the horse and its revival in the dance, or else in a mock wedding ceremony. At the conclusion of the dance the hobby-horse is offered some beer and oats to fatten it up.

In the French Pyrenees, until recently, a jolly old man would wear a horse-tub that reached down to the ground. On the back of the tub were painted two horses' legs, and out in front hung the head of a horse. But the man, whose upper body was visible above the tub, wore a top-hat. When he came to dance he scattered the spectators out of the way saying, 'Give way, lads, give way for me to dance!' The horse made pirouettes right and left, then did a jig; the dancer inside took special delight in manipulating the head and tail of the horse by pulling on strings inside the costume. The dance turned into a melodrama. An evil Moorish king, wearing a crown, arrived on the scene, followed by a princess. Someone appeared with a throne and set it down in the middle of the performing-area. The princess took her seat there, and the king tried to propose marriage. But three policemen prevented him from approaching, instead leading him to the hobby-horse. The horse made loud pronouncements against the king for his wrongdoings then, having got a confession out of the Moor, left him to repent for an hour. During this time the horse would dance; when he finished the king repeated his intention to marry the princess. The dowry was discussed in terms of macaroni noodles, jam, and gold mines on the floor of the ocean or in the clouds above. The horse presided over the marriage ceremony, and once the wedding ceremony was concluded, the dancing resumed.

King James I of Aragon celebrated his reconciliation with Marie de Montpellier with a hobby-horse dance. A young man wore a small hobby-horse on his back and performed joyous steps to the sound of drums and shawms. All the time he was dancing a dancer dressed as a knight and holding a tambourine presented the good horse with handfuls of oats which he took from the tambourine.

In Germany several dancers carrying the head of a horse performed the *Schimmelreiter* dance, or the 'dance of the rider of the white steed'. The dancers entered people's houses on Winter's Eve along with several youths pretending to be women. Once inside the house, they performed noisy and farcical dances, sometimes knocking over the furniture until they were bribed with a bit of food to make their way out of the door and into the next house.

In India and Pakistan communities performed dances with hobby-horses. These were often connected by wedding festivities, but in the state of Rajasthan (formerly Rajputana) they re-enacted the wars between the Hindus and the Muslims.

As far away as Java and Bali in the South Pacific the hobby-horse dance is performed. In the Balinese horse trance-dance, called *sanghang djanar*, the dancer starts out riding the hobby-horse. But as he enters more deeply into trance he becomes the horse – prancing, galloping, stomping and kicking. In the yellow horse trance-dance, two hobby-horses walk on coals made from coconut husks. Like a horse they kick and knock out of the way the larger pieces of coal, then stomp on the smaller pieces with their 'hooves'. If a spectator is seen smoking a cigarette the horse-dancers take notice and chase them away from the performance area.

For members of the Bambara in the Republic of Mali, a wild ride on a divine and chaotic hobby-horse marks the culmination of the sixth and final state of a life-long initiation process, of which the penultimate stage, the *Tyiwara*, has received brief comment in Chapter VII. The mount of the masked rider on his 'horse' is seen as a kind of epiphany during which the initiate engages in sublime spiritual union with God. In the course of his journey he also returns to innocence and spiritual infancy, comically expressed in an earlier phase of the ceremony when the candidate indulges in joyous capers, buffoonery and plain horseplay.

The six initiation societies, called *dyow*, work collectively to liberate and revive a man; individually each stage is devoted to the discovery or rediscovery of the strands of consciousness winding through a man's life and destiny. The programme of instruction begins when a child is not yet circumcised and continues well into middle age. A candidate progresses to the next successive stage of initiation only after he has, among other things, mastered the masks and dances associated with that society; the dances and their accessories become increasingly more unwieldy and difficult to present with requisite grace and authority. Candidates spend much of their time preparing their costumes and perfecting the choreography. Groups of initiates compete with each other during two annual festivals. It is interesting that the gestures and attitudes of the dances specifically relate the human body and mind to the behaviour and spirits of animals. Each society is associated with certain organs of the human anatomy, and each is in turn connected with an animal and the various physical, moral and mental qualities it is believed to embody: the necessary point of departure for admission into a brotherhood is predicated by an awareness of man's partnership with the animal world. The earlier stages of initiation are linked with lower parts of the body, the later with sense organs in the upper part of the body, where the higher levels of consciousness are believed to reside. The ankles, foot and leg are connected to the first society of initiation, the *n'domo*, and the hyena is the associated animal. Contrary to expectation, this gluttonous animal has positive connotations of power, balance, knowledge and intuition; but like the uncircumcised child it also represents an androgynous state, naïvety, inarticulacy (its mask often has no opening for the mouth), and incomplete wisdom. The hyena is the one who steals small objects: he is clever enough to take without being caught, but stupid to steal small objects of no value. The children's masked hyena dance is followed by running about, scaring people, and stealing objects like buttons and beads.

The last of the *dyow* societies, in which the hobby-horse figures, is called the *kore dugaw*, meaning literally, 'the vultures of *Kore*', the god of vegetation. The initiatory process, extending over a two-year period, leads the candidate to the final summit of knowledge. Accordingly, the eyes and brains are the parts of the body associated with this society, as well as the wrist, which corresponds to the subtle skill of making the spirit manifest through actions; the comportment of the wrist is carefully scrutinized in the candidate's dance motions, since a sure handling of the wrist is an indication of ability to work, as well as a sign of an autonomous control of the reins of destiny.

In the last phase of *kore dugaw*, described by Dominique Zahan in *Sociétés d'initiation bambara*, the initiate is considered 'cavalry officer', and once he has completed the ceremony, he is the 'chief of a great army'. His war horse is a crazy-quilt hodgepodge of hundreds of elements tied to a hobby stick, made of kapokier wood. The pole is normally a dozen centimetres thick, and a metre long. The objects attached to it are truly bewildering in their diversity: skulls of rats, ducks' beaks, sparrow hawks, panther claws, feathers, bones, shells and vegetable materials. These objects represent man and woman, kitchen utensils, the technical arts, weapons, food, furniture, the major constellations, sky and earth, animals and plants – in short, all that constitutes the initiate's universe. On his head he wears a horse mask, also made of kapokier wood. It is sculpted in a trapezoidal shape; the mouth is rectangular, as are the eyes; between them sits the nose in relief; the long ears stand erect. The dance display of the hobby-horse, mask and trinkets consists of high jumps and kicks, prancing, bucking, rushing and retreating, ranting and raving. Special tunes and drum rhythms imitate the sound of galloping hooves as the horse races against the wind. Mounted on horseback, the entire cavalry afterwards canter off for a wild and tumultuous ride, often in the direction of a neighbouring village in quest of 'grain'.

The principal associations of the hobby-horse are grain and wind. The wind, a metaphor for the horse's most exhilarating attribute, swiftness, is the symbol of man's intelligence. It confers on the rider mobility and the power to penetrate everywhere; he can ascend to the topmost branches of a tree or descend to where the millet is being prepared. Like the wind, he can sweep under the grain, whisking it away from those foolish enough to have left it in the open air. The theft of the grain is seen as acquiring a portion of the wisdom of God: it is the grain which the creator did not see fit to reveal to lesser mortals. The hunger of horse and rider symbolizes a quest for ultimate knowledge about the secrets of the universe, and the grain is the initiate's remedy against death. Death is the last and most important attribute of the Bambara hobby-horse: the search for knowledge is also a contest to possess the secret of immortality. In the dance, the desperate kicking, running, rushing, jumping and bucking of the hobby-horse represent to the Bambara a warrior coursing into battle on his steed to fight for the life which has no end. The candidate who goes on to penetrate the secret of immortality ascends to God through the celestial skies, as if borne on a winged horse and swift winds.

61 Dogs and their wild cousins, the wolf and jackal, frequently appear in myths and legends of most cultures. In North American Indian folklore the wolf is the guardian of the warrior and is often depicted on dance masks. A dancer with an elaborate transformation mask depicting wolves is suspended from ropes in preparation for a dance.

62, 63 In his journal, Captain Cook spoke of the dual nature, man and beast, of the Indians of the North-west Coast. Such an impression might be gained from transformation masks. This dramatic wolf mask opens to reveal a human face.

64 Dogs and death are commonly linked in myth and legend. In the mythology of the American Indians of the South-west, the arch-trickster Coyote is the harbinger of death. A masked Coyote dancer is shown on this Mimbres funerary vessel from New Mexico, 1100–1250. The central hole was made to 'kill' the spirit residing therein when it was buried with the owner.

65 The traditional contest of the Yoruba of Nigeria in which youths leap from a mound is echoed in this dance mask where the spotted feline attacks between the horns symbolizing the antelope, while a youth performs acrobatic feats above.

66 Bronze panther or leopard mask from Benin, Nigeria, *c.* AD 1500.

67 The Egyptian deity Bes, often depicted with feline attributes, dances on a panel of the chair of Sitamun (tomb of Yuia and Thuin, *c.* 1400 BC). His knives are for protection and the sound of his musical instruments is intended to ward off evil spirits.

68 Jaguar dancer on Mayan cylindrical vessel from Mexico.

69 The lion dance takes place at the Chinese New Year. Such dances were intended to rid the countryside of pests and vermin. In this Singapore lion dance the dancers surge at the spectators and then retreat.

70–74 Horses are noted in mythology and folklore for their strength, energy and speed, but they are also known for their ability, through disciplined training, to perform or 'dance'. *Opposite* (*above*), hobby-animals take part in a medieval chain dance. *Opposite* (*below left*), hobby-horse dancer from Aix-en-Provence. *Opposite* (*below right*), Roumanian children perform hobby-horse dance. *Above*, in this engraving the discipline and control which can be achieved by horses is evident in the croupade and ballotade, which are preparatory exercises for the supreme achievement of the 'cabriole'. *Below*, engraving by Jacques Callot of the horse ballet performed in Santa Croce, Florence, for the arrival of the Duke of Urbino in 1616.

75 Ceremonial bird dances reflect man's desire to emulate the graceful and liberating flight of birds. John White's painting (*c.* 1585–90) of an American Indian bird prophet imitating the bird affixed to his head.

76 Bird dancers figure in the Japanese courtly dance, the *Bu-gaku*, as depicted in this historical painting by Hanabusa Itchō.

78–80 *Above left*, realistically dressed Indian peacock dancer. An association with courtship and marriage lies in the natural habit of the peacock displaying its beautiful tail features for the peahen. The hornbill is also associated with marriage on account of its natural instinct to mate for life. *Above right*, hornbill feathers serve as fans in a dance from Sarawak. *Right*, Hindu dance drama featuring Garuda, the mythical bird god, portrayed with hornbill features.

77 The eagle dance of the Pueblo Indians of North America. The eagle is identifiable with the Thunderbird, believed to be the sower of thunderclouds and therefore the bringer of rain.

81 The carnival which sweeps through South and Central America at the beginning of February is an exuberant display of masks, dances and mocking processions. A carnival dancer almost takes flight with the wide-spanned wings of his bird costume.

82 Bird dancers with moveable beaks, from the North-west Pacific, appear to be sharing a lighthearted moment with their photographer, E. S. Curtis, whose pictures, despite their posed qualities, are the most evocative testament of the vanishing Indians of North America.

XII Flight: the Dances of Birds

The bird throughout the history of religion has been a symbol of the imprisoned human soul escaping from the body after death to fly off to its heavenly reward. The flight of birds is a talent coveted by earth-bound mortals who interpret soaring as a liberation, inasmuch as it is a negation of gravity which connotes levity of spirit. The acrobatic dancer like the bird is a highly privileged creature: he has a distinct control over gravity, and in his leaps can create the illusion of flight. In classical ballet the impression of being airborne is referred to by the technical term 'ballon', gracefully defined by Isak Dinesen in her short story 'The Poet' as 'a lightness that is not only the negation of weight, but which actually seems to carry upwards and make for flight'. This concept of weightlessness is dramatized in the 'Dancers' myth (see Chapter I), in which the children of Bear Lake begin to rise mysteriously towards the heavens in the midst of a dance. They become heavenly dancers, taking up their place next to the angels. For angels are but bird-people suspended in immortal dance; in the words of the four-teenth-century Old Dutch hymn cited earlier: 'In Heaven There Is a Dance'.* An anonymous Spanish poet of the fifteenth century brings together the association between the dancer, the bird and angels: '. . . And where you dance it seems to me/ As if, in a tall wood// A thousand birds of dawn/ Awake to greet the day . . .// So angels dance to music/ That god makes merrily!'

In animal myths dance often belongs exclusively to the province of birds, as Coyote painfully learned in the Zuñi folktale 'How Coyote Joined the Dance of the Burrowing-owls'. What is some-times called 'dance' in bird myth turns out to be flying games. These joyful and light-hearted displays are calculated to arouse envy in those who cannot dance. Indeed, birds do seem to make

---

* 'Choirs of angels' originally referred not to the angels' function as singers but rather as dancers, in the ancient Greek sense of *choros*, 'a band of dancers', from which 'choir' is derived.

natural dancers, the way they hop around, pecking at their food while their heads bob up and down; or the way they leap and glide from branch to branch in the park, and sweep high into the sky. Some birds actually have fancy courting dances; or rather, it should be said that among the mating rituals of animals, those of birds most obviously suggest to the human observer a dance. Bowerbirds, it will be recalled, construct what the Australian Aboriginals call 'dance-huts' to display their feathers, and the stilt-birds of that same region turn out in great numbers for mating quadrilles. Nor is the mating dance of birds bound to earth. Pairs of grebes skim across the water towards each other, meet, rear up, and seem to dance on the water's surface. The skylark performs its mating dance airborne, soaring hundreds of feet up in the air, all the while accompanying itself with a tune. The pavane, *Nachsteigen*, and crane dance of Zaire are but a few human dances modelled on birds' mating displays.

Birds come well equipped with dance costumes. Their plumage, often very beautiful and exotic, highlights their nervous and graceful movements. People use the feathers of birds to render themselves more attractive or terrifying in their dances. The eagle head-dresses of the North American Indians make the chief an imposing, larger-than-life man. In their war dances, the Indians summoned the spiritual strength of birds in feathered head-dresses and they fought arrayed in plumage. According to Herodotus, the Libyan tribes of North Africa used ostrich feathers for light shields, and something similar to what he describes has recently come to light in a fresco from the excavations of the volcanic island of Thera in the Aegean.

The movement of birds has inspired several ballets, including *Firebird* and *Swan Lake*. The latter is probably the most popular in the classical repertoire; it is also the ballet which has most convincingly adapted the movement of an animal to the choreography of ballet. There is something perfectly natural about the way the dancer portraying the Queen of the Swans glides from bird movement to human movement when allowed to become a woman each midnight until dawn through the magic of the sorcerer Von Rothbart. The choreography for the Swan Queen fully exploits the imitation of a swan's wings to capture the pathos of the swan maiden, at one moment protecting her cygnets with outstretched arms, at another smoothing her wing feathers with her soft cheek, at another reaching towards her lover with arms that enclose like wings, or retreating in panic with frantically beating wings. In *Firebird*, too, the magical bird of fire which helps Ivan overcome evil is half bird, half woman. But whereas the Swan Queen is pathetic, the Firebird is triumphant, dancing exuberantly in a series of swiftly executed leaps that display joyful liberation in flight.

The bird is citizen of both land and sky. Ready accessibility to the upper ether makes the bird a perfect messenger of the gods. Throughout history the movements and behaviour of birds have been studied and interpreted by professional classes of seers. In Aeschylus' *Prometheus Bound*, Prometheus catalogues his gifts to mankind; he pauses on the craft of bird-divination: 'I ordained in exact manner the flight of birds with crooked talons – which fly to right by nature, and which to the left, and which are hostile to one another, and which sit together.' In ancient Athens the owl was the prophet. *Glaukopis*, literally 'owl-faced', was the animal epithet of Athena, and the wise bird served as emblem of her city on coins. Owl dances are spoken of frequently in Greek literature. The *skops* had little to do with prophecy, but was rather a humorous dance in which the piercing gaze and the twitching of the owl's neck were reproduced. According to a late source, bird-hunters mimicked the bird to hypnotize their prey. Also of humorous intent were the theatrical dances of comedy. In comedies such as Aristophanes' *Birds*, choruses of dancers disguised as birds provided a zany moving backdrop to the satirical drama in which the winged attempt to establish a utopian form of government in the skies. Aristophanes knew his birds well; there are some thirty species described with great accuracy of detail. Greek vase-painting provides clear evidence for cock dances which were performed to the strains of the flute.

The ease with which the bird can travel from one world to another is coveted by the shaman. Throughout shamanistic cultures the bird is associated with the medicine-man both in concept and in fact. Joseph Campbell, in the first volume of the *Masks of God*, states that the essence of 'the shaman's power rests in the ability to throw himself into a trance at will. Nor is he the victim of his trance: he commands it, as a bird the air in its flight. The magic of his drum carries him away on the wings of its rhythm, the wings of spiritual transport. The drum and dance simul-taneously elevate his spirit and conjure to him his familiars – the beasts and birds, invisible to others, that have supplied him with his power and assisted him in his flight. And it is while in his trance of rapture that he performs his miraculous deeds. While in this trance he is flying as a bird in the upper world . . .'. In the underground galleries of the Palaeolithic caverns birds are frequently depicted: owls, wild geese, cranes, even penguins. One of the famous Lascaux cave paintings in France portrays a bird sorcerer, a shaman who has fallen into a deep ecstatic trance after his dance: he has a bird head and next to him lies a staff crowned by another bird. Recent excavations in China have revealed drawings of shamans disguised as crane-men. Today the shamans of Siberia wear bird costumes and claim descent from a bird mother. Yakut shamans are remarkable for their imitations of birdcalls, and to represent their ascent to the heavenly realms they imitate the flight of birds. In the South American *Palicur* festivals, the spiritual power of the bird is transferred to the dancer through the feathers of the headgear which shamans carry on a pole crowned with a dance rattle; like the dance the vertical pole describes the flight plan of the shaman to heaven.

Many cultures have bird ancestors who are imagined to have been the original rulers of the universe. Yoruba dance masks incorporate elements repellent to the witches of the night. They are believed to be reincarnations of the first rulers of the universe: birds who drank men's blood with sharp beaks. A creation myth from the Toma tribes of Guinea tells how in the beginning the *ouenilegagui* bird transferred its power to human society. Now when the power of the birds needs to be summoned, Bird Men of the Toma tribes dance. It is required on two critical occasions: after the death of a *zogui*, an initiate of the forest spirits, and when candidates are escorted to initiation ceremonies.

Because of the lofty territory birds occupy, they are often associated with the stars, the rain and clouds, and the wind. In some cultures, it is thought that the birds sowed the sky with stars in a kind of planting dance; the Tungus of Siberia refer to the 'Milky Way' as the 'Birds' Way'. According to an African belief, when the woodpecker pecks at a tree, it is inviting the rain to dance; and certain African tribes beat the woodpecker drum in their rain dances. The Thunderbird is thought responsible for sowing the storm clouds, and the Pueblo encourage this action in their imitative eagle and Thunderbird dances. The mere flapping of birds' wings can create wind. The Micmac Indian tribes tell a story about a time when they could not go fishing for several months because of persistent storm winds. The cause after a time was discovered when a member of the tribe saw a huge bird flapping its wings on a promontory jutting out into the sea. When the bird was captured, however, the air grew so calm and still that scum covered the sea and it stank badly. The tribes were just as badly off as before. So they agreed among themselves to release the bird if it promised to beat its wings gently. The Kwakiutl, who have a similar myth, learned to dominate the winds with a ceremonial dance mask made from feathers. At the top of the mask is a movable ornament with four arms tipped with feathers; the dancer could make the feathered arms whirl at any speed he chose by running a disc connected to the movable ornament along the ground.

An extremely dramatic bird dance is the acrobatic Mexican flying-pole dance called *voladores* ('flyers'), the survival of an ancient Aztec custom. During the Aztec 'centennial', four to five dancers wore the costumes of eagles and macaws, the birds sacred to the sun. The performers were escorted in a torchlit procession to an open plaza, in the middle of which stood a towering pole surmounted by a platform. One of the dancers perched on top of the pole while the other four, suspended at the waist by ropes, flew around the pole exactly thirteen times. The thirteen revolutions of the four dancers represented fifty-two years, the duration of the Aztec 'century'. The dance was performed at the end of the cycle of years when there was great anxiety about whether the sun would continue to shine, since according to Aztec prophecy the world was to come to a violent end during the performance of a *voladores*. The successful completion of the dance was a sign of confirmation that the next cycle of fifty-two years would begin and an occasion for ecstatic celebration and joyous thanksgiving to the sun.

Today *voladores* has survived in the mountainous regions of the states of Puebla and Veracruz and in the highlands of Guatemala. In the forest a tree is felled for the dance, and sacrifices of turkeys and hens are offered to the freshly hewn pole. The pole is then specially wound with ropes and erected in a ceremony. At the top rests a two-foot platform on which each of the dancers in turn performs a dance imitating the movements of a bird scratching the ground. To fly around the pole the bird dancers launch themselves with ropes tied around the waist; gradually they descend in thirteen revolutions until they skilfully touch the ground feet first. Four is the traditional number of performers among most tribes, but the Otomi prefer six, one of whom is a Malinche, or transvestite. The costumes vary from tribe to tribe. The Huastecs dancers disguise themselves as sparrows, while the Otomi, Zotonacs and Aztecs wear a fan of feathers in conical hats.

Voladores is usually preceded by other dances, including *quetzales*, in honour of the magnificently coloured quetzal bird. The *quetzales* dancers perform simple steps in one, then two lines, and finally both lines weave in and out in serpentine configuration. The dance above all displays the stunning plumage of the bird, recreated through a large, multicoloured wheel called the *resplandor*. This splendid disc is made of feathers, coloured streamers and ribbons attached to a cone-shaped hat. An image of the quetzal bird crowns the head-dress.

The Hornbill

Writers on natural history from Pliny the Elder onwards have been drawn to the exotic hornbill, because of both its prominent beak and its unusual mating habits: most varieties of hornbill will pair off for life. When the female of the African variety is pregnant the male immures her in a hole of a tree with mud and saliva; he makes allowance for a window through which he presents food and water, and even flowers. The mating behaviour of the hornbill is interpreted by certain pygmies belonging to men's societies in traditional Zaire as the separation of the sexes and the strict division between male and female territory. The dance is accordingly performed in the forest by members of the men's societies, who wear enormous and colourful masks emphasizing the hornbill; raffia covers their bodies from head to foot to strengthen their identity with the forest, which is a man's territory. While the maskers dance, a chorus of men shout invective at the women, warning them to keep to their duties in their huts.

According to Senufo mythology, the hornbill was one of the first five animals to appear on earth; it was also the first creature to be killed for food; later it was chosen to carry the souls of the dead to the underworld. Among the masterpieces of African art are the large Senufo sculptures of the hornbill. These stylized statues, which highlight the long beak by making it curve onto the belly, are over four feet high. In spite of their considerable weight the statues were carried on the head of initiates to represent the original and vital forces of the universe.

In the Bambara cycle of agricultural dances the *kono*, performed by older groups, is often the first masquerade. *Kono* represents the hornbill, which is prized by the Bambara for its subtle intelligence. It takes two dancers to manoeuvre the costume, consisting of a conical wooden frame and covered with a cloth. Out of the top of the frame one can see the hornbill's head rotating from side to side as the bird's big lower beak claps open and shut. The head is supported on a pole which one of the dancers bobs up and down; the beak is manipulated by a string hidden in the back of the head. When it opens its beak a loud squawk comes forth: the Bambara believe that the hornbill announces the start of the planting season.

The rhinoceros bird, a variety of hornbill found in Melanesia, is a favourite bird in the mythology and dances of New Ireland. She is patroness of the dance, and whenever the men perform, they hold a wood-carving of the bird's beak tightly clenched in their teeth. The native inhabitants of New Ireland in general take an active interest in their exquisite natural surroundings in their daily lives: it is just as much a matter of course to acquire exact knowledge of the lore of plants and animals as it is to be familiar with cooking and the raising of young. In particular, tribal members have an affinity with birds and bird-lore. They know, for instance, the haunts and favourite fruit-trees of the cassowary and hornbill, the exact time the megapodes lay eggs, and the location of stagnant pools where the birds of paradise display their exotic plumage. The thirst for bird-lore is in part motivated by the practical need to hunt birds which supplement a mainly vegetarian diet. But the fascination with birds is also aesthetic. The colours and plumage are woven into ceremonial masks, and their shrill and piercing calls are incorporated in their 'yodelling' songs.

Tribes in New Ireland are divided into moieties named after bird totems. The rhinoceros bird is worshipped as a totem, yet she is the butt of jokes, since she symbolizes human vanity and weakness. A charming myth tells about the origin of the rhinoceros bird's cry. One of the bird's enemies, the flying squirrel, owned a magnificent Jew's harp. But he no longer took delight in playing it and so decided to trade it off for something which the rhinoceros bird might have. Before he ever had a chance to propose a deal, however, the rhinoceros bird swept down from a high branch, and snatched the harp away from the flying squirrel. The bird alighted in the topmost branches of the tallest tree and there exhibited his booty to all the creatures of the forest by giving a concert. And they all so much enjoyed the way the rhinoceros bird played the harp that they commenced dancing. But the flying squirrel had an ally, a very small bird, whom he sent to collect some thorns. When he returned, he whispered something into the ear of the bird, who flew away. While the rhinoceros bird was in the midst of performing a the little bird pricked her in the anus with a thorn. The harp fell out of his mouth onto the ground, and the flying squirrel quickly retrieved it. The rhinoceros bird, who was in great pain, had lost not only the harp but control of her bowels as well. And she emitted a piercing cry that shook the branches and leaves of the trees in the forest like a clap of thunder, and all the creatures were badly frightened. And that is how the rhinoceros bird got her cry.

In New Ireland the ability to dance well is a highly coveted talent; the virtuoso dancer is regarded by the tribes as 'the finest thing in the world'. Another rhinoceros bird myth tells about how the kingfisher fancied herself to be the prima ballerina, a position normally reserved for the rhinoceros bird. The birds, as usual, had all painted their faces white with chalk (as indeed the women of New Ireland are required to do when they dance) and then paired off in rows to begin. The kingfisher suddenly started dancing. This was unusual and out of turn, since the rhinoceros bird always led the dance. But all the same the birds followed in step, except the outraged rhinoceros bird. She got a mirror, and holding it firmly in her beak, marched straight up to the kingfisher to show her how ridiculous she looked: for in her haste to lead the dance the kingfisher had forgotten to chalk her face, and she looked harried and haggard. The kingfisher was mortified when she saw her face in the mirror, and all the other birds derided her with squawks.

An imitative rhinoceros bird dance called the *segombal* mocks the prima ballerina. The dance is performed by several men paired off in lines. With the beak of the bird clenched between their teeth, the dancers incline forwards, their arms crooked behind to represent wings. Simultaneously the dancers imitate the bird hopping from branch to branch, plucking off all the fruit it desires. Always mindful of its safety, the bird is shown bobbing and twitching its head back and forth. The dancers do this very realistically: they turn their heads backwards and forwards, then left and right, keeping one eye half closed and the other trained in a specific direction. True to life, when an 'enemy' does appear, the dancers flap their arms and utter the piercing cry of the big-nosed bird.

Birds in Hindu Dances

In Hindu mythology gods move through the agency of animal vehicles. Often birds serve. Karttikey, god of war, rides a peacock; Brahma rides an ordinary bird; Vishnu chose for his vehicle the half-human Garuda, resembling an eagle.* In the island of Bali,

* In Hindu mythology Garuda is an embodiment of the sun. As Vishnu's vehicle Garuda is represented as half man, half bird, with a golden body, white face and red wings.

an enclave of Hindu culture, the Garuda is one of the sacred Legong dances. A female dancer portrays the bird-man. Her costume consists of real birds' feathers affixed to the ordinary Legong costume and attached to the dancer's back. Two enormous wings are fastened to the arms. Tufts of red-yellow, green and brown feathers sit at the base of the spine; on top of the head-dress is a white lily. In Bali Garuda is the storm-bringer.

In Hindu sculpture a dancer in flight is variously suggested – by depicting a leap or loss of contact with the ground, or by a bird vehicle like Vishnu's Garuda bird, or simply by giving the dancer a pair of wings. An unusual temple frieze from India (twelfth to thirteenth century) shows nine celestial dancers performing a hand-gesture dance. Instead of hands their arms end in the heads of long-necked peacocks; the right leg of each dancer is elevated, another indication of being airborne, according to the canons of Hindu sculpture. The dancers are the Apsaras. Born from the ocean of churning milk, they soon became the favourite dancers of the god Indra at his court. The Apsaras sometimes live in the waters with the plants and trees, sometimes on land with the peacocks and arjuna trees. They entice and beguile men with their smiles and dancing, but a self-disciplined man (*Arjuna*) is not tempted by them.

Bird Dances in Ancient China

'Heaven commissioned the swallow/ To descend and give birth to Shang'.*

In ancient China beliefs about real and mythical birds – the swallow, owl, divine pheasant, crane and egret – are interwoven in poetry and dance. The swallow, for example, was believed to have been the founder of the royal Shang dynasty; it was also the primary symbol of fertility in the great springtime dance festival, called the Royal Festival of the Return of the Swallows. In Chinese legend the earliest people were known as the Lords of the Birds' Nests. People in those days lived in birds' nests to avoid the dangers of beasts and monsters threatening them on the ground. Later men learned to protect themselves with weapons and were able to live on earth. During the following period, referred to as the Great Ten, lived ten ancestral emperors, the greatest and the last of whom was Yu. During the reign of a previous emperor, Yao, there

---

* From 'Swallow Ode', Sacrificial Odes of Shang, from the She King, or *The Book of Poetry*, in *The Chinese Classics*, ed. J. Legge, Hong Kong University Press, 1960. Vol. IV.

had been a great deluge. Yu's father had been ordered to dam the waters with dykes, but he had not succeeded. Exiled by Yao's successor, Shun, he was killed on the Mountain of the Plume. When his body was slashed open, it turned into a yellow bear.

Yu took over his father's work. Instead of trying to dam the flooding waters, Yu cut deep riverbeds into the earth and succeeded in redirecting the paths of water. Yu also mapped out the lands. He invented the smith's craft of forging iron, by pounding the anvil. This suggested to him the invention of the dance drum. With this drum Yu was able to capture harmful animals, such as the Three Miaos, horrible winged creatures. He could tame up to one hundred animals at a time, and a mythical dance was called the Dance of the Hundred Animals. His technique was simple; he beat loudly the dance drum and made the animals obey the strong rhythms.

Yu was mostly human, though ugly and lame; and he had a large raven's beak for a nose. He himself danced exceptionally well for his lameness, taking on the form, like his father, of a bear, or sometimes that of the divine pheasant.

One of Yu's enemies was the owl, a one-footed dancer with a human face. Originally the owl had been a dance drum. According to legend, Drum and Tiger attacked the Red Barge on the Yao River. The emperor exposed the corpse of Red Barge and demanded that the murderer come forth, whereupon Tiger changed into an eagle; and Drum into an owl with red feet. For his wrong Yu punished the owl. He forced him to perform a dance of submission and ever after made the owl the emblem of the smiths, whose pounding anvils sound like the distant thunder. Of all the creatures, however, the owl is not afraid of thunder, because in his pounding dance he invented thunder and lightning.

Two colourful Chinese legends tell about the invention of dance instruments by musicians who were companions of Yu. One musician, the crocodile K'ouei, was himself a drum. The first dance songs were invented when he beat his stomach with his tail, breaking out in fearful laughter which sounded like thunder. Another musician invented a song for the stringed lute so beautiful that the divine pheasant and the phoenix rose up and danced. The divine pheasant is an enormous bird of paradise, azure in colour and having eight wings. Her beak is that of a bird, but the face is human. A bit like the lame Yu, the pheasant also is one-footed. The pheasant, too, is a wonderful dancer 'who doesn't walk or strut along the ground but always flies'. She is the double of Yu the

Great. Whenever Yu takes up the drum he leaps through the air like the eight-winged pheasant. His performance takes place near the Mountain of Plumes where his father's body turned into a bear. At the top of the mountain Yu collects the feathers of the pheasant, and in his dance Yu imitates the way she beats the drum with her wings. Yu gives his soul to the dance, since it keeps all the forces of nature in order while blessing the earth on which he treads.

The divine pheasant appeared on the ceremonial dance robe of a marriageable Chinese princess. When the magpies made their nests and the chickens began to hatch their brood, the song of the pheasant in the land was the call of the young men to the girls to come out and dance. A fragment from a Chinese poem from the *Che King* addresses a mythical bird, the Song-sseu, which had a human head and the body of a female pheasant. 'Mountain pheasant with your long tail,/ Pheasant plumes borne by the dancers,/ The girl's chariot is decorated with pheasant's plumes,/ The girl's robe is decorated with pheasants.'

At the beginning of the Chinese New Year, when the snows melted and the rivers flowed again, the ancient Chinese gave thanks. Gifts were offered to the king, the first husbandman, and the ministers of agriculture, to the one hundred seeds, the workers of the fields, and to all the animals. There were dance and song contests between youths, and marriage vows were exchanged at this time. The festivals were held near a mountain, next to a river. Along the riverbanks boys and girls gathered orchids, and, waving them about in their hands, drove away evil influences. The fragrance of the blossoms, it was believed, helped to unfreeze the earth after the cold winter frosts. The festivals gave all an opportunity to gather together after several months of isolation; it was a time of great abandon, and people went literally mad for a while.

One of the most colourful and dramatic festivals was the Royal Festival of the Return of the Swallows. Swallows appeared in the spring season, heralds of joy and rebirth. Every year they arrived punctually in magnificent, thick flocks that momentarily clouded the sky, on the day of the spring equinox. The swallow was protector and legendary founder of the Shang dynasty, and it was natural to give thanks in song and dances to the fertility powers of the bird. A myth which appears in Marcel Granet's *Danses et légendes de la Chine ancienne* accounts for the origin of the swallow's life-giving charms.

K'o had two wives, Chiang Yuan and Chien Ti, both of whom conceived miraculously. The pregnancy of the latter occurred when the two young ladies were bathing in the river by the rising ground of Yuan, and a swallow dropped an egg which it held in its mouth. The egg was five colours and very beautiful. The two women struggled for possession of it, to put it under cover in a jade basket. Chien Ti obtained it first and swallowed it, whereupon she became pregnant. The child she bore became the father, centuries later, of the founder of the dynasty of Shang.

No imitative dances of swallows are known to have taken place at the spring festivals. There were, however, dances in honour of the return of the swallows, and animal dances which gave thanks to those animals protecting the fields. The people presented themselves before the masked dancers imitating, for example, the cat which ate field mice, or they paid homage to the dancer of the leopard, a predatory animal which tracked down the wild boar, ravager of crops.

A central feature of the festival was the courting dances and love-songs of youths. The call for a mate, as in the poem to Song-sseu, was expressed through the love of birds. The divine pheasant of Yu appeared on the ceremonial dance robes of the princess, and among the common people the male invited the girl to dance by holding out an egret plume. The Chinese character for the marriage vow was two hands clasped together; it was also the symbol of a bird being sought as a mate by another bird. Love-songs inspired by the spring festival and the return of swallows to the land evoked birds as love-charms. 'My lord, oh, what pleasure./ His left hand holds the egret fan;/ His right hand calls me to the dance./ Ah, what is not my joy!' 'The Gourd' mentions the appealing cry of the partridge and wild goose. ''Tis flood at the ford when the waters rise./ 'Tis the cry of the partridge calling!/ The waters rise and the axle is not wet./ The partridge cries, calling her mate.// The cry of the wild-goose is heard,/ At day-break, when dawn appears,/ The man sets out to seek a wife,/ When the ice has not yet melted.'

The symbol for the marriage vow and the mating of birds also expresses a soldier's oath to his lord. The burial of the ruler was like a wedding because the king's servants and military retinue were expected to be united with him in the tomb. A haunting aspect of certain burials was the dance of the white crane dancers, who led the people to their final home with the king. In this setting the crane is a symbol of longevity and afterlife.

A vassal of the king felt a strong allegiance to his master, both living and dead. When a king died his body was laid out on a bier with all the possessions he had won through wars and with presents from his vassals. Below in the court an effigy of him was covered with the flag of death and his coat of arms. The entire ceremony was a triumphal union of forces over death. The vassals banded together to drink their last cup of wine, saying, 'Alive all pleasures are shared; dead, we shall share our mourning', an echo of the bride's wedding vows, 'Alive our rooms are apart, dead we shall share a tomb!'

It was in the court around the effigy of the king that the dances took place. At their conclusion, some of the king's most faithful servants were expected to follow him into the burial chamber, a series of underground passages staked out like a labyrinth. A royal decree said, 'For the Son of Heaven (the Emperor) it is said, the human victims killed to accompany him to the grave shall be at most several hundreds, and at least a few dozen.' The Duke Wou was accompanied by 66 people; the Duke Mou by 177. Ts'in che Houang-ti was accompanied by women only, and a machine was constructed to close the door of the tomb behind them.

The practice of human sacrifice could apply to the funerals of noblewomen as well. Granet cites the case of the daughter of Ho-lu, King of Wou from 614 to 595 (?) BC. The princess was so outraged at an offence perpetrated against her by her father that she committed suicide. The offending act was to have offered his daughter a fish, after having eaten half of it himself! The king had his daughter buried in as sumptuous a manner as possible. Workmen cut an underground labyrinth for her tomb, which was furnished with the most precious of objects. When the burial preparations were ready, several dancers began performing the crane dance in the market-place outside. An order was sent out to the entire populace to witness the spectacular dance. And it was somehow arranged that all the youths and maidens of the capital of Wou were made to follow the crane dancers, like the Pied Piper of Hamelin. Once they were inside, the great bronze doors of the tomb were shut and sealed for ever.

About the crane dance itself, there is little available information, except that it required two groups of eight dancers, all dressed in white. The dance was accompanied by a tune called the *tche pure* ('the fire-bird of summer'), which had been invented by a musician named K'ouang of Tsin. When his master had drowned in the river P'ou, K'ouang was ordered to play a tune. The music made two groups of cranes rise from the watery grave. As they rose, they stretched their long necks and sang; and as they stretched their wings, they began dancing.

Epilogue: the Dance of the Butterfly

Her spirit was really that of a butterfly, so confessed a woman to a monk in a Japanese Noh play. To prove it she danced in the Imperial gardens as a butterfly. The classical dance of the Butterfly, known as *Bu-gaku*, is derived from India, China and Korea, but Japanese versions were developed and enjoyed great popularity in the ninth, tenth and eleventh centuries AD. The plot of the Noh drama concerns an itinerant monk who stops to rest at a deserted palace. At night, under moonlight, a woman appears to tell the monk about the Imperial palace in its heyday – how the gardens were once luxuriant with flowers, and how music, dance and feasts enlivened the court. After a time the woman reveals that she is in reality the spirit of the butterfly who frequented all the flowers, except the plum-blossom. She petitions the monk to be led to Buddhist enlightenment, where she may experience communion with all things. At this moment the woman is transformed into a butterfly with variegated wings. While the monk recites the 'Lotus of Truth', the butterfly maiden sings and dances.

The finale of the drama consists of the chorus's song describing the dance of the butterfly – how in springtime the woman's soul wandered in the Imperial gardens, and how, to the accompaniment of the yellow birds, the Japanese nightingales, one could see the butterfly dancing among clouds of blossoms, making the petals fly like snowflakes. The cycle of seasons rotates from spring, to summer, to autumn; now in winter only the frozen white chrysanthemums remain; but nearby dances the butterfly, like a turning wheel; she dances towards her enlightenment, the dance of Bodhisattva, the dance of the immortals. Little by little, she withdraws from us: 'See her wings wavering with whirling circles of mists,/ See how her figure gradually disappears in the morning haze.'

As she is about to achieve enlightenment and immortality by joining the celestial dance, she vanishes from mortal view. Like the parents of the children of Bear Lake in the 'Dancers' myth, dancers of eternity lie beyond grasp or vision; once having experienced apotheosis, nothing can persuade them to return. This point becomes even clearer in an alternative version of the 'Dancers' myth told by the Luiseno Indians, in which a band of dancing maidens are fleeing from their vicious pursuer, Coyote, when suddenly a rope drops from the sky. As the maidens climb to safety, they sever the trailing rope, preventing Coyote, author of death, from following. For earthbound creatures access to the land of the blessed is severely restricted: the rope is cut.

A Japanese Kagura *dancer performing the* Kocho (*or Butterfly*) *Dance*

SELECT BIBLIOGRAPHY

GENERAL WORKS

A. Folklore and Mythology

BONSER, WILFRED, *A Bibliography of Folklore* (London 1961)

BREDNICH, R., ed., *International Folklore Bibliography* (Bonn)

CAMPBELL, JOSEPH, *The Masks of God*, vol. I: Primitive Mythology (New York 1959)

GRAY, LOUIS HERBERT, *The Mythology of All Races*, 13 vols (Boston, Mass. 1916–64)

LEACH, M., ed., *Standard Dictionary of Folklore, Mythology, and Legend*. Especially articles on dance by G. P. Kurath (New York 1950)

THOMPSON, STITH, *A Motif-Index*

B. Dance, Religion, Art and Ritual

BOAS, FRANZ, *The Function of Dance in Human Society* (New York 1944)

— *Primitive Art* (reprinted New York 1955)

BOWRA, C. M., *Primitive Song* (London 1959)

CAILLOIS, R., *Masques* (Musée Guimet, Paris 1959)

FÉLICE, PHILIPE, *L'Enchantement des dances* (Paris 1957)

HAMBLEY, W. D., *Tribal Dancing and Social Development* (London 1926)

KIRSTEIN, LINCOLN, *Dance. A Short History of Classical Theatrical Dancing* (reprinted Brooklyn 1969)

LABARRE, WESTON, *The Ghost Dance. The Origins of Religion* (Garden City 1970)

LANGE, RODRYK, *The Nature of Dance: An Anthropological Perspective* (London 1975)

LEEUW, G. VAN DER, *Sacred and Profane Beauty*, tr. D. Green (London 1936). Chapter I

LÉVY-BRUHL, L., *Primitives and the Supernatural*, tr. L. Clare (London 1936). Especially Chapter IV, 'Ceremonies and Dances'

LOMAX, ALAN, *Dance and Human History* (film, Choreometrics Project, Columbia University)

LOUIS, MAURICE, *Le Folklore et la danse* (Paris 1963)

NICOLL, ALLARDYCE, *Masks, Mimes and Miracles* (New York 1931)

OESTERLY, W. O. E., *Sacred Dance* (reprinted Brooklyn 1968)

PREUSS, K. T., *Der Unterbau des Dramas* (Leipzig 1928)

RIDGEWAY, WILLIAM, *Dramas and Dramatic Dances of Non-European Races* (Cambridge 1915)

ROYCE, A. P., *The Anthropology of Dance* (Bloomington and London 1977)

SACHS, CURT, *World History of the Dance*, tr. Bessie Schoenberg (reprinted New York 1963)

WOSIEN, M.-G., *Sacred Dance* (London and New York 1974)

C. Man and Animals

ARMSTRONG, E. A., *Bird Display and Behavior* (reprinted New York 1965)

BARRY, GERALD *et al.*, *Man and His Language* (London 1965). Chapter II on codes and signals in the animal world

CLARK, KENNETH, *Animals and Men* (London 1977)

DARWIN, CHARLES, *Expressions of the Emotions in Man and Animals* (London and New York 1873)

FRISCH, KARL VON, *The Dancing Bees*, tr. D. Ilse (London 1954)

GROOS, KARL, *Die Spiele der Tiere* (Jena 1896)

—— *Die Spiele der Menschen* (Jena 1899)

HALDANE, J. B. A., 'The argument from animals to men; an examination of its validity for anthropology', Huxley Lecture (London, 1956)

KLINGENDER, F. D., *Animals in Art and Thought to the End of the Middle Ages* (Cambridge, Mass. 1971)

LaBARRE, WESTON, *The Human Animal* (Chicago 1954)

LOMMEL, ANDREAS, *Masks: Their Meaning and Function*, tr. N. Fowler (New York 1972)

RAWSON, J., ed., *Animals and Men* (London 1977)

SAELZLE, K., *Tier und Mensch* (Munich 1965)

FILM ARCHIVE: Institut für den Wissenschaftlichen Film, Göttingen, Germany. With descriptions in *Encyclopedia Cinematographica*, ed. G. Wolf. Contains films of many tribal and theatrical animal dances from African and Oriental traditions.

REGIONAL WORKS

I. Africa

BERNOLLES, JACQUES, *Permanence de la parure et du masque* (Paris 1966)

BLEEK, W. H. I., and LLOYD, L. C., *Specimens of Bushman Folklore* (Cape Town 1968)

COLLINSON, DAVID, 'The Dogon' (film, Part I of *Tribal Eye*, BBC)

DENG, FRANCIS, M., *The Dinka and Their Songs* (Oxford 1973)

DENNETT, R. E., *Folklore of the Fjort* (London 1898)

DOKE, C. M., *et al.*, *Bushmen of the Southern Kalahari* (Johannesburg 1937) (=*Bantu Studies* X/4 and XI/3)

DORNAN, S. S., *Pygmies and Bushmen of the Kalahari* (London 1925)

DREWAL, J. H., 'African Masked Theater', *Mime* (2), 1976, pp. 36–53

ELISOFON, ELIOT and FAGG, W., *The Sculpture of Africa* (New York and London 1958)

FROBENIUS, LEO, *Kulturgeschichte Afrikas* (Zurich 1933)

—— *Atlantis*, Vol. X (Jena *c*.1926)

GRIAULE, MARCEL, *Conversations with Ogotemmêli* (London 1965)

— *Masques Dogons* (Paris 1938)

— and DIETERLIN, GERMAINE, *Le Pâle Renard* (Paris 1965)

GORER, GEOFFREY, *Africa Dances* (London 1935)

HIMMELHEBER, HANS, *Negerkünstler* (Stuttgart 1935)

HUET, MICHEL, *The Dance, Art and Ritual of Africa* (New York 1978)

LAUDE, JEAN, *The Arts of Black Africa* (Berkeley 1971)

LEMOAL, GUY, 'Rites de purification et d'expiation', in *Systèmes de signes* (Paris 1978)

LIENHARDT, GODFREY, *Divinity and Experience: The Religion of the Dinka* (Oxford 1961)

LINDSKOG, BIRGER, *African Leopard Men* (Uppsala 1954)

MUSEUM FÜR VÖLKERKUNDE, BERLIN, *Westafrikanische Masken* (Berlin 1960)

OGUMEFU, M. I., *Yoruba Legends* (London 1929)

OLBRECHTS, FRANS M., *Maskers en dancers in de Ivoorkust* (Leuven 1940)

SEGY, LADISLAS, 'The Mask in African Dance', *African Art Studies* (1), 1956

THOMPSON, ROBERT F., *African Art in Motion* (Berkeley and London 1974)

VAN DER POST, LAURENS, *The Heart of the Hunter* (New York 1961)

VEDDER, HEINRICH, *Die Bergdama* (Hamburg 1923)

VINNICOMBE, PATRICIA, *People of the Eland* (Pietermaritzburg 1976)

WILLIS, ROY, *Man and Beast* (London 1974)

ZAHAN, DOMINIQUE, *Sociétés d'initiation bambara* (Paris and The Hague 1960)

II. North America

BOAS, FRANZ, *Kwakiutl Ethnography* (Chicago 1966)

— 'The Eskimo of Baffinland and Hudson Bay', *Bulletin of the American Museum of Natural History*, XV (1907)

— *Tsimshian Mythology Based on Texts Recorded by Henry W. Tate* (reprinted New York 1970) (=Bureau of American Ethnology, 31st Annual Report, 1909–10)

CATLIN, GEORGE, *Illustrations of the Manners, Customs, and Condition of the North American Indian. With Letters and Notes.* 2 vols (London 1876)

CLARK, WISSLER, *The American Indian.* 2nd ed. (New York 1922)

CURTIS, EDWARD S., *The North American Indian.* 20 vols, with plates (Cambridge, Mass. 1907–30). Contains full versions of dance origin myths

CUSHING, FRANK HAMILTON, *Zuñi Folk-tales* (New York 1901)

DENSMORE, FRANCES, *Music of the Acoma, Isleta, Cochiti and Zuñi Pueblos* (Washington, DC 1967)

DRUCKER, PHILIP, *The Northern and Central Nootka Tribes* (Washington, DC 1951)

HAMILTON, TYLER, *Pueblo Gods and Myths* (Norman, Oklahoma 1964)

KURATH, G. P., *Music and Dance of the Tewa Pueblos* (Sante Fe 1970)

LAUBIN, REGINALD and GLADYS, *Indian Dances of North America* (Norman, Oklahoma 1976)

WATERS, FRANK, *The Book of the Hopi* (New York 1963)

WHERRY, JOSEPH H. *Indian Masks and Myths of the West* (New York 1969)

WOODCOCK, GEORGE, *Peoples of the Coast. The Indians of the Pacific Northwest* (Bloomington and London 1977)

III. Central and South America

GRAY, LOUIS H., *The Mythology of all Races*, vol. 11 (13 vols, Boston, Mass. 1916–64)

MARTI, SAMUEL and KURATH, G. P., *Dances at Anáhuac* (Chicago 1964)

RECINOS, A., ed., *Popol Vuh*, tr. Goetz and Morley (Norman, Oklahoma 1950)

SAHAGUN, BERNARDINO DE, *Historia General de las Casas de Nueva España* (Mexico City 1829)

STEWARD, JULIAN, ed., *Handbook of South American Indians* (Washington, DC 1946–59)

VAILLANT, G. C. *Aztecs of Mexico.* (Garden City, 1941)

WAUCHOPE, R., gen. ed., *Handbook of Middle American Indians* (Austin, Texas 1964). Especially Vol. VI, Chapter IX

IV. Oceania

BERNDT, R. and PHILLIPS, E. S., *The Australian Aboriginal Heritage* (Sydney 1973)

BERNDT, R., *Djanggawul* (Sydney 1973)

ELKIN, A., *Art in Arnhem Land* (Melbourne and London 1950)

— *Arnhem Land Music* (Oceania Monographs, no. 9) (Sydney ?1957)

GROGER-WURM, HELEN, *Australian Aboriginal Bark-Paintings and their Mythological Interpretation* (Canberra 1973)

HOLT, CLAIRE, *Dance Quest in Celebes* (Paris 1936)

KIRTLEY, B. R., *A Motif-Index of Polynesian, Melanesian, and Micronesian Narratives* (Bloomington 1955)

LEWIS, PHILLIP H., *The Social Context of Art in Northern New Ireland* (Chicago 1969)

PARKINSON, R., *Dreissig Jähre in der Südsee* (Chicago 1907)

POWDERMAKER, HORTENSE, *Life in Lesu* (London 1933)

READ, W. J. 'A Snake Dance of the Baining',

Oceania, II (Melbourne 1931–2) [see also Bateson, G., 'Further Notes on a Snake Dance of the Baining', *Oceania*, II (1931–2); and Poole, J., 'Still Further Notes on a Snake Dance of the Baining', *Oceania*, XIII (1942–3)]

RÓHEIM, G., *Children of the Desert*, ed. W. Muensterberger (New York 1974)

SCHMITZ, C., *Balam. Der Tanz- und Kultplatz in Melanesien als Versammlungsort und mimischer Schauplatz* (Emsdetten 1955)

SMITH, WILLIAM RAMSEY, *Myths and Legends of the Australian Aboriginals* (London 1930)

SPENCER, SIR WALTER BALDWIN and GILLEN, F. J., *The Northern Tribes of Central Australia* (London 1904)

STREHLOW, T. G. H., *Songs of Central Australia* (Sydney 1971)

V. India and the Hindu Tradition

ARCHER, W. G., *The Hill of Flutes. Life, Love, and Poetry in Tribal India* (London 1974)

BELO, JANE, *Trance in Bali* (New York 1960)

COOMARASWAMY, A. K., *The Dance of Shiva* (rev. edn New Delhi 1968)

HÖPNER, GERD, *Masken aus Ceylon* (Berlin 1969)

MEAD, MARGARET, *Trance and Dance in Bali* (film, 1937–9)

ZOETE, BERYL DE, *Dance and Magic Drama in Ceylon* (London 1937)

— *The Other Mind. A Study of Dance in South India* (London 1953)

VI. Japan, China, and Tibet

BARZEL, ANN, *La danse au Japon* (Paris 1939)

GRANET, MARCEL, *Danses et légendes de la Chine ancienne* 2 vols. (2nd edn Paris 1959)

HALLOWELL, A. I., 'Bear Ceremonialism in the Northern Hemisphere', *American Anthropologist*, XXVIII (1926), 1–175

LUCAS, HEINZ, *Lamaistische Masken der Tanz der Schreckensgotter* (Kassel 1962)

WILLIAMS, BRYN, ed., *Martial Arts of the Orient* (London 1975)

VII. Prehistoric Europe and Africa

BREUIL, H.; *Four Hundred Centuries of Cave Art* tr. Mary Boyle (Montignac 1952)

GRAZIOSI, P., *Paleolithic Art* (London 1960)

KUEHN, HERBERT, *The Rock Pictures of Europe* (London 1956)

MAURICE, LOUIS, 'Les origines préhistoriques de la danse', *Cahiers de préhistoire et d'archéologie*, 4 (1955)

SIEVEKING, ANN, *The Cave Artists* (London 1970)

TSCHUDI, YOLAND, *Les Peintures rupestres du Tassili-N-Ajjer* (Neûchatel 1956)

VIII. Ancient Greece and Rome

HARRISON, J. E., *Ancient Art and Ritual* (Cambridge, Mass. 1936)

LAWLER, LILLIAN, *Dance in Ancient Greece* (Seattle and London 1964)

LUCIAN, *The Dance*. Loeb edn (London and Cambridge, Mass. 1936)

PICKARD-CAMBRIDGE, A. W., *The Dramatic Festivals of Athens* (Oxford 1968)

PRUDHOMMEAU, G., *La Danse grecque antique* 2 vols (Paris 1965)

SIFAKIS, G. M., *Parabasis and Animal Choruses* (London 1971)

TOYNBEE, J. C. M., *Animals in Roman Life and Art* (London 1973)

WEBSTER, T. B. L., *Greek Theatre Production* (London 1956)

— *Dithyramb, Tragedy and Comedy* (rev. ed. Oxford 1962)

INDEX